FEAR ✟ AND CLOTHING

FEAR ✠ AND CLOTHING

UNBUCKLING AMERICAN STYLE

Cintra Wilson

W. W. NORTON & COMPANY

Independent Publishers Since 1923

New York · London

AUTHOR'S NOTE:
Everyone I photographed for this book was chosen because I unreservedly
and enthusiastically admired their personal style. Any comments or captions
relating to these photographs should be read in this spirit of wholehearted
applause and celebration for true style diversity. —C.W.

For information about permission to reproduce selections from this book,
write to Permissions, W. W. Norton & Company, Inc.,
500 Fifth Avenue, New York, NY 10110

For information about special discounts for bulk purchases, please contact
W. W. Norton Special Sales at specialsales@wwnorton.com or
800-233-4830

Manufacturing by Quad Graphics Fairfield
Book design by Ellen Cipriano Design
Production manager: Julia Druskin

Library of Congress Cataloging-in-Publication Data

ISBN: 978-0-393-08189-3

W. W. Norton & Company, Inc.
500 Fifth Avenue, New York, N.Y. 10110
www.wwnorton.com

W. W. Norton & Company Ltd.
Castle House, 75/76 Wells Street, London W1T 3QT

1 2 3 4 5 6 7 8 9 0

DEDICATED TO:

THE

WILBERFORCE

FAMILY ART MOVEMENT

AND

FIRE CULT

CONTENTS

Contents

FEAR ✦ AND CLOTHING

Introduction
STARVE, SMOKE, KILL

Or: Walk a Mile in My Frankenhooker Boots
Or: Style Matters, Because Clothes Make You Psychologically Naked

*Clothing concerns all of the human person, all of
the body, all the relationships of man to body as well as
the relationships of the body to society.*

—ROLAND BARTHES

Ultimately, it comes down to this:

Style can either liberate you, or it can enslave you.

After some five years of hammering at it, I am reasonably certain that this book is mainly about personal style, and why you should want to cultivate it with harrowing urgency. Your closet is a laboratory in which you may invent astonishingly powerful voodoo. It may be used as a tool to direct yourself toward your own ideal destiny. It's geomancy—portable feng-shui, right on your body. Style is one of the most remarkably fast, proactive, and gratifying ways to change your mind, change your mood and—as a surprising result—change your circumstances. It is one of the most direct ways of exploiting the Socratic adage "Be as you wish to seem," or, more slangily, "Fake it till you Make it."

Dressing as the superhero/man/woman/drag queen/dictator inside you that is struggling to get out will, in real, definite ways, get you closer to realizing the earthly goals that image represents for you. On any day of your life, you may abruptly decide to pit elegance against despair, strap on brave new boots, stomp on the terra with a bold new footfall, and open up a whole new vista of crazy experiences.

While writing this book, I nicknamed this particular phenomenon—the ability of style to change your life—"fashion determinism." I have come to firmly believe that inasmuch as we are what we eat, we also tend to become the character in the world whose costume we are wearing.

Unlike the fickle and capricious world of so-called "High Fashion," *style* has no absolute rules.* Style exists regardless of circumstances; it does not in any way depend on how much money you have. If you want a look badly enough, you can and will find a way to create it with whatever you have available. Anyone who knows how to articulate their sense of style may look like royalty or a rock star or both in or out of their own context—regardless of how old they are, what kind of shape they're in, or whether their outfit cost them $7 or $7,000.

Style is the collision point between our fantasies of who we are, the larger realities we live with, and the way we are perceived by others. Style can be your best secret weapon in the task of knowing yourself and finding harmony in your world—or the most canny,

---

* I attempt to use the word "fashion" in this book, more or less consistently, to mean the faddish, up-to-the-minute stuff available via retail. "Style" I use as a more ephemeral term to refer to that series of choices/will to personal expression which informs everything you select to represent your world, from your furniture to your diet to your mate to your taxidermy collection.

double-agent conspirator against you in a mass-conformist brain-washing that wishes to regulate you into a cubicle, both literally and psychologically.

Your style is your visual interface with the rest of the world. We dress to define our own characters for ourselves—and to tele-graph who we want people to think we are, and how we expect to be treated. The way you dress reveals both what you know about yourself . . . and also what you don't. When you compose an out-fit, you are creating a *statement* that is, essentially, a shorthand mini-autobiography.

Sometimes your outfit declares you to be the rare and won-derful animal you are. Sometimes even your most mundane outfit blurts out embarrassing personal information you wish it didn't.

People tend to develop wardrobes that reflect both their inner and outer landscapes and weather patterns. What we wear is often an overcompensation mechanism for a whole host of neuroses, character weaknesses, social insecurities, sexual and/or body anx-ieties, and other fears and disillusionments you consider so shame-ful and gruesome that you are concealing them even from yourself (but that you are also unintentionally blurting out to the world, via your hazardously plunging neckline).

Clothing is like a vivid tabloid that society seems to have a gentleman's agreement not to look at too closely or study very seriously.

I think we can all read each other like a cheap airport novels just by looking at each other's outfits, if we know what we're look-ing at. Our clothes overshare our circumstances far more than we realize.

Fashion operates in many ways as a language. I like to say that fashion is a *language of references*. A wardrobe is very much like a *vocabulary* of these visual references.

I find that closets have considerably more going for them than body language, in terms of psychological "tells" and biographical cheat sheets. Micro-movements and tics might help in a poker game or an interrogation room—but you can glean even more subtle and damning personal information by checking out how pointy someone's shoes are, or how many pleats they wear in their trousers. Your outfit can give the clothing-attuned eye a flood of semi-impressions—a peek into your bank account, an up-to-the-minute self-esteem update, and a periscope into your bedroom (to name a few). Just as you can extrapolate a lot about the values of your dinner party host by reading the titles on his bookshelf, an outfit can sum up a human being like a two-sentence *TV Guide* film synopsis. Even the most casual mess you throw on to walk your dog on a Tuesday afternoon pretty much strips you to the wheel wells and sells you out cold to anyone with an eye for psychological fashion deconstruction.

When you first began to establish your style habits as a semi-conscious teenager, you may have thrashed around and experimented with bolder and more daring personal images that you wished to project. Later, if you didn't retreat to a log cabin to build pipe bombs, you probably got a little embarrassed and turned the volume down on yourself and eliminated the pony-skin Creepers, concha belts and white fringe jackets that were the most incriminating evidence of your Bad Self. A few years later, your closet, like most people's, probably became a more or less coherent bunch

An Alaskan kayaker's headware of choice.

of items that together comprised a suffocatingly narrow and cre-atively anorexic idea of how you think you look your best, in the most blameless way possible.

If you're like most people (and haven't given over a morbid amount of attention and credit card debt to your unending obses-sion with personal style), you might own and wear a whole slurry of clothing that doesn't actually reflect who you really are. This probably started out as intentional—you probably purchased things to blend in to your work or social environments. You prob-ably also bought random impulse items in the grip of murkier sub-conscious motivations and/or psychological blind spots (maybe your pervasive feelings of negative self-worth were momentarily sated by that orange lizard-skin belt that you've never worn with anything, ever).

Hey, it *happens*.

⌁⌁

MY ENTRY INTO THE world of luxe ready-to-wear was a fluke; actually, it was the accidental result of my own fashion determin-ism. (The story, as I heard it, was that I was recommended by my fellow Critical Shopper Mike Albo, because he had once seen me in a white pinstripe Gaultier pantsuit that I picked up at a Mon-terey thrift store for $100.) Fashion was the furthest thing from my mind, as a topic, when I began writing the Critical Shopper column for the *New York Times* in 2007. Journalistically, for the last 2.5 decades, I had gone from obsessing over the corruptions of fame to obsessing over the corruptions of politics.

At first, I tried to turn the job down—I told the editrix that I didn't feel I was qualified.

I had always cared about personal *style*—but I've always thought that looking too up-to-the-minute fashionable was the risible mark of being a "fashion victim." I had never been very interested in top designers or their musical-chair relationships with high-end labels . . . mainly because designer fashion was never something I could actually *afford*. I've never been one of the usual suspects that constitute so-called "high society": I don't hang out with socialites, I've never kept track of the ruling-class attendees of the black-tie charity gala events routinely glorified in the social pages of fashion magazines. High-end retail was basically as foreign to my world and natural expertise as high-stakes dog racing, or cold fusion.

But the goddess who was to be my most beloved editor at the *New York Times*, Anita LeClerc, believed my outsider perspective might bring a fresh angle to the column. And lo, so it was that a lower-middle-class, sailor-mouthed high school dropout given to wearing Frankenhooker garments was tapped to serve the Paper of Record as a freelance fashion critic.

It was a stunning surge of abrupt legitimacy.

Most "fashion critics" are front-row cheerleaders in support of the fashion industry and its ever-fluctuating aesthetic tyrannies; known industry professionals on a first-name basis with top designers who share a vested stake in keeping the fashion world financially healthy, and staying on its good side.

But, since I had no friends to lose in the fashion world, I was able to approach fashion from a relatively noncollusive critical perspective. Being deliriously ignorant of my topic, I really had no choice other than to use this handicap to my advantage. I did no due diligence and walked into stores with as few preconceptions as possible, and drew conclusions straight from the garments themselves, without being influenced by the celebrity, popularity, or reputation of their designers.

Many times, I ended up actually seeing the clothing of famous brands and designers whose names I was only peripherally aware of—Oscar de la Renta, Lanvin, Gucci—for the very first time on the day I walked into their boutiques to review them. I had never before (at least knowingly) seen any actual clothing by Valentino (I had never even been that far up Madison Avenue, for that matter, despite living in New York for over fifteen years) when I wrote my first fashion review, on Valentino's Madison Avenue boutique.

There is something slightly metaphysical about criticism (particularly when you have no real knowledge of your subject but you are being paid to make subjective value judgments about the beauty, validity, and/or hipness of garments priced light-years beyond your pay grade). Clothing is inherently a personal subject, so, in order to write about it, I had no real option but to do something distastefully intimate: I had to bring readers into the dressing room with me. I had to get down and dirty and *engage* with fashion, and pull my head through enough necklines for each designer to communicate to me in his/her own aesthetic sign language.

For the first two years of reviewing high-end fashion, the luxury was so frightfully alien to me that I had to aggressively downplay how awestruck I was, or all I ever would have really written was *Holy shit! I can't believe how crazy soft this thing is! Or the amazing squiggles on it! Or that it costs $4,890! And they're letting me touch it with my horrible fingers and my chipped Day-Glo nail polish!*

After writing a few articles, I found myself asking certain questions over and over (which, I would later learn, were questions that the designers also needed to ask themselves):

What is this garment *saying?*
Who is supposed to wear this thing—who is the character
     this costume was built for?
Where would they be able to wear it? *And why?*

On one of my early Critical Shopper excursions, I had what I figure was my Rosetta Stone moment, in the Balenciaga boutique. Professional fashionisti had been calling the designer Nicolas Ghesquière a genius for some time. I'd seen photos of the Balenciaga line, but I didn't really get what the big deal was.

Then I saw the Jacket, in the flesh (or the wool, as it were).

It wasn't something I'd ever want (I wrote)—*not my style at all.*

It was a classic bouclé jacket—a short, fitted, nubby wool thing that a First Lady might wear, by Chanel or Adolfo—but it had powerful differences. It had been toughened up: it was tighter, thicker, more compact. The interwoven wools were black and white, with loud sparks of fluorescent primary color going "Bang!" inside. When I tried it on, the collar was surprisingly high and elegantly rounded; the shoulders jutted straight out into hard little puffs. Many unlikely, paradoxical tightropes converged into this impossible, rowdy, schizophrenic jacket—it was like an Elizabethan motorcycle jacket for the Lady President of Tomorrow. I felt like it articulated the designer's heartbreakingly generous interpretation of female power: radical chic that still made traditional sense. It was as if the jacket came with its own brass horn section, to announce your presence in a way that was simultaneously lusty, confident, noisy, and strong—but unquestionably regal. It was an empowering structural muscle that could be used as protective corporate armor, but it was also nonaggressive: stronger for being penetrable. Mighty like a rose.

Ultimately, it revealed something stunningly simple. Like a dream, it installed new doors in an old room, and opened them, revealing a shockingly bright, open, robust new territory for feminine grace. It was refreshing and gladdening to see such courageous invention; an outpour of inspiration with such vivid affection and respect for women, and belief in them.

And it was $2,765—so there was no chance I'd ever own it, unless I went back with a gun. But I was glad it existed; I was grateful just to *see* it. After that, luxury boutiques ended up being museums for me. Fashion reviewing sank its hooks into me as a subject, because it was art appreciation, really. Like any mature art form, fashion articulates comments on the world in a distinct way that no other medium can—and in ways I found thrilling and revelatory.

As my ever-deepening fascination with fashion inevitably began to influence my own appearance, my questions started getting more personal and existential:

> What does this goddamned pantsuit actually mean?
> Why does this handbag exist?
> Why is this something I am supposed to want, and . . .
> > What does it say about me if I want it?

These questions gushed out into a whole tertiary strata of stumpers, like:

> How conscious are we about our fashion choices, really?
> How much do we gutter out into fashion choices that are
> > essentially being made for us, that don't reflect who we really are?

Designer boutiques began producing ever more dilemmas and Zen koans for me, such as:

> Do the things we wear have more impact on our lives than
> > we give them credit for?

and hairiest of all:

> What the hell is Beauty?
> And why am I supposed to think it looks like *that*?

Fashion (perhaps due to the fact that there are relatively few straight men involved with it) is certainly not *entirely* free, but is *relatively* free, of the usual hegemonic cultural influences that tend to dip-dye other media. Obviously, styles on fashion runways are never suggestions about what human beings can or should actually wear on the street every day. I like to think of high fashion as what society might look like if aesthetics were prized over military power—what the world would look like if, say, the gently eccentric (if not clinically insane) King Ludwig II of Bavaria had been driven by an ambition to cover the entire world, and not just his own immediate kingdom, with whacked-out fairy-tale castles with rooftop winter gardens, Moorish pavilions, and swan-shaped boats.

If, as philosopher-psychoanalyst Jacques Lacan surmised, the unconscious mind is structured like a language, high fashion—the ongoing spectacle of new looks stomping down Paris runways and elevated to absurd heights of importance in the pages of fashion magazines—might be thought of as a really late-night, drunk conversation between the posh cultural superego, the practical socioeconomic ego, and the stoned creative id, during which all three forces argue passionately in visual modalities. It's fascinating to see which of these impulses dominate, each fashion season—and it's always a good fight.

Like journalism, cut flowers, live theater, or virginity, all high fashion is made to perish. It's a vapory crystal-ball-gaze into the gestalt of all tomorrow's parties, right this second, manifest in looks that die nearly the second they're zipped—but they all tend to recall something. Every garment is inspired by some other garment in fashion history and by the time and sociopolitical environment that informed it.

Fashion intentionally evokes moods, and feelings. It recalls eras, attitudes, and temperaments. It remembers old movie roles; it gives Greta Garbo orange hair and open-toed boots. The fashion industry visually interprets the vibe of the moment, and informs us how to look *in on it*, or at least *aware* of it.

⊰◈⊱

I FIRST SUSPECTED THAT FASHION reflected politics right around the end of the Gulf War, when there was a brief resurgence of what I called the J-Lo Desert Storm Bootie—a kind of ersatz combat Timberland whimsically retooled into a wooden stiletto-heeled tactical boot-pump, equally unsuitable for both armed conflict and dancing. We weren't seeing the war on TV, so we weren't terribly *conscious* of it—but fashion, in its own form of gibberish, was *talking* about it.

I felt the same sense of fashion being distinctly relatable to politics after Barack Obama was elected president in 2008. The day after the election, I walked by the Manhattan Barneys and found myself quite moved to see what Barneys' brilliant creative director Simon Doonan had done in the windows.

The display seemed to be shouting something along the lines of "Ding, dong, the witch is dead." It was an explosion of images and fashion moods that had been *hidden* all through the Bush administration. It was an assortment of images culled from the late sixties to the late seventies (in short, the ten romping years of uninhibited, anti-establishment social freedom that the GOP has been scrambling to obliterate from history and cultural memory ever since). Psychedelic power-flowers framed pictures of hippie role models like Carly Simon circa 1972, photographed in a relaxed haze of hemp and sexually liberated denim. All the frail, *Rosemary's Baby*, kinder-infirmary garments were tucked away into a tiny pink coffin; the Pat Nixon polka-wear that had prevailed for the last eight years was finally back in its cold storage locker, along with the Sousa marches and patriotic barbershop quartets.

Hair was allowed to fall back down out of its iron Thatcher helmet. Bohemians were back—effortless pleasure in shredded jeans, butterfly tops, and birth control pills. The Barneys windows were telling me that human females were allowed to be tomboyish, smart, and sassy again. We were free to play both sheet music and musical sheets with rascals like Mick and Warren and Sweet Baby James, again.

The Obama inaugural was another riveting fashion moment: Our smoking-hot, fashion-forward new First Lady wore a Narciso Rodriguez creation that was mind-bending—it evoked a French maid uniform covered with blood, which I took to be a coded fashion jab at the GOP, to wit: *You pork-drunk Ivy League hillbillies sure trashed the hell out of the Lincoln Bedroom, but We the People you have spent so much energy imprisoning, impoverishing, persecuting, and oppressing are in control again now, and your eight-year frat party is over. We're taking your car keys, we're going to clean up your dead hookers, your filthy little wars, and mop up this disgusting bloody mess that once was our middle class.* Shame on you.

I pitched this book as a journey "to see if political economy visibly influenced people in different regions all the way down to their underwear drawers."

The power structures in any geographic area—corporations, religious institutions, schools, military bases, film studios, prisons—exert both overt and subtle pressures over the nearby citizenry, even if the citizens aren't directly involved with them. Over time, the people living on the periphery of any power structure gradually drift into collective tribal fashion habits that reflect these power centers, without realizing that in a different city, they might have evolved into drastically different fashion animals.

This book is the result of my chasing my absorbing curiosity about the power of clothing around the United States, into areas and states of mind I have never visited before. I went to cities I hoped would help me grasp fashion codes and signatures of the different so-called economic "belt regions" of the United States: the Cotton, Rust, Bible, Sun, Frost, Corn, and Gun Belts.

Inevitably, the writing of this book became a personal journey: a discovery of my own fashion evolution. Style is a surprisingly powerful agency or deterrent for human connection. I came to realize how certain fashion phases I had drifted into became a shark-filled moat that distanced me from everyone else—and how, paradoxically, fashion was a tool through which I could restore humanity to myself, and myself to humanity.

I am earnestly directed toward the goal of expanding fashion consciousness. I believe there is an unspeakably great benefit to unbuckling our perceptions of what we usually consider to be beautiful, and expanding these criteria beyond the narrow norms of our usual self-segregating cultural boxes and whatever fickle, airtight rules constitute the ever-mutating fashion laws prevailing at the moment.

I hope to persuade you that defaulting into an outfit the creative equivalent of a frozen pizza is in many ways as self-sabotaging as choosing to wear a prison jumpsuit. Fashion is too joyful and important a way to empower yourself. I believe you should never allow anything into your closet that is less than a *FUKK YEAH!* expression of who you really are.

For the record: I have absolutely zero interest in squeezing all humans into a sartorial world that looks like an idealized and exclusive advertising fantasy. I am staunchly opposed to all consumer brainwashing that suggests that women need to look a certain 98-pound, seventeen-year-old way—or wear anything in particular. I think beauty has more territory on earth and in a great many more people than is generally acknowledged in our pop-consumerist, youth-worshipping media.

I found, virtually everywhere I went on this walkabout, concrete evidence to support the old John Keats idea that that beauty is truth and truth is beauty. The whole consumer myth that there's only one way to look good is toxic, violent, manipulative, boring, and fundamentally untrue. If you have a strong personal style, you can swan or bulldoze your way over any trend. Authentic self-expression comes into no "correct" size, shape, or price tag. Fashion only turns you into a victim when it bullies, conceals, and exploits you. When used consciously, fashion is almost magic in its ability to *reveal you to yourself, and empower you.* As the legendary street fashion photographer Bill Cunningham once said (and has been showing fashion lovers for over fifty years), "If beauty is what you seek, you will find it every day."

You are absolutely free to use personal style as a magic bullet. Every day, when you go into your closet and choose what you wear, you have the freedom to declare your own visual agency and Will to Glamorous Self-Empowerment with a bang! Or with a subtly blown kiss. Only you and your hairdresser will ever know what your style secrets really are. Worn well, your wardrobe may transport you across cultural boundaries and class lines. I am no fan of the Cinderella myth, but I do believe that in some circumstances, the exact right new shoe might magically change your life.

You can and will become your own incarnation of virtually any heroic or mythological entity you naturally adore, but first *you need to give yourself permission.* You need to *grant yourself the authority to dress as your most realized, ideal self.*

So, in the name of fashion determinism, I ask you to ask yourself:

What is your style really saying?
What direction is your style driving you toward?
What person is your style encouraging you to become?
Where is your fashion tribe? Are you already a member of it?
Or do you need a new one?

In short:

Are those really your pants?

I may not be persuasive enough to liberate your mind (or my own) from every form of tyranny, but I pledge that I have thrown my full weight, in this book, into the attempt to free minds from any threat of victimization by fashion.

I suspect that our fashion statements may determine our destinies. The following is my report.

Heroic, from Toes to Fauxhawk. Distinct, Personal, Brainwash-free, Trend-Immune and Mighty. Witnessed in Dallas, TX.

1

SAN FRANCISCO /
THE MACRAMÉ BELT

A Closet from Which to Emerge a Butterfly

If you're going to San Francisco, be sure to wear
some flowers in your hair

—THE MAMAS AND THE PAPAS

Given that this book is largely my psychological invasion of America's closets, I think it is only fair if I show you mine first. After all, we are all at our most psychologically naked when we have our most *deliberately selected* clothes on.

While writing this book, the more I looked back at my own evolution, the more I realized that fashion was essential to every phase of my development—and that the clothing I chose to mold my character had everything to do with the environment that I was living in, and the company I kept. Whenever meaningful changes have taken place in my life, I seem to have rallied the necessary will to endure new phases first by dressing into the new part. Future selves have always revealed themselves to me in the form of bold and compulsive costume changes. Clothing brought me into rooms I would never have been in otherwise (and excluded me from places I probably would have been bored to death in, anyway).

My fashion journey began in the San Francisco Bay Area—a place which adds up to considerably more than the sum of Alcatraz, Rice-A-Roni, cable cars, sexual experimentation, plentiful drugs, and opera. It is a destination for people running away from unfabulous places, possessed by an urge to shed their skins and become people their parents would be shocked by. It is a city for major transformations, where people have always been at liberty to reinvent themselves and cycle through identities until one sticks. The Golden Gate is wide open to anyone yearning to breathe free in shinier pants. It is where I wore my formative years, and learned to be many different selves through multiple styles of footwear. To change your presentation is to force the evolution of your charac-

A denizen of SF, modeling his favorite unspecific, Korea-made sports-fan hat.

ter. To reshape your insides and give your future self a jump-start, buy new boots you think are too exciting for you, and make your personality grow into them. San Francisco is made for this experiment; you can initiate a minor ego death and resurrection just by changing neighborhoods and cutting the sleeves off your shirts.

San Francisco exerts a certain gradual, tidal pull that massages all the subtlety off your clothes. As your personal character develops, you find yourself drifting, for better or worse, into sharper and more specific costumes that describe your innermost fantasy of who you are. Do you wish to walk through life as a full-time sex fantasy, a sorcerer of Middle Earth, or an undead creature of the night? There are specialty boutiques just for you, Lady Gandalf, and dentists who will gladly mold and bond your custom perma-fangs. It is one of the few places on earth where a person really can create a fantasy avatar for themselves and live in that costume full-time—even if it involves chain mail, a 1946 Buick, pagan bloodletting rituals, white PVC nurse costumes, or all these at the same time.

Magical thinking and crazy-dreamer tendencies have encouraged generations of crackpots to run as wild as *yerba buena* over the Bay Area landscape. Its citizens are compulsive bonanza speculators and unreconstructed economic cash-bubble fiends. Gold prospectors scrambled into San Francisco in the late 1840s to change their fortunes and transform themselves into tycoons. Robber barons from the Industrial Revolution came to change their class status by abandoning the East Coast, where powerful old aristos had a padlock on the social hierarchy, and purchased huge mansions on swanky Nob Hill; high society could still be claimed in the untamed West by anyone who showed up with enough money, regardless of surname.

Some come to San Francisco to change the sex of their clothes, or to change their sex altogether. In the early 1940s, when over

9,000 gay and lesbian servicepeople were dishonorably discharged from the military, many were processed out in San Francisco— and stayed there. This sudden influx of the military's unwanted homosexuals gave the city a gay-friendly economy, and turned Babylon by the Bay (as it has long been nicknamed by more conservative American communities, and/or those that deny the existence of a full gender spectrum) into a permissive, tolerant, and relatively safe place to come out of the closet.

Upper-middle-class thrill and truth-seekers came to "the City" in the sixties to change their minds. They grew their hair, dropped out of the world of social expectations, bought love beads, and joined a counterculture revolution that seemed to be the necessary antidote to the girdle-tight social mores they'd grown up with in Connecticut or Missouri. Many adventure-seekers left their minds behind in the Summer of Love; the hangover is still alive and unwell in some of the darker corners of the city's ever-present drug scene.

My family came to the Bay Area to escape Chico, California, a small college town in the Sacramento Valley. My father, an art professor, had tenure at one of California's most embarrassing universities: Chico State, which had the dubious honor of being voted *Playboy* magazine's number one party school in 1987 (during his teaching stint, the school's annual Pioneer Days had to be cancelled when a group calling themselves the Beer Pirates made a point of permanently scarring drunk, unconscious underclassmen with a branding iron they'd made out of a Coors logo belt buckle). My mother, a classically trained concert pianist with other ambitions, started a rock band. Her gigs were advertised around Chico with posters made by my father: a photograph of my mother's abdomen with all the gig venue information written on DYMO tape labels stuck below her navel; her shorts were unzipped just enough to reveal a distinct tuft of pubic hair. (I still harangue her about this. She looks, mortified, at the ceiling. "It was a different *time*," she pleads.)

Needless to say, my mother wasn't exactly a happy faculty wife in a largely conservative town, even at a college primarily recognized for binge drinking. So, in the early seventies, my parents bought a houseboat in Sausalito, the first town across the Golden Gate Bridge, for $9,000.

Sausalito already had an established reputation for being a colorful, bohemian community. The mayor, Sally Stanford, had once been the madam of one of San Francisco's better bordellos. When Ms. Stanford visited my first-grade class, I was dazzled by her tight red skirt suit, gumball-size pearls, and stacked white Dolly Parton wig, all of which, to my childish reptile brain, said: *Power.*

The houseboat docks on Richardson Bay resemble an organized mess, an eyesore, or a romantic thrill, depending on your state of mind. A scavenger class of artists and hippies improvised homes on top of whatever floating structures they could salvage. Steel auxiliary boats, lifeboats, landing craft, and tugboats became the infrastructure for an anarchic fungus of impromptu homes. Some were little more than several sheets of warped and delaminating plywood atop a row of orange foam pontoons, bearded at the waterline with mussels and barnacles. Anything set on top might function as living quarters—a Volkswagen bus, in one case. It was a radical, deconstructionist reinvention of community. A few of the docks successfully fought off all threats of gentrification and remained, until very recently, stubbornly resistant to both progress and plumbing.

In response to their environment, houseboat men, in the late seventies, were a rather swashbuckling pirate class of hardy, self-sufficient rogues: intelligent, rowdy, and capable guys with handlebar mustaches, rugby shirts, dirty white bell-bottoms, mud-spackled gumboots, exotic musical instruments, reptile terrariums, and a lust for adventure, lager, and debauchery. A photo of my mother from those days was taken from the vantage point of someone on a motorboat. She is sunning herself, waving from the deck in a large floppy hat, smiling, blithely topless. Houseboat community residents of the late 1970s, for the most part, would not look out of place backstage today at a Motörhead concert.

An acid casualty my mother nicknamed Captain Rock 'n' Roll lived in a tiny boat in the berth next to ours. "His brain stopped in the sixties," my mother explained. The Captain's wardrobe, when he wore it, had stopped there, too: feathered fedoras, dirty marching band jackets of the Jimi Hendrix variety, old Frye boots, no shirt. His fashion evolution had abruptly stalled out in the muds of Woodstock—signifying that he was both unwilling and unable to engage in a post-1969 world. Fashion stagnation impressed itself upon me as a form of social death. (Worse still was the Captain's propensity for sunbathing nude with his various girlfriends on his roof, in direct eyeshot of our breakfast table. He and his women would wave at me each morning as I ate my toast.) The casual approach to nudity on the houseboats—my being eye-level with most of the pubic hair in Northern California—gave rise to my firm belief in the magic of garments, a nearly pathological Victorian prudishness, and a lifelong horror of nudists.

When I was six, my mother started a new band, Vermillion, with a beautiful neighbor on the houseboats. My future godmother, Margot Jones, wore enormous hair turbans and Jackie O sunglasses, drove a convertible Fiat Spider and looked like a young Diahann Carroll. Ms. Jones became my first fashion icon when she designed and made matching stage outfits for the band: poly-denim wraparound jacket and bell-bottom sets, studded with multicolored rhinestones. To my absolute thrill, she made a small, matching version for me, which satisfied an insatiable craving I didn't even know I had, until that moment: *aggressive fabulousness.*

I would change into my stunning pantsuit when other house-boat children visited me unannounced, so that I could lord my superior glamor over them.

"Are those real jewels?" a dazzled little girl asked, once.

"Yes," I said euphorically (imprinting myself with a fashion obnoxiousness I would never outgrow).

My bejeweled outfit, I felt, identified me as a *special* child (indeed, it put such a profound distance between me and the other children that they stopped coming to my house entirely).

When the band dissolved, my mother became a pianist at a restaurant in the Hyatt Regency. She advanced to wearing black satin blouses and false eyelashes and putting her hair in hot rollers most nights in order to play the piano, with an oversize brandy snifter for tips. She would occasionally come home with origami rings made from one-dollar bills, given to her by drunkly smitten businessmen.

Another remarkable fashion incident occurred when I was in first grade. I befriended a pair of blonde identical twin sisters. Their mother, Pauline, and my mother became instant friends, due to the bizarre fluke that I looked exactly like the twins—to the point that when Pauline made us matching dresses, it was impossible to convince onlookers that we were *not* identical triplets (a phenomenon our mothers parlayed into nearly three years of never needing to pay for ice cream or carnival tickets).

We sensed a trembling underground when Pauline and my mother started dressing alike in high boots, dark turtlenecks, and short plaid kilts. There was a palpable sense of rebellion in these outfits; the twins and I understood on a nervous animal level that the sight of our mothers' fully exposed knees signified something dangerous. Shortly thereafter, a newly empowered Pauline was in the midst of a divorce.

When I was ten, my sister was born and my family moved

back to land, but further assimilation into mainstream society pretty much stopped there. I had only ever gone to small satellite schools, where my friends were dweeby, concave boys who solved Rubik's Cubes in under three minutes, suffered from crippling food allergies, and made geodesic domes out of drinking straws. I was a capable Dungeon Master, played weak (if enthusiastic) Nerf football, and jumped around in helpless spaz attacks to well-worn DEVO albums.

Since my best friends were boys, I didn't want to needlessly remind them of my gender handicap, so I made my sex wholly inscrutable with short dirty hair, ever larger and thicker sweat-shirts, and down parkas big enough to sleep in.

In seventh grade, I was transferred midyear into the public middle school, where the seventh-grade girls looked like they'd been abandoned in the bathroom of Studio 54 and subsequently donated to Roman Polanski. Consciously unaware of their chest development, they wore shirts so tight and thin that the outlines of their areolas were visible. Their jeans were tight enough to give them the rather disgusting camel-toe look; they wore Cherokee heels—a popular brand of sandal with six-inch platforms formed from bone-colored, corrugated plastic. Their hair was rolled into "bitch flips"; they used black liquid eyeliner. Their leather purses contained mascara, Marlboro 100s, lighters, lip gloss, and feath-ered roach clips.

I was frightened to death of them, and they thought something was wrong with me on a gender-identity level. I did my best to adopt the costume of my new tribe, and opted to wear a somewhat less pornographic version of jeans by Chemin de Fer, the premier label of their clan uniform. (This was not a personal choice, on my part, so much as use of conformist fashion to ensure survival.)

When I reached high school, I made lame, halfhearted attempts to dress in the dominant preppy style before realizing that preppiness required a whole domestic infrastructure of socio-economic privileges which most of the other white kids had, but I had not. I could afford neither the requisite Bass Weejuns, Ralph Lauren shirts, the French ski sunglasses, nor the skis that made them necessary.

With the fate of social misfitism once again advancing inescapably toward me, I had no choice but to adapt. I followed the lead of the school's leading rebel, Mitzy, a brilliant girl from the houseboat community I had known since first grade. I had never seen anyone dressed from head to toe in black before Mitzy arrived at my door one day in a large hat, turtleneck, jeans, combat boots, and a black veil—a look my mother called "Satan's Beekeeper." The effect was earth-shattering. I shaved the back of my hair off, bleached my jeans unto the texture of string cheese, and "went punk" virtually overnight.

The punk venues in the city were in North Beach—right around the corner from Chinatown, with its shiny smoked ducks and unmistakable fish–feather–ginseng smell, and beatnik Mecca: Lawrence Ferlinghetti's City Lights bookstore, the Vesuvio Café, and the Purple Onion, one of the few nightclubs in the country brave and principled enough to let the tragic Lenny Bruce perform during the last rounds of his quixotic court battles.

The corner of Broadway and Columbus was home to the Condor, a famous strip club. The illuminated marquee was a cartoon illustration of their star performer, Carol Doda, with blinking red nipples. Ms. Doda, before being one of the first women to have silicon breast implants, was locally famous for her nickname, "The Perfect 36," given to her by a San Jose radio station after her alleged hourglass measurements, 36–24–36 (considered the feminine ideal, in her heyday). Years after Carol Doda (whose bust was then a famous 44) was forced into retirement, the Condor was briefly famous again when its manager died *in flagrante fabuloso,*

THE CHARACTER: SWEET, WARM, HARD MOCK-MACHISMO

From the Freddy Mercury 'stache to the Wonder Woman with a Whip (?) and Bio-hazard tattoos, this Muffin Top is ALL THAT. Don't you just want him to strap you to a comfy armchair and feed you wild blackberry pie? SEATTLE, WA.

trapped between the ceiling, the spinning hydraulic piano, and a cocktail waitress. (Call it what you will, that guy had *style*.)

Counterintuitively enough, in becoming an overnight punk poseur, I became a more authentic version of myself. Punk rock was actually a fairly wholesome fashion choice for a girl born into my tax bracket. It spoke to something restless, impulsive, and con-trary in me (now recognized as ADHD), and seemed to be the appropriate battle attire for the war of attrition between me and my parents that had been escalating for several years. I was glad to have a good excuse to return to fashion androgyny. Punk girls *could* be pretty, but they didn't *need* to be pretty. The prevailing style, at that point, was heavily influenced by a handful of local skateboard gangs who favored Doc Marten boots, rolled-up jeans, and cheap acrylic Norwegian ski sweaters from Sears. (In a nice example of organic feminism, many boys acknowledged that they wore the sweaters in imitation of Penelope Houston, the female lead singer of one of San Francisco's best bands, the Avengers.) A fashion image from those days that was imprinted on me indelibly: two girls riding away after a punk show down Broadway on a battered Vespa P200E. Both were wearing flimsy cotton Donna Reed dresses from the 1950s with pointy flat shoes and cat-eye sunglasses at night. They were both leaning forward and cackling viciously, zooming away after delivering some bald-headed boy on the street an exquisite insult.

Once I went punk, the popular high school girls who had ostracized me earlier in the year began to give me the kind of wide berth afforded to people who are crazy or potentially violent—which was a distinct improvement in my social standing. Dressing as a criminalized person enabled me to nonverbally articulate my feelings of alienation quite eloquently. It also had the effect of moving me, in a permanent way, away from the mind-set, goals, and conversations of my more conventional classmates. I had become a public eyesore, a truant, and a "bad influence"—a "there but for the grace of God go you" object lesson that the gym teacher took pains to point out as a warning to other girls flirting around the fashion gateway of punk and/or Madonna wannabe-ism by allowing a black bra strap to be visible. (Being a fashion villain was, at least, more fun than being politely invisible.)

Punk, in theory, was always political. I was too naive to know why leading my friend Angus around on a leash of long fake pearls felt so deliciously wrong, but I knew it meant something.

There was a natural alliance between punk rock and the gay leather fetish scene. As high school kids, we'd make pilgrimages to the legendary Image Leather store in the Castro, to ogle the handmade bondage and discipline accoutrements—ball gags, zipper hoods, harnesses—and to breathe in that delicious "new paddle" smell. Every once in a while, the counter guys would let us peek into their dungeon downstairs, where mannequins were arranged in tableaux demonstrating the recreational possibilities of leather

suspension harnesses and full-body restriction cocoons. I didn't
understand how any of this was sexual, but as a fashion show it was
the tits.

I had the good fortune to misspend a great deal of my youth
with club kids and drag queens, whose example taught me to build
my own mythic persona from the outside in. At fifteen I made a
fake ID, in order to jive around the underground club scene that
was thriving in the South of Market area. Before it was "SoMA"—a
breeding ground for new condominiums—it was a wasteland of
defunct train yards and abandoned warehouses, and an obsessive
hotbed of street fashion, of the style more or less inspired by the
British club scene orbiting around icons like Boy George and the
legendary British artist/genius/fashion innovator (and my personal
fashion Jesus) Leigh Bowery, whom we club kids worshiped from
afar in magazines like *The Face* and *i.D.* Bowery was a revelation:
his safety-pinned cheeks and full-body sequinned manatee costumes demonstrated that fashion was a medium one could use to
be disturbing, provocative, surreal, oversexed, absurd, and fabulous—*simultaneously*. Inspired by Bowery, I did an experiment one
night by attending a club wearing a white rubber swimming cap,
just to see if it was possible to get away with. The next weekend, I
was amazed to see two other women wearing white rubber swim
caps, and I realized that the only thing dictating the limits of the
possible, in fashion, was your own willingness to rock that hub-
cap/those quilted yellow pants/those night-vision goggles.

"Fuck Sex, Let's Play Dress-Up," I wrote in Sharpie on bathroom walls.

The Haight-Ashbury has had a reputation for being on the wild
side since a citizen revolt in 1950 successfully stopped a freeway
from being built on the panhandle. As is usually the case with
neighborhoods that resist gentrification, the Haight acquired an
unsavory tang and began to decline. The old Victorian homes suc-

cumbed to rot, property values plummeted, rents dropped. Soon it was an ideal neighborhood for persons too louche, weird, and unemployable even to sustain apartments in North Beach.

If ideas about social rebellion percolated in the North Beach coffeehouses, these revolutions were prosecuted on Haight Street —arguably San Francisco's bohemian fighting zone. It is less literary and alcoholic, more kinetically inclined toward harder drugs and action. In North Beach, you played the saxophone; in the Haight, you did too much meth and used the saxophone to beat in the hood of your landlord's Volkswagen.

My nightlife habits eventually led to an enthusiastic summer of meth abuse (nightlife denizens at that time were suffering from the highly delusional mythology that meth was a healthier and less addictive recreational drug than cocaine). I moved in with my best pal, a darling, waifish, bleach-blond beauty of a girlyman and a highly charismatic star of the Haight fondly known as Tod the God, or Tod the Amana Speed Queen, who was to be one of my lifetime fashion heroes. We spent several delirious weeks getting high and getting dressed together.

Amphetamine psychosis produces rare fashion tendencies. Tod always used to say the three C's of speed abuse were "Cosmetically Correct for the Cosmos." The way he explained it: The Gods, whomever they might be (speed tends to make one come over a bit mystical) appreciated fabulousness and attention to detail. If we were sufficiently brilliant-looking, and bursting out of our own freaky mandala of fabulously curated, rare garments and accoutrements, there was a definite sense (or a shared dementia) that the flow of the universe would align itself with our whims.

If Liberace had been a homeless onion, he would have been a speed freak.

Speed freaks dress like nesting Fabergé eggs with one stupendous layer over another—except everything is ripped, full of cigarette burns, and held together with safety pins. A gold lamé dress may be ripped into a turban, held together with your aunt's rhinestone brooch. *Of course* you will wear every single plastic rosary in the ballerina jewelry box. Why wear one T-shirt when you can wear five, in a now-looking clash of designer colors? How about a pair of soiled dress slacks cut off at the thigh, with a black satin garter belt underneath and net stockings and anklets and rings on your gloves and necklaces strangling your boots and fourteen plastic barrettes in your hair? One of my favorite outfits, which I dubbed Clash of the Tartans, involved at least six different varieties of plaid.

We coveted bracelets, which we used in place of clocks: for each twenty-four hours without sleep we'd add another bracelet. Our forearms were wreathed in rhinestones, chicken bones, rubber O-rings, studded leather cuffs—sometimes halfway up to the elbow.

Which is not to say that speed-freak fashion can't go horribly, horribly wrong.

One girl we knew, who had a hooked fish tattooed on her neck, used to wear a fright wig and a white nurse outfit, the apron of which was covered with stains that were either real or extremely well simulated blood. I saw an ex-ballerina at a bus stop once with a Mohawk and her old toe shoes hanging from the epaulet of an army overcoat.

I am deeply ashamed to confess that in the name of an avantgarde "couture of cruelty," I once made live goldfish into earrings by pulling them out of the tank and sticking wires in their dorsal fins. I also sometimes wore an eyepatch, which, aside from looking ridiculous, hobbled my depth perception and was hazardous when paired with a skateboard.

Skinheads swarmed around the Haight, congregating around the Anarchist Bookstore. Their scene was anchored by an apartment belonging to a thirty-something "Bootwoman"—a Fagin-like character who sold powerful marijuana and had taken on the legal role of foster parent for an impressive number of these tall young men. They were a family unified by boots, suspenders, bad hair, bad politics, and cute street names like Creature and Dirt Head. The skinhead girlfriends were severe, angry young women who cut their hair in a "fringe"—a buzz cut with short bangs designed so that you couldn't grab their hair in a fistfight.

Once, walking to the liquor store to buy cigarettes, I rounded a blind corner and landed smack in the middle of a klatch of around fourteen jumpy skinheads. This was not good—in packs, they were more likely to swarm. I was wearing what I thought was an imitation of the great Leigh Bowery: a lurid plaid wool shirt with a zipper, a leather cop hat that had been spray-painted Day-Glo orange, blue vinyl pants, pointy black boots, and a large gold iron cross around my neck. I decided to straighten my back and walk through the gauntlet in a fake-nonchalant fashion as if they didn't exist or I didn't really exist and/or I belonged among them, because it was too late to turn around. This worked—they ignored me—so I used the same technique to avoid harassment again on the way out of the liquor store.

"You see that Nazi chick? No fear," I heard one of the skinheads say to his friend admiringly. (It actually hadn't occurred to me until then that I was dressed like a Nazi. I thought I was dressed like a gay English club kid.)

Skinheads, for all their swastikas, had nothing approaching the violent mythology and genuinely antisocial tendencies of a group like the Hell's Angels—their propensities toward chaos and hate crimes usually began as a response to wanting, very badly, to belong somewhere. The skinheads I knew were relatively literate, neglected boys with nowhere to go home. The aggressive skinhead look was a defense against feeling unwanted, weak, and alone; however, it broadcast signals which essentially guaranteed

SAN FRANCISCO: LOW TO NO INCOME. HAIGHT STREET RUFFIAN:
"SPARE SOME CHANGE?"

Haight Street is a complex time warp. Street youths combine the anti-capitalist, anti-authority sentiments of the late 1960s, the anti-grooming and retro-punk dress codes of the early 1980s and whatever narcotics happen to be in circulation at the moment to create a lifestyle of collective loitering and dedicated vagrancy.

It is a 100% recycled social scene made from the bones of past social scenes, existing in the context of a high concentration of used clothing stores, vintage boutiques, and bars where the staff and patrons appreciate big band music and dress like extras from Dean Martin movies.

Haight Street's mixed-up teenage zombies seem to have arrived decades too late for the parties they most wanted to attend. As if in permanent mourning, they wait in fashion purgatory for the past they belong in to repeat itself.

that all the human interactions they had outside of their group were anxious and negative. This seemed to have a cumulative, drip-torture effect on their personalities. Their deeply held suspicions about the dangerousness of the world were reconfirmed daily because of their tribal reputation. What began as a wayward teenage team costume grew into a grimly self-fulfilling prophecy. It would start one day with a new pair of boots and a buzz cut, and end with a young man getting his ass stomped and thrown in jail. Later, a number of Haight Street skinheads moved to the Pacific Northwest to be full-time neo-Nazis, having drifted deeper into the political hooliganism that went right along with their Docs and prison-boy buzzcuts.

The historical relevance of the skinhead subculture costume abruptly became real one day. The swastikas, originally adopted as a kind of shocking joke ornament, became the driver of the boys' symbolic bus. The hate crimes seemed to chase their chosen fashion statements as naturally as dogs chase tires.

Eventually, I was kidnapped by family members and taken to rehab. The only thing I regretted was missing the skinhead wedding, when the Bootwoman married her nineteen-year-old ex-foster child. It was reported to me that some of the other skins got rather loud around the keg, during the ceremony, and that the bride (in her cherry-red, fourteen-hole Doc Martens) whipped around and screamed, "Shut the FUCK up! Can't you see this is a very fucking important day in my life?!"

⚜

IN THE LATE EIGHTIES and early nineties, San Francisco seemed to be ground zero for the tattoo renaissance, and the facial and genital piercings that came with it.

You can read tattoos like tree rings in order to guess how many summers a girl has hung out on Haight Street. "Modern Primitive tattoos are the bell-bottoms of the nineties," my friend Angus remarked. A lot of young women became the experimental sketchpads for their up-and-coming tattoo-artist boyfriends—with mostly unfortunate results. A surprising number of comely

CREDIT: STEVE WILSON

MARCHER IN PARADE

A San Francisco citizen exercising the right to a peaceable assembly.

nymphs ended up with thick black faux-Micronesian stripes all over their arms and legs, and band logos tattooed on the backs of their necks ("future killers," in tattoo industry slang: ink above the collar, below the cuff). Though no other definite decisions had been made about their lives or career paths, it seemed urgently necessary to a great number of nineteen-year-olds to make expensive and irrevocable aesthetic decisions about their skin. Tattoos were a ritual of self-declaration—"I am" statements—but made with such a small and unintegrated number of personal "I"s as to act more as self-abnegating, "I am not" statements. These young people were culling themselves from the conventional herd, effectively branding themselves with the Coors logo, hard, dark, and early. I've always winced at the sight of these young women on warm spring mornings, trying to wear a light daffodil of a sundress when their shoulders are festooned with snakes, skulls, knives, slickness unto death. "San Francisco is where twenty-year-olds go to retire after getting their BA," another friend once said, to explain this phenomenon.

True enough: to live on Haight Street was to participate in the collective delusion that you and your peers were going to be young and hip and cute and drunk forever.

There was a distinct point in time, more or less coincidental with the collective rediscovery of the tattoo arts, when the post-punk wardrobe of my extended tribe (at this juncture, a lower Haight-Ashbury aggregate of motorcyclists, college dropouts, and would-be artists) turned as abruptly and completely black as if a wall of ink had crept up from the Pacific and saturated everything, save for occasional outcroppings of little silver skulls. It became the style known as Goth, eventually, but at the time, before it became Goth qua Goth, the local term for dressing in all black, daily, was Death Rock.

We were in our earliest twenties, and poor. If your clothes were all black, everything matched and was vaguely elegant (if you squinted). Entropy was a thrifty, built-in style; if your tights ripped into cobwebs, that, too, was a look. We lived in squalid apartments with numerous roommates. Many of us worked in nightclubs until 4 a.m. (At the time, I was a Jägermeister shot nurse—the bondage nurse outfit being the one non-black outfit I owned.) Secretly I nursed grandiose ideas that my funereal attire aligned me with beatniks, existentialists, Zen Buddhists, French situationists, 1930s movie stars, samurais, and Motörhead. (In reality, my style could probably have been more aptly described as "biker Madonna with mood disorder.")

Death Rock was a reasonable fashion response to doing infrequent laundry, and having tinfoil over your windows and rarely seeing the sun. On the bright side, our new monochrome color chart was helpful in community-building: you knew you could rely on a fellow blackly attired tribesperson to answer questions like, "Hey, where should I go to get my 1978 Triumph Bonneville repaired/get green dreadlocks/get the word 'Golgotha' tattooed in five-inch letters across my back/buy jimson weed/cast a reverse love spell for under fourteen bucks [insert your sinister demimonde activity here]?"

Death Rock branched off into the more Baroque Goth, a look with more Anne Rice à la Renaissance Faire tattered black lace bodice-ripper influences, particularly beloved of sad girls with ruffled shirts and tarot cards who wistfully changed their names to Pandora and Persephone, worked at the sex clubs on Larkin Street, and wrote vampire poetry.

Vampires and the San Francisco S&M, fetish subculture seemed predestined for each other, at least on a kitsch level. In the words of fashion historian Dr. Valerie Steele, vampires have always represented, the "erotic macabre." Goth has a big element of kinky nihilism: buckled PVC corsets and other snazzy bondage accoutrements, in concert with the usual Morticia Addams styles. Goth originated in the Victorian cult of mourning. "Victorians had a joke: when women got into fashionable mourning dress, they called it 'the trap rebaited,'" Ms. Steele told me. In San Francisco, anyway, the need to wear rotting black Victorian clothing seemed to arise organically from living in dark, rotting Victorian homes.

I worked for a summer on a theater project with the poet/ performance artist/dominatrix/Goth icon Danielle Willis. I just wore black clothes, but Danielle was a Satanic blood fetishist who had her own nineteenth-century phlebotomy kit, permanent fangs dentally bonded to her eyeteeth, and a serious drug problem. She did, however, write great articles on the ironies of Goth fashion, like "Lord Damien Stark's Makeup Tips for the Bleak":

> *Whiteface should create the illusion that you really are that pale, and not that you have a bunch of makeup from Walgreens caked all over your face. Done badly, Gothic makeup can look painfully stupid. After spending money on a decent base, take the trouble to apply it evenly. It's appalling how many Goths overlook something so basic and vital to their entire aesthetic. Equally bad and unfortunately just as frequent is the tendency to overpowder and the tendency to end one's pallor at the jawbone. I can understand someone having difficulty with liquid eyeliner, but some mistakes are just inexcusably stupid. Don't make them.*

I teased Danielle that her decorative penchant for red velvet chaises, heavy curtains, ball-and-claw side tables, stigmata, and other forms of morbid opulence didn't mean she necessarily was Goth, just Italian. She hit me pretty hard.

The Goth subculture is more than the sum of its chicken bones, vampire clichés, and existential pants; it is still a visual shortcut through which persons of a certain damp emotional climate can broadcast to the other members of their tribe who they are—a look that simultaneously expresses and cures its own sense of alienation. Looking back at my own experience, it seems that black clothes were a response to certain catastrophic events that were occurring with terrible regularity. We had all lost, or were in the process of losing, friends to AIDS, addictions, and accidents. There were always disappointments in romance, and no surplus of mental health or functional families. Boots, black, and leather provided a certain group with an emotional exoskeleton, a blustering attempt to express an edgy, careless willingness to hurl ourselves into what seemed to be an inevitable oblivion. But the writing on the collective black flag, for all our reckless posturing, may have been best articulated as: "Ow, I'm hyper-sensitive. Please don't hurt me again."

But being a Goth doesn't mean you have no sense of humor. "Gothic style should be as opulent, decadent, and individual as possible," Danielle Willis wrote. "If you're not up to making the effort necessary to carry off this most high-maintenance of affectations, try wearing plaid shirts and listening to Nirvana instead."

Haight Street, over the years, has simultaneously become more expensive and more of a slum. All the love, wishful thinking, and utopian softness of flower power seems to be gone; counterculture ideals about drugs and marginal living invariably gutter out into bad addictions and living on "spare change" donations. The street kids loitering around the Haight the last time I visited were primarily "Crusties"—bus grime–encrusted homeless kids, with heavy metal accessories: pit bulls, bandannas, facial tattoos, liquor in the morning. Desperate oblivion-seekers given to aggressive panhandling and harassing the bourgeois shoppers, constituting a walking reminder of how the Other Half was living.

⚓

FASHIONWISE, SAN FRANCISCO'S ROUGHLY 800,000 residents are perhaps best characterized by these two extremes: unchecked fashion permissiveness at the low-income end of the economic spectrum, and locked-down, ultra-conservative squareness on the flipside.

The serious retail shopping area of San Francisco is Union Square, which has the highest concentration of retail wealth and

The state bird of California is the condor.

luxury conglomerates: Saks Fifth Avenue, Neiman Marcus, Louis Vuitton, Hermès, Chanel, Gucci, Prada, swanky hotels, restaurants, and cable cars. It's the tourist-friendly zone, where the city puts its biggest Christmas trees and parking garages.

Wilkes Bashford has been the go-to fashion destination for the city's wealthiest society fixtures—Junior League and Chamber of Commerce types, socialites, political luminati—since 1966. Mr. Bashford owned and ran the store himself until 2009, and arguably was the architect of the premier look for the older, absurdly rich people of San Francisco's Pacific Heights and Russian Hill neighborhoods: hyper-expensive, conservative basics in rarefied Italian textiles by such prohibitive labels as Brioni and Zegna, that don't make a whole lot of visual sense outside of the dowdy headspace of the old-money, San Francisco society bubble, but have visually defined that super-elite clique for over four decades. Mr. Bashford was at least in tune with *fun*, however—at one point in the heyday of the store, there was a full bar on every floor (even the rich enjoy shopping while trashed). I know of no other men's shoe department where a gentleman may try on $1,450 green crocodile car shoes while downing a shot of Cuervo and listening to "Get Off" by Foxxy. My friend Angus told me about the superb customer service they had in the eighties: if you bought such shoes, and asked, someone in the store staff would actually go to the trouble of *breaking them in for you.*

For such a forward-thinking city in terms of social policy, San Francisco socialites (always photographed at opening nights of the ballet, opera charity events, AIDS galas) are remarkably square when dressed up. The women's evening-wear at Wilkes Bashford has always been reliably foofy, sparkly, and defiantly unhip—ideal banquet-wear for the derrière-garde, as it were.

If the Crusties are on one side of San Francisco's fashion yard-stick and the yawnworthy socialites are their polar opposite, the perfect middle ground, in my opinion, is represented by Modern Appealing Clothing (MAC), one of San Francisco's most beloved shopping destinations for nearly thirty years. Run with enormous wit and creativity by the eccentric Ospital family, MAC has always been dedicated to the cultivation of lesser-known designer talents and local artists, and has the rare atmosphere of a business that has been leading the way toward discovering new ways to express a consistent vision of creativity, vibrance, personality, and environmental sustainability (before people even called it that). "Our model is really the farmers' market at the ferry building," Ben Ospital told me. "The farmers honor labor. They sell the freshest stuff at its most perfect point in time. Disposable fashion is like fast food! We honor the hands that make clothes. Like 'slow food'—

we like to think of our clothes as 'slow clothes.' We're not fashion victims. You want to find that jacket that is your most perfect tomato, and wear it for twenty years. . . . If it's all going to end up as landfill anyway, it should all be really good-looking."

I bought my first good belt—sturdy, plain, timeless—at MAC's old Post Street location in 1993. At the time, I was way too broke for this reckless expenditure; it was my very first "investment" piece. I still have the belt, and I still wear it (which, according to my math, means it has not just paid for itself but is actually paying me now).

How does one reconcile the relatively expensive price of perfect tomatoes and/or perfect clothing? "We have customers who will buy a Jil Sander coat, but then to save money they'll stay home at night and learn to make beer," Ben Ospital explained.

⸙

SAN FRANCISCO CHANGED CONSIDERABLY in the eighties and nineties.

One hundred years after the Gold Rush, tech nerds from around the world in company-logo polo shirts, khaki Dockers, and cellphone belt clips flooded into Silicon Valley to partake in the dot-com boom, and created the area's disproportionate number of resident billionaires. The creaky old Victorians were bought and neurotically restored. Now Babylon by the Bay is the Vargas pinup girl of American cities; it has the unintentionally surreal gloss of TV dramas set in the 1940s: it's too clean. The vintage cars and trams are straight from the OCD collector's garage; the "painted lady" Victorians have all had a few too many cosmetic procedures; even the palm trees look moussed. San Francisco now looks like a Las Vegas luxury casino called "San Francisco" (if you choose not to see the alarming number of zombie panhandlers).

On my last few visits, I was disappointed by how mundane most fashion had become. It is, in most cases, depressingly casual. At the San Francisco Ballet in 2009, young women were standing around the lobby wearing flip-flops and hoodies. One wore what looked like an asymmetrical bridesmaid dress specifically chosen to reveal her large, spinachy-looking shoulder tattoo.

But San Francisco can't be repressed, fashionwise. The annual Bay to Breakers race is a veritable Mardi Gras of giant, jogging genitalia and other handmade atrocities in foam rubber. Political rallies are a regular Halloween dance on the steps of City Hall. San Francisco's new fashion identities will surely be in keeping with its eccentric tradition, now that it has an annual Love Parade and medical marijuana.

⁂

IN 1994 I LOADED up a U-Haul with all of my worldly possessions and moved to Los Angeles. There were boxes and boxes of everything San Francisco had given me that I thought necessary to take with me into the rest of the world: wigs, bullwhips, cigarette holders, animal-print spandex bodysuits, plaster religious statuettes, elbow-length leather gloves, animal skulls, posters stolen out of bus shelters. Almost nothing of any tangible worth or any value—but the best stuff I ever owned, the costumes through which I survived my misspent youth. The rhinestones with which I first began to decorate myself in order to assemble the glamorous character I dreamed of being, and which (after many more years, tears, and bottles of glue) I eventually, more or less, became.

2
WASHINGTON DC / THE BELTWAY

War and Pleats: I Love a Man in a
Command-Form Fashion Statement

*I don't blame myself. You see, Mr. Gittes . . . Most people
never have to face the fact that at the right time, in the
right place . . . they are capable of ANYTHING.*

—DIALOGUE FROM *CHINATOWN*

There is a scene at the end of the Cate Blanchett film *Elizabeth* in
which the Virgin Queen finally submits to her fashion destiny.
To demonstrate this, she instructs her ladies-in-waiting to visually
cancel her youth and beauty; they paste thick white makeup on her
face, strap her into her heaviest, stiffest regal garments, and pull
the frightful, tight-curled wig with the receding hairline over her
head. When Elizabeth subsequently reveals herself to her court,
everyone gasps. What she has done is terrifying: she has prosecuted no less than a complete, mindful, deliberate assassination
of her "self." Her frightful new presentation symbolizes that Eliz-

abeth has sacrificed not just her femininity and sexuality, but also her humanity, for England. Her rigid new style announces that she has fully eradicated her frail interior person, and finally accepted her awesome burden of being the full-time vessel and embodiment of *power itself.*

My first trip to Washington DC was in 1997, when I attended the second Clinton presidential inauguration. Having only lived in San Francisco, LA, and New York, I had never seen so much military personnel before—ever. The military was crawling all over the Washington Mall; clumps of sturdy young men in camouflage fatigues with light blond stubble mossing their heads and thick, utilitarian metal-rimmed glasses (frames colloquially known as "birth control" by some soldiers). Most startling of all to me were the members of the youth auxiliary corps—tiny, serious boys with hard eyes and straight backs in military parade dress, with no sense of humor or youthful playfulness whatsoever. The presence of these boys was a somewhat chilling psychological ad campaign, aimed at the children of tourists, to wit: *Jeffy here is in the Air Force. He's only twelve, but he understands the meaning of duty. He's already got medals. He's going to learn how to fly supersonic jets. He's developing skills that can tackle any threat to this great nation. Hell, he could kill you with his bare hands right now, and he hasn't even got underarm hair.*

It was interesting to learn that there were kids like Jeffy who had already abdicated their humanity in order to be hell-bent on protecting my freedom—but, I wondered, was this future leader of America really willing to die for a definition of freedom that included smoking medical marijuana, cross-dressing, and chaining oneself to ancient redwood trees to prevent them from being turned into wall paneling? Would he really be willing to fight for a religious freedom that included goat sacrifice or the use of powerful Amazonian hallucinogens? The military, entrusted with the guardianship of America's democracy and freedom, has always

been constitutionally incompatible with most of the more interesting and entertaining expressions of personal freedom. It has
never had any explicit interest in fighting the forces that actually
do constitute a threat to the freedom of American citizens, such
as poverty, corruption, ignorance, our own government, major
corporations . . . or poor fashion sense.

⹅⹆

THREE MAIN LIBIDOS SEEM to drive most human ambition
in the United States: fame, money, and power. These rampant
desires run unchecked in cities whose economies are built around
them: LA, New York, and Washington DC, respectively . . . and
they also inform the content of each city's closets.

Washington DC is the center of the nation's power; power is
the narcotic that Washington's most ambitious sociopaths crave,
beyond fame or money. Since power is essentially defined by its
enforcement, Washington is a city defined by war; the collective
mood ring, if not its actual color palette, is always on Orange
Alert. Since the closets of the nation's capital naturally reflect
the defense/security/intelligence industrial complexes that are
the prime movers of its regional economy, residents of Washington DC tend to dress very *defensively.* Their overprotective
office-wear essentially serves as both camouflage and psychological body armor. Since intelligence is power in DC, DC fashion
statements tend to be extremely conservative and deliberately
boring. There is no content that can be read in a navy blue Brooks
Brothers suit, save a certain tax bracket. It's a symbolic and sartorial corpse.

Washington DC fashion statements read like blacked-out doc-
uments released under the Freedom of Information Act, in that
they betray no relevant, timely, or interesting personal informa-

tion whatsoever. DC fashion statements tend to be almost entirely *redacted.*

The business zone of America's political power center includes the Pentagon and blocks of homogenous office buildings in the suburbs of Maryland and Virginia. The whole area is surrounded, both physically and psychologically, by Interstate 495, the Capital Beltway—which I like to think of as a metaphorical belt, not unlike the rope worn about the waists of Hasidic gentlemen that symbolically separates the top half of their bodies from the lower. The Beltway separates hearts from minds, reason from dialogue, men from women, and power from the wretched refuse and teeming hordes that compose most of the American citizenry.

⊣⊞⊢

IN JULY OF 2005, *Rolling Stone* assigned me to the White House press corps for five weeks. It was a tense and divisive time. The second term of the Bush administration was kicking into third gear, Valerie Plame's CIA cover had just been exposed, and this outrageous news cycle had just been deliberately derailed by the nomination of Justice John G. Roberts to the Supreme Court. There was a larger-than-usual helping of snappy young Republicans humming around the White House—young women with prematurely wide, matronly hips and undersized cheerleader features, dressed in A-line Lady Bird Johnson–style dresses, with tightly twisted hair knots and pinkly detailed Coach handbags. Guys in their twenties were proudly shorn into a roundheaded military look, and wearing wraparound Oakley sunglasses, boxy dark suits, and the periwinkle blue shirts that were, that spring, the reigning uniform of the GOP camp (I nicknamed them "Blueshirts"). They seemed to share an abrasive, stinging kind of confrontational cleanliness, as if they had all just graduated from Brigham Young University with their virginity intact, and celebrated by being shaken and poured into the nation's capital from an icy tumbler full of Pine-Sol, pumice, and the New Testament.

As is my usual lot in life, I was being thrown into Washington DC entirely ignorant of what I was about to be covering—so, to appear less out of my element, I nervously decided to arm myself by blowing a bunch of money (that I didn't actually have) and investing in a proper pinstripe suit.

At some point in time, there must have been some patriarchal conspiracy—a backroom deal between the Freemasons, the Mafia, Italian wool manufacturers, and the Council on Foreign Relations—that has made it virtually *impossible* for a lady to find a commanding, off-the-rack pinstripe suit in a simple, well-tailored-yet-unslutty cut. I trolled the better department stores only to find suits for women that all seemed to be awkwardly cut in inferior fabrics, and/or larded with ruffles or ribbons or some other ghastly feminizing element that robbed the lines of simplicity. I was no more able to find skirt suits in the right grey flannel or three-season Italian cashmere than I was in worsted Kevlar or 80-grit sandpaper. I finally broke down—I had no option but to get down and dirty and have a suit custom-made—but it didn't come without a fight. The tailor, a Korean man, informed me that even the suiting material I'd managed to buy on the Internet and bring to him—a lightweight indigo wool with faint white pinstripes one inch apart—was ordinarily reserved exclusively for menswear. He told me that female suits are far deadlier than the male: men, apparently, are easier shapes to drape in pinstripes. The creation of a bespoke women's two-piece requires the highest-level black-belt skills, in terms of the tailoring arts. I declined to accept this verdict as an incontestable law of nature, and bared my teeth over interminable delays in delivery—but ultimately, I got the suit in time. I believe the poor man truly suffered for it.

(And nothing feels quite so importantly badass as your first lethal pinstripe suit. Like a first motorcycle jacket, invest in the best one you can buy without ruining your credit or going to jail, and then *submit*—let the transformative effect of it swallow you whole. That is how you fall through the looking glass into weird new phases of adventure.)

One pair of black Prada slingbacks (bought for approximately the same price as the whole damned suit), a nerdy pair of glasses, and a necklace and earrings made of 10mm "fuck-you" pearls later (eBay), I felt sufficiently camouflaged to hang out with my journalistic superiors in the James S. Brady Briefing Room.

But even my proud and hard-won pinstripe costume could not prepare me for sitting in the same room as Fox News's Carl Cameron.

Other reporters might show up for briefings looking dead-line sleep-deprived, windblown, or slightly hungover—that Woodward-and-Bernstein-as-played-by-Redford-and-Hoffman look that says, *I am carrying the fire of such important, time-sensitive information, so I obviously can't be expected to button ALL the buttons on my shirt, and this was the only tie I happened to have wadded up in my glove compartment.* Carl Cameron, in contrast, always looked as freshly clipped, manicured, and clear-eyed as if he'd just slept eight hours at the rectory, drunk a warm cup of nourishing electrolyte broth, and been ritually bathed, powdered, and tweezed by a team of executive choirboys. It was a level of ultra-conservative, hyper-conformist super-grooming I have never witnessed before or since—a radically professional, germ-free appearance that I could only picture being equaled by an astronaut, or a baby in an intensive care unit. The effect is uncanny—Carl Cameron's personal presentation conveys a total self-abnegation and control-freakiness that could conquer any obstacle to professionalism, from lint to sorcery.

PAT NIXON: THE LOOK THAT DENIES THE LATE 60S EVER HAPPENED

Exemplary of the freeze-dried, de-clawed, prim, undersexed, shellacked, deodorized, submissive, tranquilized, yang-free, imperial establishment matron style that always seems to crawl back into women's fashion during republican administrations, and tends to coincide with tighter restrictions on women's reproductive rights, upticks in racism and Bible-thumping, and the economic rape of the middle class by "unforseeable" stock-market calamaties that somehow still always seem to massively benefit the nation's richest 1 percent.

If your goal is to work in or around the government, the unwritten rule, as it is in most professions, is to dress for the job you want, as opposed to the job you already have. In Washington DC, this hierarchical imitation-as-flattery-as-day-look has created a negative fashion feedback loop. The higher DC residents ascend professionally, the more deeply and successfully they submit their closets to this uniform super-conformity. Type-A go-getters in the nation's capital must look dissimilar from the whole, but somehow magically *more so*. Like Carl Cameron, they must stand out *just enough* from an otherwise identical crowd by being the cleanest, most twinkling headstone at Arlington.

After the White House stint, I ended up spending nearly five years regularly loitering around Washington DC for one reason or another. I was insatiably curious about the metabolism of the defense industry, having caught what the locals call "Potomac fever."

Airtight fashion laws are a natural extrusion of Washington DC's locked-down, security-addicted, collective mind-set. Proper clothing is an initiatory wall of fire that everyone has to pass through; the "right clothes" are one of the prices of admission. Democracy may or may not end at the footsteps of the capital . . . but it definitely ends by the time you get to the coat-check.

One of the best anecdotal examples of this is when Google cofounder Sergey Brin arrived on Capitol Hill one day in 2006, believing his worldwide clout would be a sufficient door-opener for him to casually drop in and meet members of Congress. "The visit, which was reported in the *Washington Post*, was hurried, and, in what was regarded by some as a snub, Brin failed to see some key people," Ken Auletta wrote in *The New Yorker*. "It probably didn't help that his outfit that day included a dark T-shirt, jeans, and silver mesh sneakers." The blog "The 463: Inside Tech Policy" corroborated Brin's fashion faux pas: "We still hear from Hill staffers about so and so big name tech CEO who dared wear jeans (with a sport jacket and loafers) in their office back in the 1.0 age, and how their boss quietly fixated on the breach of etiquette."

Such is the inviolable nature of DC's fashion totalitarianism.

Capitol Hill didn't care that Sergey Brin was potentially the biggest asset in the Western world for an upcoming cyber-war with China. Anyone who has managed to rise to a prominent position in the realpolitik machinery of the free world needs to *see the stripes on your necktie first so they know you're safe to play with*. It's a military town, and Brin's way-too-casual-Friday look was perceived as a severe breach of protocol. The attitude to this buffoonish invasion, loosely articulated: *Oh, so—you must be Mr. Special Internet Genius? Well, perhaps when you're swinging on the big tire in your California jungle gym you can wear flip-flops and a Levi's loincloth. "Thinking out of the box" might be a swell advantage over there in Silicon Valley or Asperger's Island or whatever you kids call it, but in Washington DC, by God, our sandbox is called* the Middle East, *and we have these things called* security clearances *which mean that* we are the only real grownups on earth who know the horrible truth. *And we've got news for you, Captain Imagination: There is no "out of the box." Anywhere. You're always in the box.* The more you think you exist outside of the box only shows how tragically ignorant you are of how deep the box is, and how inescapably in the box you really are. *Enjoy your plane-trip back to your own personal fairyland, where there's cups of crayons in the lunchroom so you can be creative on your place mat. Now if you'll excuse me, I've got some death to deal out.*

⬦⬦

IN ANY CITY, REGARDLESS of its smothering collective fashion tendencies, you will encounter a handful of style superstars— persons savvy enough to manage to obey the fashion laws of their tribe, while, however subtly, letting their fashion freak flag fly.

Since he was married to my best friend, Mitzy, it fell to Sean McFate, a professor at the National Defense University and former 82nd Airborne paratrooper, to impatiently educate me on an endless variety of obscure military and defense-related topics about which I knew absolutely nothing. (Behind the Beltway, if you are not wholly conversant in a phone book's worth of three-letter government acronyms and you haven't internalized entire tree graphs of military command structures, you are considered to be too

stupid to keep breathing.) Sean had been a program manager for
DynCorp International in Africa, and spent several years training
armies in Liberia for the State Department—but he is also an avid
opera buff and a fabulous dresser, so I begged him for his help in
interpreting the sartorial codes of his city.

"President Kennedy said that DC is the town of 'Northern
charm and Southern efficiency.' You could extend that to its fashion as well," Sean told me, over one of a series of lunches I bribed
him with.

Sean explained that the dress code for men in Washington
DC—the inflexible look of a God-fearing, free-market capitalist policy wonk, generally speaking—is Brooks Brothers "trad,"
or traditional preppy. Paleo-conservative, ruling-class menswear
is the look of inherited money—the musty, straight-from-Dad's-
attic look: Harris tweeds, argyle cashmeres, regimental ties, and
buttery Oxfords. The effect of a well-done, aggressively natty
trad ensemble is effete, patrician, and almost hostile: disdainfully
smart, fretfully natty, and prohibitively elitist in its airtight thread
counts. It's a look that says: *After I smash the goose-feathers off your
shuttlecock, I intend to privatize your rainwater. Boola boola!*

Since the main culture of Washington DC is military, there
is a propensity for the culture to regard itself as *essentially* male.
Military men, after all, have formed their closest emotional bonds
while being shot at with other men. On the battlefield, a soldier's
courage is the sum of his virtues in action, magnified by his love for
his fellow soldiers—a spectacular, profound, adrenaline-pumped,
hero-on-hero love that non-life-and-death transactions with over-
familiar women involving laundry, cat boxes, and minivans really
can't compete with.

As a result, the estrangement between Mars and Venus in
Washington DC is particularly pronounced. DC, at its social
core, is not unlike an ancient Greek or Roman society where real

love is exclusively man-on-man—the admiration and approval of other men is the most meaningful social currency. Women, with their kooky, foreign, emotional demands, ultimately represent a bothersome and disposable home front. There is the same kind of surprisingly strong, unspoken undercurrent of latent homosexuality that one might find in an all-male prep or boarding school—a taboo some men brazenly challenge, when the weather is warm, by abandoning all sense of sartorial discretion, by exploding into a veritable Mama's Boy regatta of flamboyant candy-colored seersuckers and violent floral neckties. It is intended to be a show of fearlessly secure machismo, à la the old Gallant South. But to an outsider, especially one from New York, it tends to look just the tiniest bit *gay*.

Due to a combination of Christianity, Mormonism, alcoholism, and the inherent hypocrisies of conservative politics, sexual mores behind the Beltway seem to be permanently stuck in a bizarre pantomime of a conservative "family values" mind-set that factually expired somewhere back around 1961 (if it ever factually existed anywhere, at all).

Take a bunch of married, unreconstructed neurotic ex-military bull elephants, and throw them into the bar at the Hay–Adams with a bunch of smart, comely twenty-five-year-old Capitol Hill staff girls (also drunk, and prized for their ability to do their jobs in five-inch Louboutin heels), and you get a level of repressed sexual tension that whiplashes Taliban-style into an uptightness about female clothing cranked up to eleven. There is an excruciatingly narrow margin for acceptable female dress; all women, no matter how attractive or plain, no matter how many postgraduate degrees they have or how well they fly fighter planes, walk an inescapable fashion tightrope. Their style will fall into the binary categories of either "dowdy" or "slutty"; there are virtually no fashion grey areas.

"For women, it seems to be a real pickle," says science and technology defense analyst Dr. Guy Incognito (who wouldn't let me use his real name, even though he is a dear friend). "If you're hot, you can dress up and get the attention of the men, but not their respect. You'll get daggers from other women. If you dress down, you'll be viewed as brain-damaged by the men, and patronizing by the women. If you're not hot, and you dress up, you'll be seen as over-reaching and possibly announcing yourself, à la savanna baboons, to be in oestrus (seeking baby and/or promotion). If you're not hot and you dress down, you're just homely, which is functionally the equivalent of being brain-damaged in this city."

The default answer to this no-win fashion conundrum, for an alarming amount of working women, is to buy their wardrobes at Ann Taylor; a label so ubiquitous in Washington DC it might as well be tattooed on the C7 vertebrae of every woman under sixty. The line has always offered tasteful middle management office clas-sics in wool with just enough spandex to vaguely suggest a Sarah Palin strip-o-gram. My shorthand for the look was always "capital-ist burqa" or "corporate office submissive": cubicle-wear of so-so quality for the single girl in her late twenties whose self-esteem has been almost beaten to death by the beauty industrial complex, and whose decent education has been punished with a thanklessly demanding office job. She's a can-do Cinderella who has always had to change the oil in her own pumpkin and is too overworked to have a healthy social life outside the workplace. Her outfits must therefore be corporate-respectable, yet body-conscious enough to attract a nice tax attorney husband.

The Ann Taylor ethos rubs me the wrong way for the same reason I don't like white women singing "Summertime" or winos drinking cooking extract: too much vanilla will make you go blind. But the brand is the retreat position for the schizophrenic DC work environment, where female sexuality is both an asset and a liability.

Washington's permaclass of wealthy Georgetown establishment socialites has always ruled the roost on DC's domestic front. The older rich ladies are the keepers of the social rulebooks—and the keepers of all the best HUMINT (human intelligence) and RUMINT (rumor-based intelligence) in town. These are the Mean Girls who make or break political aspirations, who get to wear big hats at polo matches, make disparaging comments about social climbers, and police the actions and/or styles of younger, more fertile women.

For a large part, the formalwear created for these women (one of the global teaspoonful of humans capable of affording such garments) is girdled and privileged, highlighting a state of voluntary submission to the patriarchs of their tribe. Their look is an orderly, anger- and yang-free approach to the complex abyss of femininity, drawn from the late 1950s to mid-1960s, when husbands were playboys and closet homosexuals and wives attended luncheons and kept up with correspondence until trotted out for state occasions.

Rich Georgetown ladies tend to drift into that Pat Nixon look that denies that the late sixties ever happened. Their clothes evoke a demure, under control, decidedly non-rowdy, submissive type of woman who appreciates her role as an ornament of great value, and sits prettily and quietly in Gulfstream jets. It is the look of mothers of brides, and Hong Kong billionaires' wives. The hard hair and brocade jackets are a throwback to the freeze-dried, declawed, prim, undersexed, shellacked, deodorized, imperial establishment matron style that always seems to crawl back into women's fashion during Republican administrations, and tends to coincide with tighter restrictions on women's reproductive rights, upticks in racism and Bible-thumping, and the economic rape of the middle class by "unforeseeable" stock market calamities that still somehow always seem to massively benefit the nation's richest 1 percent.

During the darker years of the Bush administration, it struck me that the cut of most women's clothing in retail fashion inventories eerily evoked *Rosemary's Baby*. It was all baby-doll dresses and little pastel blouses with Peter Pan collars and smocking over the collarbones. Child-women were infantilized and bowed up until they resembled decorative, virginal Easter eggs. All the high heels seemed to evaporate from department stores in favor of quiet little ballet shoes that might enable a wife to tiptoe out of the dining room so that the men, freshly cigared, could talk like grownups.

There is an indulged weakness evident: the ideal society wife is made into a streamlined, luxury toddler. Many pieces evoke the Pampered-with-a-capital-P innocence of the nursery, yet defy the vigor of either youth or sex. In the baby-doll dresses, there is no ironic infantilism (that flirty, kinderwhore cuteness that winks at pedophilia), but a kind of learned helplessness that waves a limp hand at actual infirmity—the kind of silky pink bedjacket garments one imagines Sunny von Bulow wore to sleep through parties.

The creations of designers who cater to First Ladies, such as Valentino, Oscar de la Renta, and newcomers like Derek Lam, tend to be nostalgic and never challengingly hip. It is a clean, monarchic glamor. The brands have a tenure granted by the designer's perennial alliances with actual monarchies and the otherwise untouchably rich. In iconography alone, such brands are pure currency: Jackie O both mourned JFK and married Onassis in Valentino.

When I was first allowed into an Oscar de la Renta boutique, reviewing retail for the *New York Times*, I found the garments mind-blowing. I clutched the insanely craft-saturated sleeves and stared into them like kaleidoscopes, wondering, "How many nuns went blind?" Layers upon layers of meticulous, eye-crossing detail created a mesmerizing depth of texture. There was so much going on: whole landscapes and leitmotifs wrought in black beads and marabou feathers; drapes and pin-tucks of such alien perfection and accuracy that the dresses looked like they were built by the Pixie Corps of Engineers.

It was there that I saw the point of it all.

Clothing this advanced just might guarantee a lady the center of attention, in most rooms—even if she lacks charm, looks, and substance. It is the haberdashery equivalent of a Maserati; people are likely to be a bit hypnotized, no matter how unspectacular the driver may be.

⌘

ONE OF THE BASIC elements of psychological warfare is to look intimidating to the enemy, and one of the unintentionally hilarious aspects of Washington DC's inability to psychoanalyze itself becomes manifest when powerful, high-visibility women dress, either consciously or unconsciously, in clothing that resembles Fascist dominatrix regalia. As Pat Benatar pointed out, love is a battlefield, and sex is a weapon—apparently, when you mix too much power with a whole lot of oil money and pent-up aggression, there is an inexorable pull to leather. While there is much to be said from the standpoint of pure style about the sexy cuts of Nazi uniforms—several of which were actually designed by Hugo Boss—when female senior defense officials dress up like She-Wolves of the SS, it tends to make the rather discomfiting suggestion that when America is done looting the Middle East, it intends to invade Poland. (Let us never forget that stunning outfit then Secretary of State Condoleezza Rice wore to stomp around the troops at the Weisbaden Army Airfield in 2005: an ankle-length, band-collared black military-inspired trenchcoat with epaulets and knee-length stiletto jackboots. It's the outfit that would have happened if the Marine dress uniform was redesigned by Hugo Boss for *Matrix 6: The Empire Steps On Your Face with Its Boot Forever*.)

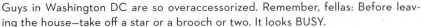

Guys in Washington DC are so overaccessorized. Remember, fellas: Before leaving the house—take off a star or a brooch or two. It looks BUSY.

The real rock stars in Washington DC, however, are the top military officials. Generals, in particular, are notorious peacocks. They are massively vain. "They need to be complimented on their plumage," my friend Mitzy informed me.

The peacock metaphor extends to the wives of decorated military men—who, like peahens, seem to be genetically preconditioned to total invisibility in order to better highlight the glory of the male. The Beltway is host to a disproportionate amount of middle-aged women with premature salt-and-pepper hair, orthopedic-looking shoes, and box-shaped floral print dresses as shapeless as oven mitts. Many Washington women end up taking a fashion approach not unlike that of the flounder, who undergoes a period of metamorphosis in order to camouflage itself to look identical to the ocean floor, and thereby be invisible to predators (the predators in this case being other Washington DC wives, and their tendency to morally police one another).

Frump has a stranglehold on most middle-class wives and mothers behind the Beltway, but wives of military officials tend to become even dowdier, as if every shiny bauble that ever comes their way is automatically sacrificed to the virile human Christmas tree of a husband they're politely standing behind. (Even all the lipstick, rouge, and eyeliner in the house eventually goes on the old soldier, especially when he starts appearing on TV as a mouth-piece for the Pentagon.)

Retired military men tend to enter the private sector, because working for private defense companies is, in effect, the only cushy retirement plan—the only golden parachute available for silvered paratroopers. An old colonel's task, once out of the military, is to exploit his military career connections on behalf of his new employer and convince his old cronies in the Pentagon to bend the federal budget around to acquire the new battle gadgets he represents.

Once an officer retires, however, a whole change of fashion life must take place; a man who has lived the bulk of his life in uniform is now forced to go shopping for civilian-wear. For the most part, asking these men to enter retail clothing stores and dress themselves is a bit like releasing an overly socialized Holly-wood chimpanzee into the rainforest where it must hunt and eat other chimps. The lifelong conditioning necessary for successful self-dress simply *isn't there.*

"It can be so painful to watch the retired army colonel begin 'The Transformation,'" says Dr. N., a major defense intellectual. "The awkward first suit. The Saturday trips with the wife to Jos. A. Bank. It's really all too painful to contemplate."

"The retired military guys try to imitate the Boston Brah-mins, but remember—they're imitating imitators who don't get it either," said Sean McFate. "Most of these guys are to the right of center—think NRA. Ex-military men impress one another by wearing their résumés. They are older. Most have glasses that tint automatically. They'll wear a knit polo shirt with the logo of an embassy they've visited in the recent past—and their copious belly will fill out the entire extra-large shirt so that it's stretching, and their belt buckle will be surging under the weight at a 45-degree angle. Then they'll have a cheap sports watch, to indicate that they're athletic. They'll have a baseball hat with something like a ship they served on," McFate continues. "The thing about private defense companies is that you are the rank you left the military with for life. If you left as a colonel, you'll always be a colonel. You will get commensurate responsibilities and authorities that go along with that. You can make the argument that fashion buttresses rank and authority structures in contracted companies."

I was curious about what our active military was actually wearing into battle, so in 2008 I attended the SoldierTech expo on the top floor of a Sheraton hotel overlooking the Pentagon.

After 9/11, hundreds of billions of dollars were thrown by the Pentagon to private defense contractors with the explicit intention of "overmatching the adversary" (read: outspending the enemy) with cutting-edge technological battle gear. Our troops were envisioned as "Future Fighters." It was optimistically projected (by companies that had received federal money to develop these things) that by 2008, U.S. soldiers were going to be clad in bulletproof uniforms that automatically tracked their vital signs and reported them to commanders and medics, who would digitally monitor their health. These *Iron Man* uniforms would also regulate the soldier's body temperature, control bleeding, and "provide nutrients." This suit, including kit, was supposed to weigh no more than 50 pounds. (It wasn't on the battlefield by 2008, and still isn't.)

In real life 2008, a soldier's kit consisted of a night-vision device, a combat helmet, Interceptor body armor, knee and elbow pads, protective eyewear, and an M4 carbine tricked out with various scopes and thermal aiming devices. For the wars in Iraq and Afghanistan, a soldier's kit would ideally weigh around 75 pounds. In reality, they often weighed up to 105 pounds.

Studies have shown that a soldier's performance level starts to noticeably decline if he is carrying more than one-third of his body weight. This is acknowledged by both the contractors and the military, who confess they have been woefully unsuccessful in reducing this burden. The "magic number" for the weight the military is allowed to lard onto an infantryman is an informal but generally acknowledged 86.5 pounds—roughly the weight of a ten-year-old child, distributed onto the body as ergonomically as possible. This 86.5 pounds is broken down into an endless long-division of grams, all exhaustively accounted for on the soldier's body, or more specifically his "trade space," as soldier's bodies are somewhat ghoulishly called by the private sector that caters to NATO's ever-improving style needs.

The problem is this: whenever a technological advancement enables a part of the kit to shrink, get lighter, or move to a more ergonomic part of the soldier, a piece of trade space opens up. The private sector, irresistibly drawn to this patch of technological nudity (and the potential moneys they can siphon from the defense budget for filling it) unfailingly comes up with a new, can't-survive-without-it technical "capability" to fill this void. The new thing, it is complained, often weighs a *teensy* bit more than the gadget whose trade space it is replacing. The result: our soldiers have been getting incrementally heavier, not lighter, in thrall to the military's shopaholic lust for new gadget-accessories.

I had to ask about the actual real-war ramifications of the army loading down our troops with excessive war tchotchkes, so I asked

Major Tevye Yoblick, a watch officer of domestic operations at Fort Belvoir who lived and worked in Iraq for nine months as part of a military transitions team.

"You start to overwhelm the soldier," said Major Yoblick. "Now we have 40 pounds of equipment over 40 pounds of body armor. By the time I layer on all my body armor, pouches, radios, ammo, etc., I can barely move. You end up wobbling along. Twenty years ago soldiers would dive behind cover. Now soldiers trot from one source of cover to another because they're so weighed down. The urge to lie down is now secondary to going into a crouch behind a Hummer. I am not going to do 3- to 5-second rushes unless I have to. Gone are the days when you could set a base of fire and have guys flank around an enemy position quickly. We don't move fast anymore."

Heavy kit, Yoblick adds, also results in more injuries: "If you put 60 to 80 pounds on a guy, and he falls, he can break an ankle, a leg, a wrist—because he's that much heavier. Multiply that by rough ground, and someone shooting at you. Plus, a gallon of water weighs 8 pounds, and a soldier needs a certain amount of gallons per day. Water can't be dehydrated."

The Department of Defense spends over $2 billion a year on military uniforms. Military uniforms are, by law, manufactured in the U.S., but there are only a handful of manufacturing facilities that hold the contracts—namely LION Apparel, American Power Source, Point Blank Solutions (a subsidiary of DHB Industries), and Eagle Industries. The Department of Defense always gives its uniform contracts to the lowest bidder; these companies then enjoy state and local subsidies and tax breaks. The minimum-wage employees of these facilities, the bulk of whom are African American women, make a salary that puts them below the official poverty line. Most have no health care benefits, and over half of full-time military uniform makers with children rely on Medicaid and food stamps to survive.

HOW TO DRESS LIKE TODAY'S DISCRIMINATING FIELD MERCENARY
Commentary by Sean McFate, Former Merc

❶ Oakley sunglasses

❷ Oakley tactical boots

❸ Fatigue Trousers: "Everybody who's anybody wears a brand called 5.11 'Round Robins.' You carry a special hunting knife inside of your right pocket, with the clip out. The blade is about 6 inches long. The pants have a reinforced inseam, so the knife doesn't wear out your pocket so much.

❹ SUUNTO Diving Watch: "It's a thief magnet, but it looks really awesome. It's got a huge dial , it does all sorts of things that are too complex to really work – an altimeter, a compass, multiple time zones."

❺ "In the jungle you want long sleeves for bugs, also for sunshine and critters and vines. The seasoned merc will have a long-sleeve safari shirt. You want light material that can dry quickly after rain, and you don't want too many pockets – that looks too Calvin Klein."

ON BELTS:

"I wear a very hardcore web belt. You could hang a tank off of it if you wanted to. It has a very heavy buckle. You can use it as a weapon – take it off and smack someone upside the head, and at least stop them. You can also use it at night to seal doors, for security. When I was in Burundi, they had sliding doors and I would cinch them at night with my belt. Off of your belt, you have a holder for a small mag light, and a Gerber multi-purpose tool. Not a Leatherman – a Gerber has bigger pliers. You have to clean your weapon with it, so you've got to have a good pair of needle-nose pliers, scissors, screwdrivers – Phillips and standard, a knife, a file and a bottle-opener for beer. That's the bare minimum. Some of these multi-purpose things become ridiculous. The younger merc will go out and get the super cool thing that probably costs like 600 dollars, but you don't want to be ostentatious with your multipurpose tool. When I look at younger mercs, they have so many attachments, I'm like, 'Do you really need that extra-small screwdriver?'"

Q. More attachments just make you gay?

"Yeah, exactly."

How to dress like today's discriminating field mercenary.

(The executive levels of these operations tend to do quite well, however. In 2005, the impresario of DHB Industries, David H. Brooks, held a bat mitzvah party for his daughter on top of Rockefeller Center, which the *Daily News* reported to have cost

$10 million. 50 Cent was flown in to perform at the event via company jet. Mr. Brooks does, however, have an enviable sense of personal style: the *New York Times* reported that he changed, mid-party, from "an all-leather, metal-studded suit into a hot-pink suede suit.")

❧

BY THE SUMMER OF 2008, the Bush administration had successfully depressed most of the free world, and I became interested in the peace movement, particularly Code Pink, a group of radical female antiwar activists who became famous for crashing into Congress to protest to the war in Iraq while wearing outrageous pink tutus and tiaras.

It was a swampy 92 degrees the June day in 2009 I went to report on what was supposed to be a large protest in Lafayette Park, in front of the White House.

It wasn't the sight I was expecting—no pink was visible. A couple dozen peaceniks were straggling about on the frying sidewalks. Several people in wheelchairs—war veterans with sooty combat jackets—held hand-scrawled sentiments against the war in Iraq on pieces of cardboard. One guy was wandering around wearing an OPEC sheik costume. The White House across the street looked cool, mutely elegant, and unperturbed in the shade behind its black iron gate.

I approached the most starkly committed-looking peacenik on the scene, a small, intense hunger striker with Rasputin-blue eyes and the words "WAGE LOVE" tattooed across his nose in block letters. His name, he told me, was Start Loving; he was visibly frying on the sidewalk next to a sign reading "Wage Love Vigil Day #132." His pink scarf, he explained, was to show solidarity with Code Pink. "They're the only group that I know that is worth a damn in this [peace movement]," said Start Loving. "One member told me the other day that she was getting discouraged. I immediately started to cry because if those guys give up, we have no hope. They're the only game in town."

I visited the Code Pink house on Capitol Hill, a brick row house which served as the Washington headquarters for activists from Code Pink's 250 local chapters around the globe. Inside, the atmosphere resembled a grubby, renegade sorority installation. The basement, I saw, was where the pink happened. It could have been the underground headquarters of Barbie's Rebellion— stacked to the ceiling with crates of pink garments, racks of tutus, storage boxes full of tiaras, glitter tubs, glue guns, pink paint, big picket signs, papier-maché heads; a confetti of pink sequins freckled the indoor-outdoor carpet. Upstairs, earnest young interns in shorts and tie-dye T-shirts were sitting around on pink couches, typing furiously on laptops. The mood was a bit dour—despite enormous efforts both on and behind the scenes, Code Pink was sharply aware of its failure to influence Congress to stop funding the war in Iraq.

Executive committee member Gael Murphy sighed. "We're feeling our tiaras have lost their glow, and that our predictable attention-getting and disruption has run its course," she lamented. "Our visibility, our pink, our street theater, is to get [the message] into the media that there *is* opposition, that there *is* an antiwar movement. . . . But we're being trivialized."

Medea Benjamin, cofounder of Code Pink, is a small, wry, wiry woman who once worked for the United Nations, and looks more like a member of Congress than someone who would disrupt their proceedings and shout at them in the halls.

"I'm a very serious person," she insisted. "Did I ever think that at fifty-six years old I'd be wearing tiaras and going to Congress and holding up signs?"

Code Pink did get attention, with their colorful antics. "That's right," Benjamin agreed. "Without the tiaras," she told me pointedly, "*you* wouldn't be here."

But a successful peace movement—like the movement against Vietnam—depends on a cultural zeitgeist to support it. In a post-MTV climate, a counterculture is paradoxically only credible when the mainstream media pays attention to it. Lack of media coverage and its result—an inability to get exhausted working people off the couch to join the fight—was taking a toll on Code Pink. "We have had eight demonstrations of over 100,000 people, some much larger, that got virtually no [media] attention—and no response from the White House," Benjamin explained.

This, I thought, might be the sharp double-edge of the pink glitter tiara.

I had to wonder, given my convictions about fashion determinism, if Code Pink was failing to maximize the use of fashion as a means of getting media attention for their message. To effectively fight a culture war, particularly in the censorious climate of a largely monopolized media, you need the right weapons. From a semiotic marketing perspective, Code Pink was inadvertently hobbling themselves with their own sartorial attack. Symbolic fashion references work on codified psychological levels in the unconscious reptile brain that are reductively simple. Viewed in this frame of mind, Code Pink was showing up uninvited in Congress (code: Daddy's office) looking like spoiled little girls in Disney princess costumes, and disrupting the "adult" proceedings by throwing inappropriate tantrums (code: spoiled infants). What does a civilized society do with spoiled babies, but ignore, spank, or remove them? Even when they were armed with serious, valid messages and legitimate white papers, Code Pink's natural political allies in Congress didn't feel comfortable standing next to them on camera—because being aligned with Code Pink, in public, was visually *embarrassing* for members of Congress who had been conditioning their professional wardrobes in the style-voodoo of truth-camouflage their entire political careers.

Washington DC wasn't about to stop having a superficial frat-boy mentality just because Code Pink was *morally right*, any more than these guys were going to let their mothers kiss them on the field in front of their friends after losing a high school football game.

Code Pink, thankfully, is still alive and kicking. As of 2014, they were still sticking their glittery magic wands into the gears of empire, most recently to protest the use of UAV drones.

But they really make me wonder: in order for people to give peace a chance, do peaceniks need better ballgowns? If a top couture luxury designer like Louis Vuitton started supporting Code Pink by clothing them—if TV stars and supermodels were compelled to support Code Pink because their protest-cessories were designed by Alexander Wang—wouldn't it be virtually impossible for our prurient press *not* to give them more coverage? How much more potential support might they then get for a serious antiwar movement?

I am loath to give any propers whatsoever to the Third Reich, but they undeniably knew a trick or two about the art of spectacle. What if, in order to atone for having designed those natty brown shirts and Hitlerjugend uniforms, Hugo Boss was required to turn Code Pink into a fashion spectacle with equal oomph? (In a truly just world, war profiteer David H. Brooks of Point Blank Industries, which DHB changed its name to in 2007, would be forced to provide appropriate couture for Code Pink. He should at least donate to them his pink suede suit.)

⁂

UNTIL THE VISIGOTHS SACK the city, one must participate in Washington DC's fashion strictures to properly play the
game. There are always ways to sneak in a bit of flair, however,
even within the most draconian fashion laws. Sean McFate, my
DC fashion hero, was kind enough to walk me through his style
motivations for the outfit he'd chosen for his speech at the United
Nations the next day.

"Tomorrow, I'm going to the UN to talk about peace-building
in Liberia. I'm gonna wear stuff that is meant to be disruptive, just
for my own amusement. I'm not trying to send a subtle middle
finger to anybody—this is just for my own secret humor. Since
I'm a known African mercenary, I will be wearing an Armani suit
with fashion-forward banker pinstripes—which you would never
see at the UN. It's to show I'm simpatico with Goldman Sachs: private military contractor, war profiteer, Goldman Sachs—there's
a linkage there.

Dr. Sean McFate's ruling-class accoutrements, and their subtle ironies.

"I'll wear a plain white shirt and an Hermès tie, because that's the secret power tie of all men in the Western world. It's an Hermès tie with somebody in Paris's idea of what African masks look like, all over it. For the pièce de resistance, I'm wearing cufflinks. The former minister of defense of Liberia, Charles Taylor's 'Teflon minister,' told me to go see a friend of his to have these cufflinks made. If somebody gets offended, I'll say that I got them when I was in Liberia: they're a tribute to Liberia. You could look at it two ways. I'm a colonialist mercenary, or I'm a USA development person who's sympathetic and in touch with the culture of Liberia. I'm supporting local economies. I can't really be accosted for supporting local indigenous artistry."

I asked, do they have blood-diamond eyes?

"No, I didn't want to be vulgar!" Sean laughed. "But they are made of blood gold."

3

UTAH, HO! / THE CHASTITY BELT

Here Come the Brides

⌐—

I had never been to Utah, when I went in 2010—nor had I spent any time doing anything but flying over or driving through America's midsection. I figured I was in for a mind-set (and fashion bent) unlike the coastal areas I was accustomed to, but I hadn't the foggiest idea how different they might be.

Shortly before my trip to Utah, I was a guest on a political talk radio show. An older lady I'll call Brandee called in from the heartland to berate me. "You're so left-wing I am surprised you don't fall off the edge of the *world!*" she shouted as an opening salvo.

"Thank God we fought the Crusades or we'd all be speaking *Arabic*," she spat, before going on to lament my failure to recognize that our "radical Muslim" president, "Barack *HUSSEIN* Obama," was obviously on a covert mission to force good Christian Americans to convert to Islam. She pronounced his middle name in two hissing, heavily accented hate-bullets—*Huss-SAAYNE*—to underline the sheer *obviousness* of the president's secret Islamist mandate, and how blisteringly stupid I was not to recognize this.

Brandee would have been a riot if she had been played by Amy Poehler—but she wasn't, and she brought home for me the fact that people like her actually exist: angry, rigid folk that literally believe, with unwavering obedience, everything that the Bible and Fox News tell them, and likewise trust any form of idealism stamped with the Christian/conservative/Republican brand names she trusted. Brandee's brain had clearly been put through the conservative myth-chipper so many times it was mulched to a self-affirming groupthink pulp, designed to reduce every complex issue down to a stark, polar battle of Good vs. Evil.

Our nation's political dialogue in late 2010 had taken this sharp turn into a place where it wasn't even issue-based—it was just feverishly emotional, and increasingly compressed into bizarre bite-sized slogans like "Buck up or stay in the truck."

Flying into Utah, the Great Salt Lake looked breath-freezingly clear and clean—the frozen bits seemed to make frozen jigsaw shapes, black on darker black, textured like one of those silk and raised-velvet pseudo-hippie scarves I might have bought my ex-mother-in-law at Chico's.

I was the only person wearing all black on the entire plane.

Many of the families traveling with small children on the plane to Salt Lake City looked barely older than children themselves. The young mothers were pale and baby-fat zaftig; the shell-shocked-looking young dads looked barely old enough to require regular shaving. These kids were given to wearing similar alternative rock-esque gear to analogous twenty-somethings in other cities: jeans, hoodie sweatshirts, burnout T-shirts spangled with brand logos in glitter and Gothic lettering. But for Utah residents, these items contained a new dimension I hadn't seen before. The clothes of the under-thirty were distinctly *light*— they favored whites, pinks, pastel colors. Their outfits resembled something an upbeat religious youth auxiliary of the the Lawrence Welk Orchestra might wear, after an aggressive rhinestoning by Ed Hardy.

On the plane to Utah, I also noted that I had never seen so many unusual things attached to people's heads in the same place before.

Every baby under the age of two seemed to have been born already sporting fuzzy animal ears. One young dad was wearing a white crocheted faux-Rastafarian hat that I figured would only really look proper on the ghost of Marvin Gaye, during his Annunciation. My stewardess was wearing a kind of bridal, beaded headband with a baseball-size cluster of seed pearls. Two rows ahead, a passenger was wearing an ivory satin, bead-encrusted headpiece—another bridal-decoration on a non-bride. Two rows behind me, a girl was wearing a white knit headband with a woolen rose, for more of a "Bride of the Gnome Shepherd" look. There were so many head-flowers and pearly knobs hovering just above the seat backs that the cabin seemed to have been spun into a giant bridal garden by Vera Wang. The Utah residents seemed to be collectively attracted to headgear that symbolized a kind of luminous, fluffy virtue: a *halo effect*.

On the drive from the airport I noted that one of Utah's more popular bumper stickers read: "Buck Ofama."

My first stop in Utah was to be Park City, a ski town forty-five minutes outside of Salt Lake City, invaded by filmmakers and their ilk annually for the Sundance Festival.

I occasionally got the feeling that the local residents don't actually like the Sundance visitors all that much—particularly when I was walking down the side of the main road late one morning, coffee in hand, and a monster truck full of spirited local ski rats deliberately skidded into a large pothole in order to drench me in an icy wave of slush. I could hear them laughing as they squealed away. It certainly didn't improve my all-black avant-ski look, but

I understood their need to lash out: they were the locals, and I clearly resembled the obnoxious invaders from the entertainment industrial complex, who held lavish events on their turf to which they were never invited.

As a political activist, Robert Redford has always dug in his boot heels and fought a good fight on behalf of the environment. But I have always reflexively hated the *Sundance Catalog*, which I have long regarded as being aimed at rich white ladies who love things that *look* natural and ethnic, as long as they are not *actually* natural or ethnic. Their absurdly expensive, Italian merino cognac suede shearling Western apparel is maddening enough without the faux Native American frontier jewelry: turquoise and macramé creations, with sterling bars engraved with New Age slogans like "Smile" or "Peace," in Comic Sans font (made by a tribe of "Sundance Artisans" possessed of "diversity").

I noticed that Gilt Group, the online shopping phenomenon, was offering their own Sundance Collection, specifically aimed at attendees: tarty little tartans for that laborless day-labor look; furs and furless furs, thick earth-tone cashmeres, stiletto-heeled boots with waffle soles in front, just in case a hot little urban cowgirl needed to do a little boiler maintenance in her faux log-cabin ski lodge with the ersatz-Navajo throw pillows, or drive her four-wheel-drive Lexus to the Whole Foods to buy more Duraflame logs.

There is a main shopping strip in the middle of town, with the usual tourist-area surfeit of T-shirt stores. These shirts and coffee mugs, in large number, tended to feature depictions of the enviable life of a rascally cartoon moose who was apparently the official mascot of Park City, UT. This moose—a Joe Camel, frat boy–type scallywag, was living the ski bum dream-saga. Over blocks' worth of T-shirts, he could be seen wearing sunglasses, smoking hand-rolled cigarettes, shredding on snowboards, elbowing up to a bar with a frothy lager, hitting on chesty blondes wearing bikinis and skis (who were clearly excited to commit unspecified acts of bestiality with this suave, turtleneck-wearing party moose).

A film festival during winter in a mountain ski town presented a fascinating sartorial problem for film industry people. To wit: how do you indicate and telegraph your LA genius (read: sex appeal) in parka weather? How do actors, whose work primarily depends on their ability to look good while naked, indicate this fact while dressing for 15-degree evenings?

Ingenious solutions for arctic underdressing were found. Occasionally some starlet or socialite would stalk into a screening— late, so as not to arouse the adoration of too many fans—wearing a spaghetti-strap dress and five-inch Louboutin stunt-heels. This raised intriguing questions, like, how did she get across the black ice in the parking lot? Was she carried? How does she escape? Does she run directly from the exit door into an armored sauna?

I summed up the fashion code for the Sundance Festival as "alpine Brentwood"—a regional fashion phenomenon epitomized that year by a number of tall, coltish young ingenues working a particular waifish, Zooey Deschanel womanchild look: brightly colored-tights under juvenile miniskirts, pixie hairdos, tiny jackets, and boots. These outfits would have been perfectly innocent and legitimate if the weather was 50 degrees warmer—but it wasn't. This day look was clearly intended to suggest that these elfin young beauties with their bangs in their eyes were so *ethereal*—so knock-kneed and free-spirited and feebly adorable—that they had all *accidentally* tottered out into streets lined with five-foot snowbanks in clothes insufficient for human survival. After a few hours, it seemed obvious that their haplessly insufficient covering was in fact *intentional*; they were shivering like waxed chihuahui in order to inspire the notion, in the males of their tribe, that they were *in dire need of physical protection.* Actors, of course, are professionally sensitive people, and masochistic tricks are their trade.

The actresses were literally *dying* for some hot young director to be seized with a caveman-like impulse to drag them into one of the local boutiques and force them to wear an actual coat. If they had been responsibly dressed for the weather, they wouldn't have been looking hazardously vulnerable enough—they wouldn't have been *trying hard enough to get work,* playing kooky-yet-lovable leading ladies. Their fashion statements were supreme sacrifices of comfort that whimpered: *Cast me: I have no sense of self-preservation whatsoever, and I need a gallant, BMW-driving prince to save me from hypothermia. Also, I can cry real tears, and I am willing to be topless.*

On the opposite swing of that style pendulum were the smart, over-thirty women of the film profession—directors, producers, and other Future Penny Marshalls of America—who were sporting an "I am obviously not trying" assortment of sensible parkas, old plaid flannel shirts and chronic bitterness culled from the Janeane Garofalo collection. Their fashion statement, as well as I could decipher it: *I am here to work, and I hate you. I hate snow, I hate festivals, and all I really want right now is to be back in Culver City with my recently adopted special-needs dog, watching all seventy-four episodes of* Battlestar Galactica *for the third time.*

James Franco was the man of the moment that year, having recently received an abundance of kudos for his portrayal of a mountaineer forced to saw off his own arm for survival. He was hopping around the festival spreading his pervasive boyish charm, earning one fan at a time, politician-style. In fealty to his professional dominance, other actors seemed to be dressing directly from James Franco's personal wardrobe, as if to say, "You can't have Franco, but hey! I am a viable sub-Franco to cast in your next production." Franco and the unlicensed phalanx of non-Francos were all sporting a carefully casual look that suggested an impish conflation of James Dean and Daniel Boone: plaid Woolrich hunting jackets with the collars turned up; unruly hair, newsboy hats, work boots, carefully distressed jeans, omnipresent telephones. It was a dress style suggestive of *action*—real, kinetic he-man work, like bear-baiting, lumber-jousting, or self-amputating. It was not particularly suited to what they were really doing, which, in large part, was sitting in leather armchairs chairs in the Sundance lodge headquarters in front of the fireplace, reading copies of *Entertainment Weekly.*

Style-wise, the writers, Hollywood's most tortured yet narcissistic underclass, all seemed to have emerged fully formed from the knit stocking cap of a Wes Anderson underdog. Writers tend to be ectomorphic fellows. They are noticeably less virile and robust than the actors. To compensate for their lower sexual stock-market value, they employ intrigue, by being visibly more eccentric: straggly beards, Elvis Costello glasses, a carefully selected Pantone spectrum of layered, wash-faded shirts visible under professorial blazers in balding corduroy. Male writers truly in need of attention occasionally wore kooky winter hats—an occasional Peruvian knit with earflaps, sometimes featuring a scraggly pom-pom. Their style intends to project *sensitivity to content*—an *in-touchness* with their feminine side (or at least enough to write female dialogue). They carry dog-eared books, magazines, and scripts under their meatless arms and shuffle around, hunched beneath the agonizing weight of their incredibly massive brains and deep, tortured souls. Their whimsically mismatched gloves are actually a *cri de coeur,* lamenting: *O, Fortuna! I am barely making six figures a year! Even after selling both the screenplays I wrote in grad school at NYU! Kill me quickly and mercifully . . . not tonight, but soon . . .*

Occasionally a writer would stand out by having an ego collectively heavier than the rest. He would stomp in hours too late for breakfast, and seek his first coffee of the day bedecked in a *silver* parka, which bellowed, "Beware and submit, beta males, for I can actually *ski,* and I obviously engaged in heterosexual *sex* last night. Therefore, I am the only genius in the room comparable to Norman Mailer."

I thought I was going to see a lot of worst-case-scenario entertainment industry fashion: that Ron Howard default look that workhorsemanly producers tend to wear at film festivals and theater workshops. It's a uniform, of sorts: a baseball hat with the Dreamworks logo (or its factual equivalent), a letterman jacket with cheap black leather sleeves and the Paramount logo on the back (or its factual equivalent), a polar-fleece zipper jacket, over a polo shirt bearing the embroidered logo of an NBC cancelled sitcom. *I am an industry veteran,* this look confesses. *Yes, art IS commerce. I have no unseemly opinions that might impede my ability to write dialogue for seven seasons of* iCarly. *I set no fires, kill no hookers, make no art, and I will never inspire anyone, even my own children, for the sake of whose private education I will continue to deliver utterly predictable creative output, on time. Whatever project I am on, rest assured it will be safely mediocre and sponsor-secure by the time I take my clean, dependable fingers off it.*

(I found myself very pleasantly surprised, however, to see a couple of these guys wearing impressively detailed, hand-knit, Nordic après-ski yarmulkes.)

Tech guys of the film industry seem to look and act like band roadies. They have darker, dirtier parkas, deeper hangovers, and detectable body odor. They look like they haven't slept six contiguous hours in the last eight years. At Sundance, packs of fourteen or more of them seemed to be crashing together in small rented timeshare condos surrounded by spent beer cans, crushed coffee cups, pizza boxes, and wadded paper napkins. They look much older than they actually are, from spending too much time in vans. Their jeans, shoes, and hair are *actually* filthy—they come by their grime honestly, through hard work and deep resentment.

≈

WHILE ON TRIPS, I had been buying random clothing objects that I would never ordinarily buy, expressly as personality stretchers.

To hang around Sundance and force myself to be more social, I brought a gold leather jacket that I'd found a couple of months previously in a Rhode Island consignment shop. It's a lurid, bright metallic eighties-redux-of-the-1930s jacket: dolman sleeves, a drop waist with a hip snap for a blouson effect in back, and a wide, deep black fox collar. It looks like something Joan Collins might have worn to drop by Liberace's house to borrow a cup of Xanax. It really needed to be worn with a velvet turban, a hot pink satin gown covered in bugle beads, and a gun to young Ryan O'Neal's head. I felt like a glitzy jackass in it, but I discovered the jacket wasn't nearly as outrageous as I imagined once I started walking around the festival in it. One forgets that one might be wearing a jacket made of severed koala heads and blue fire and still be invisible in the midst of young actresses who are actively freezing to death.

Attention is the biggest commodity in Hollywood, and if I wanted to compete for it, the bar had already been set: with anything less than a reckless swan dive into the lap of pneumonia, a girl was simply invisible.

■ ■ ■ ■ ■ ■ ■ ■ ■ ■ ■ ■ ■ ■ ■ ■ ■ ■

WHAT I ACTUALLY KNEW about Salt Lake City Utah: almost nothing. I was approaching American cities the same way that I did designer boutiques—with as little an impression as possible going in. There is always some level of informational scum that rises to the top of your consciousness about any area, due to whatever tragedies, disgraces, and/or perversions they hosted that made it to the top of the news cycle—and whatever prejudices members of your family might hold.

My mother had strong opinions about Mormonism stemming from her experiences as the piano teacher of a particularly gifted young Mormon lady. "Mormon women are supposed to have five children. *Five*. I heard from a doctor that by the time those women are on their fourth pregnancy, they all come in for Valium prescriptions." She always had suspicions about religions she perceived as being particularly strict about controlling women's sexuality. "There's usually something very sexually *murky* going on under the surface," she would say, cocking an archly penciled eyebrow.

I naturally assumed that Salt Lake City was conservative, and that its center of gravity was the Mormon Church; I knew that the Mormon Tabernacle Choir was considered one of the chief wonders of human noisemaking. In my early childhood, Utah was proudly represented by the handsome Osmond family, their billowing hair, gleaming cliffs of teeth, and matching white suits. The Osmonds seemed to be a virtuously airlocked, closed set of a supertight family, collectively bent on creating the wholesome televised mythology that they shared an *even tighter* family connection than seemed to be possible in real life. They were so mysteriously close, it looked a bit sinister to me even as a first-grader. "Wait," I'd ask my mom. "You mean that guy is singing a love duet with his *own sister*?"

The previous year, during the trial of Yearning for Zion ranch leader/polygamist Warren Jeffs, I had been obsessed with the aggressive style of his sister-wives. Their identical high-collared, heavyweight poplin dresses with starched box pleats in a sterile rainbow of colors rarely seen outside of hospitals (powdered-egg yellow, incubator pink, industrial blue, the aquamarine of medical plastic) seemed to have developed like great folk art: without reference to anything outside their own hermetically sealed mythology. Their style code was a riot of contradicting messages: muscular-obedient, predatory-submissive. With their princess sleeves defensively puffed up to their ears and their shellacked, French-braided angel-hair teased halfway to heaven, they looked *bristled up*, like threatened raccoons or menaced blowfish. Their hackles were permanently *risen*. Like the uniforms of Hasidic Jewry, the sister-wife look was intended to declare their separation and difference from the rest of society. It was primed and pumped for cultural combat; very *Little House on the Fuck You*. Every time I found footage of them leaving the courthouse I would shriek with fashion ecstasy; as soon as daylight hit their faces, they would wrap on the same Oakley fly-eye sunglasses I knew were favored by Special Forces operatives and soldiers of fortune. In my mind's eye I always envisioned the sister-wives walking in a hor-

PARK CITY, UTAH: ROSEMARY SHOWS YOU HOW IT'S DONE, FOREVER

All a lovely color-coordinated lichen-green and ivory. She works in any decade, any time, any place. Timeless, sharp, elegant, practical. You can't see the grocery cart she's pushing, but if she looks like a million bucks just buying frozen peas, you can only guess what kind of swanky outfit she pulls together for special occasions. Princess Grace couldn't have put together a superior snow-day look.

izontal row in slow motion, à la *Reservoir Dogs*, their brown suede Hush Puppies hitting the ground in time to the opening licks of "In-A-Gadda-Da-Vida."

Salt Lake City had also planted a flag in my consciousness for being the place where angelic, blonde fourteen-year-old Elizabeth Smart had been kidnapped at knifepoint straight from the bedroom she shared with her nine-year-old sister. The tragedy was like manna from heaven for the supermarket tabloids, who had been stuck since 1996 in a rut of nostalgic keening over the unsolved murder of JonBenét Ramsey. There was a new underage blonde victim in town, and the tabloids spent the better part of a year wallowing in a wrongful lather of outrage, crammed with visuals too perfect to be believed. It was as if the central casting gods suddenly took pity upon the *National Enquirer*. Elizabeth Smart was a Class-A archetype of virgin innocence. Since she was an accomplished harpist, there were many iconic photos of her wearing a long white dress, posing with her heavenly instrument, smiling an open and unself-conscious smile, sometimes gazing upward toward a divine light.

The story became even more sensational eight months after her abduction, when, instead of her body being found (as is grimly expected in such crimes), Elizabeth Smart was miraculously found and returned to her family.

Then the horrible details came out. The Smart girl, after being abducted at knifepoint, had been taken as a "bride" by a berobed street person with messianic delusions who called himself Emmanuel, in a bizarre drug and sex ceremony, with the full complicity of his wife and apostle, the perfectly named Wanda Barzee. Emmanuel wasn't aware that his child bride had been featured on *America's Most Wanted* the same week he brought her to a house party full of tattooed burlesque dancers. His hostesses thought there was something distinctly bizarre about the young girl who followed

Emmanuel around, wearing long robes and a veiled face, trying to encourage other women to become her savior's "vessel."

Elizabeth Smart's cultural training hadn't given her any anti-bodies to combat this particular violation; she was utterly primed to be an obedient wife. Certainly her survival instincts kicked in and made her believe it was her destiny to be the second wife of Emmanuel the prophet (which was not as outrageous a cognitive leap to make in Utah, around Church of Latter-Day Saints circles, as it would be somewhere with a less magico-realistic cosmology—say, among a bunch of Minnesota Lutherans).

Elizabeth Smart was lost in plain sight for eight months.

What I found to be the most terrible part of the saga was how easily people were *unable to see Elizabeth Smart* once all of her fashion indices and accoutrements were taken away. Without her harp, blonde curls, and virginal white dress, suddenly nobody had any idea who she was, despite her image being on the covers of countless magazines and newspapers. Dressed in a Bride of Crazy Religious Street-Person costume, even *Elizabeth Smart herself* didn't know who she was. Elizabeth Smart had endured the most intense case of social brainwashing via fashion victimization since Patty Hearst. All *perception* of Elizabeth Smart was removed when her costume changed.

I read that shortly after she returned to her family, she had asked if she'd be allowed to play herself in the inevitable TV movie. This seemed horrifying at the time; nobody wanted her to go through a traumatic re-creation of her kidnap/rape for any-thing so gauche as the small screen. But I thought it was logi-cal and pragmatic of her to assume she'd play herself, given the culture we live in. She wanted a proper dramatic catharsis—and for exactly the right reasons that classical drama existed in the first place. She wanted to see the three-act structure, and she wanted to see her journey resolved, the one way society has made available to her to experience these things within the human community.

I think Elizabeth Smart understood, on a subconscious level, that hers was a public ordeal that demanded to be seen to be understood—that it was, in large part, *a costume drama*. One day she was an angelic girl with a harp; the next day she was veiled religious weirdo, chosen to wander the streets of her own city with her husband the Jibbering Prophet and her sister-wife Wanda Barzee.

⚎

MORE THAN 11,000 FLIGHTS—including mine—were cancelled over the weekend of February 1, 2011, due to blizzards, so I spent a couple of days trying to decode the regional fashion of Salt Lake City proper.

I was stuck for three days in a hotel that looked like it had been designed by the architectural wing of Muzak—geriatric and sterilized, like all the bass lines had been replaced by string arrangements, and the oboe had smothered and replaced the saxophone. The room had an interesting view—the cold, flat city felt like it was sitting at the bottom of a bowl of blue-white mountains— and the strangely outdated decor seemed to spring from this isolated, snow-driven purity. My suite had a kind of adult-infantile, wilted-debutante, *Green Acres*—era Eva Gabor princess-telephone theme. There was an actual Kleenex-box cozy, an electric brass chandelier, and beige vinyl wallpaper printed with a white filigree design—the same Levitz French Gallery will to fanciness that, I supposed, inspired such classics as the Buick Regal and better country-western wigs.

Decor and fashion are relatable to sharks and relationships in that all must move constantly or die. Wallpaper only ages as well as fabric prints. It is very difficult to freeze your aesthetic clock and still serve the fickle demands of allure. Unless your wallpaper and/or pants are of a piece with your own totally committed flavor of batshit whimsy and uniqueness (like Leigh Bowery's *Star Trek* themed living room, or the wackily inspired Madonna Inn in San Luis Obispo) you mostly can't rely on patterns you bought twenty years ago to still possess the same energetic punch they did when you first admired them.* In most cases, they will look stuck— aesthetically constipated.

On the block near my hotel there were pawnshops and something I had never seen in any city before—used adult magazine stores. The prevailing logic seemed to be that inhabitants of Salt Lake City may or may not have purchased pornographic materials in a Sanka-cranked moment of weakness, but they were too incredibly decent to have ever actually *utilized* them for the gruesome purpose of masturbation, and they were therefore still recyclable, and cootie-free.

Salt Lake City women of childbearing age tend to be blonde— not in the aggressively cheap, bleach-white way that I am, but in the really expensive, "my hair is naturally triple-shaded in this two-hundred-dollar, foil-process" way. The blonde processing my hotel reservation was an ice-cold, Young Republican press secretary-type, to whom God had apparently given the superhuman ability to sum up my character with a single glance at my black, urban, crypto-sadist outfit and stare directly into my pupils. Her gaze contained the subtext: "You are a godless urban whore, obviously sent by the Goat Lord to test my patience and my vigilance against undead, unmarried, pill-snorting, serial thrill-

---

* Unless a look comes back the exact same way as it did the first time, twenty years later (usually there are subtle variations indicating irony), the signifiers of said pants and/or wallpaper are symbolically flipped and relegated to the netherworld of self-parody. "Camp" successfully reanimates any look, no matter how outdated, much in the way that William Shatner resurrected his own career by creating a persona that gleefully undermined his old persona.

aborters like yourself. After Judgment Day, I will rain gasoline down upon you, to reinvigorate the fires of your eternal torment."

I was unable to talk her into giving me a free room upgrade, even though the hotel was over 50 percent empty. (It occurred to me that the exact flavor of her derision was very much like that of certain Middle Eastern cab drivers who have had the apparently vast displeasure of transporting me home late at night from various wine bars.)

Stylewise, women's fashion in Salt Lake City is characterized by "modesty"—a very loaded word when applied to religious people and womenswear. The women and young girls wore long skirts, far more than in other cities—ankle scrapers. There was nary a visible knee in town for girls of any age.

My baseline research technique—my quick and dirty means of aggregating sartorial information to take a city's fashion pulse— was to visit the best high-end consignment shops (where rich ladies thin out their closets and earn funny money for extras like dog jewelry) and the low-end, hard-luck thrift stores on the poor side of town. This way I was able to gather a general notion of an area's tastes, across the economic spectrum.

I chose the Deseret Industries Thrift Store, which seemed to be the largest and most exhaustive secondhand clothing store in the Salt Lake area.

My first impression, skimming through the racks, was of a weirdly persistent infantilism visible in the women's clothes. There was a spellbinding glut of adult women's fuzzy flannel pajama bottoms with cartoon illustrations on them: happy cats playing team sports, top-hatted snowmen skiing on candy canes, frolicking dogs and reindeer, snowflakes and Christmas ornaments. I found an adult-size pair of polka-dotted footie pajamas, which, unlike the ones I had found the previous year in New York at Comme des Garçons, were not in the least bit ironic.

From mass-produced textile prints, one can often derive the same thrill one gets from viewing bad art, when a design unintentionally blurts out the exact opposite of what it intends. One extremely strange print featured what appeared to be blue, stillborn baby teddy bears with icicles protruding from their skulls—which seemed to articulate the unspoken, unresolved id of the pro-life atmosphere.

In terms of women's clothing—a Salt Lake City girl in her twenties is given the narrowest possible window of self-expression. She is supposed to go straight from virgin to matron with no stops and no dancing and no passing Go and no knee-showing in between. The entire Mormon style seems built around tamping down women's sexuality into the smallest, most joyless, utilitarian, entirely male-dominated portal: child insertion and child delivery. Women are essentially baby vending machines.

A connection appeared for me between the ladies on the plane wearing knit flowers on their heads, and the babies wearing fuzzy animal ears. It seemed to me that the women in Salt Lake City who hadn't gone completely retrograde unto rejecting their entire upbringings and becoming inked-up Gothic Jezebels mostly seemed to confirm my suspicion that a great many Salt Lake City women elect to wear *grownup variations of baby clothes.*

Due, I supposed, to a nearly fanatical reverence for Christmas, there was an enormous section of festive holiday garments. I discovered that in Salt Lake City, festive means *vestive.* It may be an intrinsically conservative place, but women's holiday vests are *totally off the motherfucking chain.* There were hundreds of handmade vests, wrought in obsessive-compulsive hand-stitched appliqué, suggesting the kind of cloistered sexual frustration that produced masterpieces like the *Book of Kells.* There were entire cottage scenes with intricate flower gardens and purebred dogs. One was chock a block with patchwork velvet Christmas Cats. One crocheted vest verging into the realm of soft sculpture featured 3D bumblebees and sunflowers as big as your fist. All the vests resembled something your grandmother's church group might have buried their only suspected lesbian in—but the workmanship was awe-inspiring. I thought they should have a huge editorial fashion spread devoted to their glory, if not an entire magazine (perhaps the as-of-yet uninvented Condé Nast publication "Harlequin and Toadstool.")

Another rack contained a broad array of what I concluded had to be Mormon "temple garments," because I couldn't imagine another context in which they made sense. They were shapeless, off-white or pale yellow, angelic smock-nightgown things—not wholly unlike bridesmaid-wear, but built as sturdily and washably as nurse uniforms in thick poly blends.

The multiple racks of used, sensible low-heeled white dress shoes suddenly made more sense. There were rituals going on in this town all the time, requiring costumes that could be easily laundered, and I would never know what they were. But these garments comprised a hefty percentage of Salt Lake City's thrift surplus.

I realized that I could not wear a long pastel floral dress and feel like anything but a potential victim—such dresses can only be properly accessorized with abstinence and harps. This look centers around literal virgin-worship—hence the necessity of bridal day-wear and halo flowers. The print on your pajamas is the wallpaper for the nursery of your infantilized adulthood, where you stay . . . forever. It would require a fourteen-year-old Elizabeth Smart mind-set, pre-kidnapping—a teenage experience totally devoid of black leather, rebellion, and pop-psychology. A total submission before God and Dad and husband and state, forever and ever, amen.

The Deseret Thrift Store proved to be a source of total sartorial revelation: I ran into the only Goths in town. They were a couple, clearly suffering after a long night of godlessness. The young lady had a severe wedge hairstyle that was black in the back, orange-blonde in front. She told me she was a "dancer," pronouncing it in such a downturned way as to have preinstalled, fingerless airquotes. Her boyfriend, a weedy, green young man with vintage oval glasses, hair like a wet nutria, and Frankenstein creepers, told me he was in two bands—one called Redemption, one called Zombiance.

"Redemption—is that a Christian band?" I asked.

"Nope. I laugh at the magic underwear," he said, with the brave defiance of those who have intellectually abandoned their religion yet still fear its concepts of sin and retribution. I had forgotten the other famous Thing about Salt Lake City—the Mormon muslin underwear that never comes off. I asked where one might go to find a set—Victoria's Lament?

The great advantage to being a certain kind of fashion dork is that you make natural friends wherever you happen to see one another, anywhere on the globe. On my last night in town, I ended up in a conversation with a waitress who I thought looked super-cool with her dyed auburn hair, severe bangs, cool vintage glasses, and plaid pencil skirt—she was clearly a member of my fashion tribe, and in this least likely of places. It was a great relief to me; we greeted each other like I imagine the only two black guys in Utah would, if they ever saw each other.

I gave her a rough outline of my research project, and why I was there.

"Oh God," she enthused, grabbing my sleeve, and dropping her voice to a conspiratorial whisper. "Before you go, you really have to go check out the children's clothes in the store window across the street. Those will tell you *everything* you want to know about Salt Lake fashion."

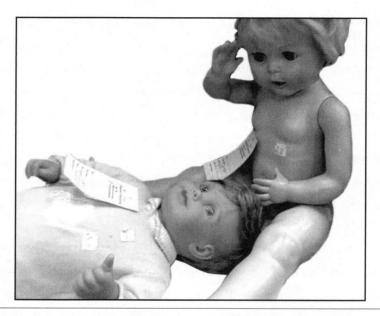

PERHAPS THE FILTH IS IN MY MIND ALONE, (BUT . . . REALLY?)

I am going to go way out on a limb, here, and suggest that if this is the kind of accidental expression of sexual angst you can find in the toy display case of a Mormon thrift store . . . perhaps a weency bit of sex education in Utah schools might not be the worst thing that could happen. I mean, look how dilated the little guy's pupils are.

So, after dinner, thus advised, I wandered across the street.

And there it was, in the window.

Knee high. A mannequin about the size of a six-year-old girl, in a ruffly white tulle creation that gave off every possible signal and indication of being (at least to the eyes of an outsider like myself) a kinder-polygamy wedding gown.

⧓

ON THE PLANE HOME, I reflected that Salt Lake City has a kind of bipolar fashion approach. It's not really as simple as dress codes of the faithful vs. dress codes of the faithless. The dominant dress code is intended to read as innocence, but what it really declares is submission to Men, God, and the State.

The fashion statement for Salt Lake City, boiled down to its crudest binary essentials, is *Yes Daddy/No Daddy*.

After her ordeal, Elizabeth Smart appeared to have processed her terrible experience as well as anyone could have possibly hoped. She was very poised and firm in court, frank and clear about her terrible experience. She sounded grounded, strong, and sane—a recovery she attributed in one interview to knowing herself as a member of her own family.

But I hope that she remembers that it took the critical eyes of a house full of tattooed strippers to make the call that finally returned her to her family, and her senses. It was the subculture outsiders who were able to see through the veil that made Elizabeth Smart invisible, even to herself.

4

JACKSON, WYOMING /
THE FROST BELT

Sled Dogs, Cowboys, and Wolf-Fur Codpieces

My aunt who lives in Jackson, Wyoming, couldn't understand why I wanted to come there to look at fashion.

"There's nothing in Jackson but fleece, fleece, fleece," she wrote. She had sent along an issue of *Wyoming Woman* magazine, ostensibly to discourage me from bothering with Jackson.

"You Know You're a Wyoming Woman If . . ." began a list:

- You think lingerie is tube socks and flannel pajamas
- You often see people wearing hunting clothes at social
  events
  and
- You design your child's Halloween costume to fit over
  a snowsuit.

Carolyn Johnson, a rancher interviewed in the magazine, articulated the sartorial thrust of Wyoming women thusly: "Women

ranchers are a mixture of blue denim and lace . . . People think
that ranching is a romantic way of life. But when you're wearing
insulated overalls and muck boots and are tired and dirty, it's not
always pleasant . . . Ranchers also need to be feminine—a lady and
a wife. You can be both."

I was unable to grasp the logic of simultaneously being a lady
and a wife, but she definitely had me at "muck boots." Paired with
the opportunity to witness the beginning of the International Pedigree Stage Stop Sled-Dog Race—"The Super-Bowl of Mushing,"
according to its own official program—I figured Jackson would be
a fashion show I couldn't afford to miss.

"In Jackson," said my sage cab driver from the airport, "everyone has an advanced degree and a dog. They also say that in Jackson, men are men, and so are a few of the women. It's where the
Mormons come to party, because God can't see over the Tetons."

The Tetons, he informed me, were so named by French trap-
pers, because they look like tits.

Jackson is a well-heeled resort town, where the bulk of the
economy stems from recreation for the wealthy: skiing and dude
ranches. There are the usual commercial features of any rich
enclave—bistros and boutiques—but all are blinged out with a
distinct Western theme. The dog race would start in the town
center, under a monolithic arch composed entirely of tangled ant-
lers. The tourist-focused art galleries are full of bronze Reming-
ton cowboys twirling lassos at full gallop and portraits of noble
hunting dogs. All of Jackson seems to be reclining in a cozy lodge
amid bone chandeliers, knotty pine floors, and folksy ceramics.
Sofa cushions are invariably woven into Native American–esque
textiles. The landscape makes the art of the late Thomas Kinkade
look slightly less like the squirtings of a blueberry syrup–poisoned
mind: there really *are* places in the world where log cabins brim
with amber-colored light in luminous mounds of pristine snow

against a purple horizon, and nobody locks their doors. (I figured this was because it was really just too fucking cold. You have to be somewhat well-off just to afford survivable heat. Whatever criminal underclass there might have been has been literally *frozen out*.)

I'd always been close to my kid uncle Rick, who was a teenager when I was born. He had been sorting through a minor identity crisis shortly before my trip, so he volunteered to be my research assistant. I'd watched him go through many fashion transformations over the years—from plaid-shirted Colorado boy to intrepid hitchhiker to Volkswagen bus hippy. As he became a builder of houses and boats, he became a swashbuckling, gumbooted houseboat pirate, and spent most of my childhood as a freewheeling connoisseur of international ladies and a terror of Sausalito pool tables. When I was twenty-one he fell in love, got married, and abruptly transformed into an ideal Devoted Yuppie Dad in clean polo shirts who drove my cousins around in a Subaru station wagon for two decades. I thought he did the parenting job a little *too* well—in sanding all the rough edges out of his wardrobe, it seemed to me he had rubbed off too many vital parts of himself, like a Victorian lady who amputated her toes to fit into conspicuously narrow boots. I hoped to convince him that he had only temporarily stunted himself by wading around in the shallow end of his closet for too long without getting his head wet.

I thought there was potential for a fashion breakthrough with Uncle Rick. He had recently laid the groundwork by making the Midlife Move Unthinkable and buying a tangerine orange 1957 Chevy truck. There was forgotten territory in him. I wanted to bully him into a cowboy outfit that would help him find it again.

A quest began in earnest to find Rick's declarative and empowering new fashion statement in Jackson's western apparel stores. For two days, I helped Rick reevaluate his wardrobe by shrieking things like, "Don't ever wear those shoes again! Those are the shoes of a simpering, emasculated half-man!"

Jackson's shops tend to sell a lot of mukluks, moccasins, and the kind of blatantly murderous furs that would get you lynched by PETA—Chinese rabbit pelts dyed burgundy and Kool-Aid purple, knitted into a kind of death angora. There is a sickly unspoken knowledge that these items came from unspeakable fur concentration camps where the tangy colors were probably squirted directly into the rabbits' eyes before the animals were peeled by dope-sick child slaves. But the weather awakens an atavistic need for fur. Jackson is so fucking cold, it stirs within the DNA a genetic memory of flint being knapped and mammoths being slain in the name of basic survival and bedspreads. Fur doesn't feel like a lazy, irresponsible fashion faux pas in this climate: it feels like blood is going to be allowed to continue circulating in your body.

⊰⊱

THERE ARE MANY STORES run by historian/collectors, trafficking in rare and genuine articles handmade by America's original inhabitants—Plains Indians living in harmony with the land, possessed of their unique artistry and a rich culture that Americans completely annihilated, and now fetishize.

I had recently read about the history of Pendleton Woolen Mills, which was very much entwined with that of Native Americans, who, in the pre-Columbian era, made their own blankets out of bark and fur. Pendleton, sensing that they could build a new market, unveiled their jacquard looms in Oregon in 1909, and sent designers on research trips to live with various Native American tribes in order to find out what colors and patterns they preferred.

It was an early example of the devastatingly seductive power of capitalism: Pendleton so nailed the Indian blanket market that

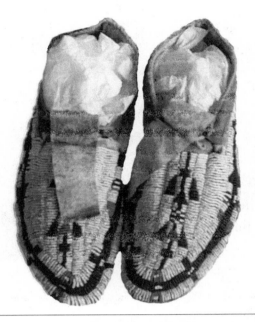

OUR GHASTLY AMERICA: HISTORY!

European settlers murdered the indigenous Plains Indians and vanquished their culture. Now we've decided that the normal stuff Indians made by hand to wear in their everyday lives—like their PARTY SHOES—are FUCKING PRICELESS WORKS of MUSEUM-QUALITY ART, which is now fetishized and hoarded by rich honkies ostensibly descended of the same people that genocided the Native Americans in the first place because they were a bunch of nude heathen layabouts who wasted their time putting zillions of beads on their shoes when they should have been more like the decent Puritans who were industriously killing them and stealing their land.

not only did all other Indian blanket-makers go out of business, but the Native Americans themselves pretty much stopped making blankets, because there was no point to such vexing labor. Pendleton blankets were wholly integrated into the very marrow of traditional Native American culture. Native American babies were wrapped and christened in Pendleton blankets. You'd wear a Pendleton blanket to dance in tribal ceremonies, you'd receive them as your wedding dowry, you'd pay down your debts with them. When you died, you would be wrapped in a Pendleton blan-

A Jackson, WY, store owner models his native day look. Pendleton Blanket Coat, Wild Bill Nietzsche 'stache, and a turquoise bolo the size of an omelet pan. This look takes a LIFETIME to acquire.

ket, and/or one would line your coffin. (These same patterns have been recently resurrected by hipster businesses like Opening Ceremony, and a whole new generation of rich white kids is sporting Navajo weaves on their car coats.)

The great thing about flea markets and consignment stores is that there is always hope of finding a holy grail—something that really belongs to *you,* that had been previously owned in error by someone else. Such finds are only possible in the gestalt of that particular nexus: a place where someone has recently *let go* of some precious, impossible-to-find object at the same serendipitous moment that you arrive to seize your rightful ownership of it.

I found such a grail in Jackson—a pair of short, black vintage cowboy boots with square toes that I'd been dreaming of since high school but never actually found. The only remaining boots intact from that era that I had ever seen were in child sizes; the rest, I assumed, had been loved and worn to death. The consignment store owner told me that it had taken a lot of wheedling to get the previous owner to release them. She didn't *wear* them, the woman explained. She was a hoarder with hundreds of pairs of classic cowboy boots, who just wanted to *own* them. The boots, the store owner felt, deserved to have a natural, useful *life*. I couldn't have agreed more.

One particular store—a combination of antique rummage and secondhand cowboy apparel—ended up cracking Wyoming fashion for me like a geode.

I didn't know people like this actually existed anywhere but in John Wayne movies—a magnificent, 100 percent solid, authentic American cowboy who had literally just come off of horseback after finishing the morning rounds on his ranch. Every detail of his cowboy outfit was perfect, beautiful and true, right down to his down to his Wild Bill Nietzsche mustache: he wore a plaid wool Pendleton shirt under a charcoal-grey, lapeled, silver-buttoned Filson Mackinaw vest, replete with a silver watch chain and a dangling 1897 fifty-cent piece.

I was helplessly drawn to him and flitted around him like a porch-light moth, insatiably curious about his every glorious detail. He explained quite plainly and humbly that he was a fourth-generation resident of Wyoming; his family, he said, were the second documented settlers of the Wyoming territory.

I began to mortify him by worshipping him openly.

I gushed over his red silk neckerchief. Compliments seemed to sting him like gooey wads of pink jellyfish; he had to swat and shiver them off. "Well, it gets pretty cold up here, what with the wind and the snow!" he protested.

"His clothes make *sense*!" cried another cowboy in the shop, leaning on the counter like an extra in *High Noon* in a woolen vest

Ladies, be strong: Introducing an Incredible, Genuine, One and Only 100% Authentic Wyoming Cowboy and Fashion God.

and a black ten-gallon hat, stepping in as protection from my hail of masculinity-impairing compliments. "They're not just *fashion*."

Oh, but they were singularly outrageous, world-stomping fashion.

His silk kerchief wasn't knotted, but held around his neck by two ends being pulled through a cylinder of antler-bone. He seemed to wince at my joy after he explained that of course he didn't *buy* it—he'd *made* it. "We cut these because it's faster than tyin' 'em! I don't own any other clothes!"

"Not a tuxedo?" asked my uncle slyly.

My hero made a face like he'd just been asked if he'd ever done the hula-hoop in a ruffled brassiere.

"Oh *no*," he said, waving the idea away. "I've seen 'em on TV."

"You know, they're pretty comfortable," my uncle continued, enjoying this new form of cowboy torture. "Some of them are like pajamas."

Then I saw them. The cowboy's boots were brain-exploding knee-high wonders wrought in rubber and leather and God. I

The pointy toes of these devastatingly cool boots came out of ACTUAL STIRRUPS connected to an ACTUAL SADDLE ON AN ACTUAL HORSE.

controlled an overwhelming desire to fall to my knees and grope them.

"What are *those*?!" I shrieked, pointing at his boots. "Do they actually exist? Can a human being actually *buy* them?!"

"Oh yeah," he said, visibly alarmed. "Schnee's."

(I later found the website: Schnee's, a store based in Bozeman, Montana, is an outerwear source "for the Montana lifestyle," where hunters and serious cattlemen may find chore boots, Rifleman shirts, Fenceline ranch pants, oil-based paraffin-treated cotton duck chaps that "offer excellent protection from rain, mud, snow, and briars"—and also cowboy-centric accessories like bison cellphone holders. My hero had been sporting the 14-inch Schnee's Western Pac Boot, which, I later read, was lined with wool felt and had vulcanized Goodyear rubber soles that "won't clog up when used in the barnyard." The pointy toes—a fashion detail which made my nose projectile-bleed with pleasure—were "made to fit into standard stirrups.")

"My hat was made right there in that room!" he said, pointing to an open door in the back of the shop in a bald attempt to direct my lavish attentions away from him. "Ten years ago! And I've been wearin' it ever since. Every day. I've never had to get it worked on or anything. I've been in some of the worst rainstorms you can imagine, and I never had to put a condom on it."

My eyes got wide; my uncle began giggling. My hero blushed redly and I got a finger-wagging from the other cowboy for being so absurd as to not recognize that a "condom" was the standard name used to refer to a kind of weatherproof, ten-gallon shower cap designed to protect one's *hat*.

"Hat never lost its shape," muttered a woman, emerging from the back room. She was Carol, the store's proprietor—who, the gentlemen explained, was a renowned master of cowboy hat shaping. In the past, she had made hats for Robert Duvall and Kevin Costner, and had made all the hats for a Broadway production of *Annie Get Your Gun*. She had also built my hero's hat from scratch, ten years previously.

"A good hat'll last you a good ten, twenty years," said the Other Cowboy. (Out of respect for his sensitivities, I resisted telling him that he was living proof of my contention that a fat, black, Burt Reynolds à la *Smokey and the Bandit* handlebar mustache is, almost without exception, the best facial hair possible on a male human being—unless that male is John Waters.) "People go out and buy those cheap, cardboard hats," he added, his tone wreathed with shame at the idea.

I got an uncanny tingling sensation in the intuitive zone of my brain—and I suddenly knew that this was the Moment. Destiny had obviously led my uncle and me to this exact establishment, that we might purchase the genuine cowboy hats that would be essential to our sartorial and personal evolutions.

From a healthy selection of used cowboy hats hanging on the

wall, I selected a black Resistol "self-conforming" number with a wide brim and red piping. It was, Carol explained, quality 4X, made of a combination of rabbit and beaver felt—a very decent hat, but not ultra-swanky. Hat quality, Carol explained, can go up to 100X, which would mean it was 100 percent beaver fur—and, like the beaver, entirely waterproof.

"You're not gonna wear that hat in New York," cracked my cowboy, as Carol expertly steam-shaped the Resistol around my head.

"Oh, just watch me," I said.

"I wore my hat in San Francisco once," he said, a little darkly. "I couldn't wait to get out of that city."

I did an inner spit-take. I had no doubt that my boys back home had got the wrong idea about my cowboy—they must have appreciated him to the point of tripping off some serious alarms. Someone really should have told him, before he visited my hometown, that in San Francisco entire bars were built around the fetishization of his day look.

Once my Resistol had been properly bent and steamed, it looked and felt as if it had grown onto my head as organically as my ears.

It was Uncle Rick's moment of truth. I helped him select a somewhat boxy, camel-colored hat neutral enough to contain the potential for a number of different personalities. Unmolested, it naturally looked like the kind of quietly refined cowboy hat a gentleman rancher might wear to a formal tailgate party. If the lid was punched up and dimpled at the top, Rick might resemble a Royal Canadian Mountie; the brim might also be bent up on the sides for a more park rangerish, Smokey the Bear-cum-Flying Nun-like effect.

Once it was preliminarily attached to Rick's head, Carol set upon the hat with her steam machine. My hero and Burt Reynolds

This silly hat my niece made me buy just reminded me that I'm handsome!

thoughtfully squinted in silence at this millinery sorcery as Carol squeezed the hat into personae of her choosing. I waved off the first two shapes, which I didn't feel quite collaborated with Rick's face. I knew there was a divine equation somewhere in the hat—that the right shape would resonate like a gong.

"You think we could try squashing it down a bit, flattening out the crown in front and making it a bit more like Larry Hagman in *Dallas*?" I asked.

A few gusts of steam later: *Kaboom.*

The right hat can be serious voodoo when the cosmos demonstrates it is yours—your head and the hat seem to instantly embrace, and beneath this union you may find yourself instantly transformed. It is a phenomenon I can only compare to that momentous day when a shy, innocuous boy arrives at his high school mid-semester with a bold new haircut, and the female species to which he has been invisible for the whole of his young life suddenly performs an abrupt hormonal shift of groupthink and launches overnight into a unanimous scrum to win his attention. When my uncle saw himself in the mirror with his newly Hag-manized hat, he *brightened up.* His expression, which had been burdened with uncertainty for the last ten or so months, suddenly opened like a dusty barn door, and a long-suppressed Colorado boy I hadn't seen since my early childhood rolled out of his char-acter, intact—like an old motorcycle he'd forgotten he owned but had been waiting for him in pristine condition. This old part of himself, rediscovered, seemed to instantly commence kicking him in the ass from an as yet unimagined new future. He was visibly reminded that he wasn't old or dead yet. My uncle imme-diately started to walk like a taller and stronger animal who liked the smell of himself again. The cowboys all agreed: this was a great hat victory.

My uncle left the next day to go back to California. He sent me a text while he was strolling around the airport. To his enormous surprise, he was suddenly visible to women again. All morning in the airport, females had been hitting on him like big sacks of hammers. "A stewardess even gave me a *seat upgrade!*" he enthused. "It's the hat! You're on to something with this fashion thing. I mean . . . it's *crazy!*"

Swagger restored. An old groove remixed. I felt like Lassie after cleverly fetching insulin to save the diabetic girl.

⚍⚎

SOMETIMES IT IS DIFFICULT to envision the multitude you may contain until you leave home and decontextualize yourself. Sartorial habits become entrenched along with all your other habitual synaptic ruts. If your wardrobe is too familiar, you never

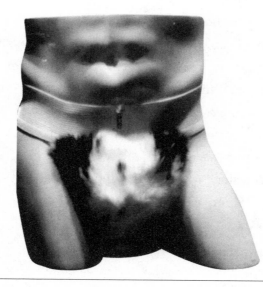

Jackson, WY: Home of that FUR CODPIECE you've always been looking for . . .

really get a vacation from your own personality. You can forget there's other rooms and other engines to play with.

I used to have a ritual with an old colonel with a lovely baritone voice—I'd sometimes call him late at night just to have him sing me "Streets of Laredo." There is something ineffably poignant in the song that always makes me cry.

> *I can see by your outfit that you are a cowboy*
> *I can see by your outfit that you're a cowboy too*
> *You can see by our outfits that we are both cowboys*
> *If you get an outfit, you can be a cowboy too*

After Wyoming, I knew I could never be authentic just by wearing the outfit. But a girl can dream, and incorporate more cowboy into her boots.

5

MIAMI / THE SAND BELT

Nudes in Jewelry

〜

I had never been to Florida before spring break, 2011.

Previous to my visit, the most recent imaginary Florida in my mind had been informed by Manhattan retail environments.

Once, in the men's department at Dolce and Gabbana, I studied a white disco suit with black lapels. It looked like something a Medellín cartel member might wear to a midnight showing of the sing-it-yourself *Saturday Night Fever.*

"Where does this suit actually *go over?*" I asked the salesman.

"Well," he said, with evident distaste, "I suppose you could wear it in *Miami.*"

I happened to overhear another young salesman working at the Helmut Lang/Theory store in SoHo, talking about his Floridian origins. He was similarly snarky about his hometown.

"Ha!" he scoffed. "South Beach is like this: You live in a crap house in a crap neighborhood, but you always park your Bentley outside in the driveway."

I preferred to believe the more rich and whimsical retail visions of Florida: the wacky Palm Beach—inspired home decor of Jonathan Adler (white on white on cane on bamboo faux-Chinoiserie, on primary-colored throw pillows decorated with sarcastic pills and owls).

In my childhood, I imagined Miami as a pastiche of half-remembered pastiches informed by reruns from the Magical World of Television. Oversaturated, preadolescent fantasies in hypercolored seventies' film stock. A high-feverish, hallucinogenic color palette—rapturous tropical mornings on an infinite lawn, mirrored beads of dew steaming into soft turquoise heat. Florida was a place where blonde genies in midriffs and harem pants rolled up onto the shores of Cape Canaveral in decorative bottles, to live in chaste

domestic harmony as the magical slaves of handsome astronauts. Monochromatic pantsuits and moral justice prevailed to the toe-tapping rhythms of the Frank De Vol orchestra. Sins were cleansed with canary yellow Handi Wipes and pump-action Fantastik.

Chiffon halter-topped palazzo-pantsuits guest-starred on *The Love Boat.*

There was Orlando, the Magic Kingdom, where super-talented children were groomed into Mouseketeers, then child TV stars, then pop superstars (before LA transformed them into drug addicts, then centerfolds, then public enemies).

The yacht-rock aesthetic dominated the eighties—the Duran Duran, *Miami Vice* look—straight guys of excessively female vanity with big frosted blow-dried hair in baby-pink suits worn sockless with tank tops, loafers, and eyeliner, accessorized with cocaine, palm trees, and yellow Lamborghinis.

My favorite imaginary Florida was informed by the Lilly Pulitzer store on Madison Avenue. Ms. Pulitzer was a woman who began an empire with naught but with two empires. Her mother was a Standard Oil heiress; her husband was the grandson of the publishing Pulitzer. Her clothing business began one whimsical afternoon in Palm Beach when, as a bored young housewife, she set up an orange juice stand (her husband owned many orchards). She had her dressmaker create a batch of bright, simple shifts in prints that would hide juice stains, and a fashion sensation was born—especially when Jacqueline Bouvier Kennedy, Ms. Pulitzer's pal and schoolmate from Miss Porter's terrifying girls' prep school, wore a "Lilly" dress in *Life* magazine.

Ms. Pulitzer's prints came from her own paintings, and it must be said that she was quite a decent painter. A few of her oils hang on the walls in her Madison Avenue store: dangling wisteria, lily pads, daisies, gooseberries, oh my—all painted in a lusty, fauvist style, in yowling colors. This unchained melody of prints was applied with abandon onto decades of casual resort wear, in every cut necessary to turn your relatives into the Von Trapp family singers.

Ms. Pulitzer's menswear is what I like to call "Golf Bastard chic." There are mind-boggling pants, and absolutely terrifying sport jackets—a veritable massacre in sherbet. I imagined the men's section was what Anita Bryant's linen closet would have looked like after Hurricane Andrew: violent mangos, pinks, and aquamarines starched into jackets of such *telenovela* bedspread intensity they might cause even Ricardo Montalbán to run screaming toward the volcano. A particular vintage pair of slacks featuring lurid, efflorescent hydrangeas in double-knit polyester would be impossible to accessorize with anything short of "the Full Cleveland" (a white Naugahyde belt and shoes).

I asked for help.

"What kind of men buy these jackets? Mobsters? Gay guys? Gay mobsters? Game show hosts?" I asked the fresh-faced salesgirl.

"Honestly?" She hesitated, looked around, thought about it, decided I was OK.

"*Gentiles*," she stage-whispered, hilariously.

I stayed at a self-described "gay hotel" in South Beach, mostly for the kicky disco-ball interior. Every room featured, over the bed, an enormous photo portrait of Elizabeth Taylor as Cleopatra. (She was, after all, the ultimate queen.)

I was having drinks with my friend and traveling chum Dr. Amanda Parkes on the porch of our hotel when two smoking-hot, wholly oversexed-looking twentysomething girls crossed the street in front of us: long, ironed hair, teeny-tiny metallic dresses, yards of shiny waxed legs, nosebleed-high hooker heels, breasts augmented unto near verticality.

"My God, look at those spectacular whores!" I squealed in delight.

Not in that dress you don't.

"Ha! Be cool. Those aren't whores," scoffed Amanda. "Those are just regular girls, going out for the night."

I was dumbfounded.

Their outfits were 100 percent semiotic hooker, right down to the two-girl, Doublemint twin, doppelganger effect. Their fashion was employing all of the signifiers of prostitution and nothing else—there was no other guiding style principle whatsoever. They were like cartoon hookers. It reminded me of that old argument about how to distinguish pornography from art: you don't know how, but you know the difference when you see it. I couldn't see any difference. The way they were dressed rendered all the signifiers of hookerdom totally meaningless. I could see this creating problems, to wit: if you're a hooker in Miami, *what the hell do you wear?*

By the end of the weekend, I realized that those girls were practically Amish in restraint compared to the rest of the girls in South Beach, who walk around casually in restaurants and sit on barstools wearing mini-monokinis the spatial equivalent of two gold Band-Aids and a cork, with five-inch heels, art nails, and body glitter.

I realized that the fashion statement of South Beach, due to both its brevity and content, was a SEXT.

To better understand the glitzier end of the Miami aesthetic, as seen in the bars of the more upscale art deco hotels, it helps if you've spent a few late nights in Rome. Once, in an underground restaurant at around 1 a.m., I saw a pack of *La Dolce Vita*–living twenty-somethings arrive in a red blur of rumbling little cars. I guessed they were young Italian TV stars or jet-setters. Their guiding fashion mandate seemed to be Nude But Over-Accessorized: gownless evening straps with metallic zebra stripes. Charm belts and denim fishnets. Mahogany groins emerging from white silk fig leaves and feathery tattoos. Seven-inch heels adding height to 22-karat toenails. Everybody seemed drenched with gold chains, as if they had just escaped from the maximum security sex-mall at Caesar's Palace.

An absurdly upscale shopping mall in Bal Harbour was a good place to observe the enormously wealthy ladies of Miami. These women have collectively allowed one another to do too many cosmetic procedures to themselves, so as a tribe they tend to look similarly strange: hoisted eyebrows, motionless heads, over-fattened lips, worn-out hair. They indulge a collective affection for bling: white jeans, spangled flip-flops, spangled belts, low-neck T-shirts, Fendi bags, white sunglasses. They own too much gold to care if you think their dresses are too short for their age; they are the type who contends that the only good iguana is a pink belt.

These women often have entourages of overtanned young gay men, who hang around them wearing pastel shorts, Tod's loafers, yachting shirts, and Louis Vuitton sunglasses. The occasional husbands resemble understudies for the cast of *The Sopranos*: cigar-smoking men with thick, hairy necks, much older than their wives.

There was, I noticed, little conversation between men and women. The women talked to other women, and to their gay male friends; the husbands were silent, or speaking to other men. In the Hermès store, which sells saddles and whips, I saw two old fat white men in boating attire steering very young black girlfriends around by their elbows; one was smiling while his *petite amie* tried on the Hermès equivalent of a slave bracelet.

The shops feature a lot of top Italian brands, shoes of incredible price with no hope of physical endurance: cobwebs made of gold string with seven-inch heels, pearl-encrusted silk peep-toe booties in beige satin—things you'd wear once then hurl off the yacht deck at a raft full of Cubans (or your husband, as he snuck into the dinghy to rendezvous onshore with his little black mistress).

The Design District of Miami is home to Art Basel, that big contemporary-art-world, insular, incestuous jet-set scene which obsessively follows itself to its own parties, polo matches, international Gumball Rally events and biennales all over the world. As a result, art-world people and the retail areas that cater to them tend to more or less wear styles within the range of a very limited aesthetic, whether they are in San Francisco or Paris or Istanbul. That particular commercial scene prefers expensive, laid-back hipster chic, totally devoid of Swarovski crystals: Rick Owens, Maison Martin Margiela, Lanvin.

The boutiques of these designers often affect a self-consciously art studio–esque aesthetic—many are lousy with taxidermy. Whole sections of shoes may be slathered in gesso. Furniture is often Saran-wrapped. These boutiques are invariably run by very young, overeducated, beautiful, scowly, totally unhelpful, bipolar shop girls who are hysterically miserable working retail, because they are impatiently waiting for the world to make them famous artists or models or muses themselves. They deeply resent not being their customers and having to sell them impossible jackets, such as the one represented that spring by Maison Martin Margiela's "Defile" collection, which was made of deconstructed blonde wigs.

Still, what became the biggest fashion revelation during my trip to Miami was the contents of my own suitcase.

Amanda and I were in our hotel room unpacking our clothes. Everything she brought was context-appropriate—weightless little things in shades of canary yellow and fluorescent papaya. Amanda looked at the pile next to my suitcase and asked, "Jesus . . . is there *anything* you brought that isn't black?"

And I looked at my stuff and I wondered . . . Shit. Is there anything I *own* that isn't black?

You never really know what you look like until you leave home and decontextualize yourself.

SOUTH BEACH: SERVING SUGGESTION

By my own metrics, my wardrobe was psychologically ridiculous. My total mistrust of God, country, sex, and my fellow human beings was literally right on the floor of my hotel room. All my clothes were black, shiny, barbed, spiky, predatory—absurdly contrary and menacing. I obviously had some issues to address. Basically, my fashion statement boiled down to one word: *No.*

This was on my mind when I wandered into the Dior store and struck up a conversation with Francine, the gorgeous French-woman working there. She had wonderful orange-pink hair, false eyelashes, no lipstick. I complimented her use of color; she complimented my lack of it.

She smiled. "I felt very conservative when I moved here from Neuilly-sur-Seine. You can't wear little skirts there. You can't bend over in a tiny skirt in the subway! Here, you go straight from the beach into the city, one block." She gave a Gallic shrug. "Why would you camouflage yourself?"

"I've been dressed in black for so long that I'm not really conscious of it anymore," I lamented. "Around here, I feel like I'm attending a children's birthday party in a latex ski mask."

"Tsk. You are from New York, so you wear black! If you lived here, your personality would discover colors."

This logic was so kind, I considered moving to Miami. Perhaps some of my fashion neurosis is regional: I've contended with life in New York for so long that my wardrobe evolved into something resembling an angler fish, or a bar-fighting nun.

I thought back to the Lilly Pulitzer store, and her paintings. Today, she would be an Art Basel celebrity, but when she was around, things were different. An heiress didn't become a famous painter simply because she could paint.

What was most interesting about her paintings, I realized, is that they look ever so slightly . . . *unstable.* I couldn't decide if Ms. Pulitzer's paintbrush managed to express a wealth of poised, controlled craziness—or a crazed, controlled wealthiness.

A photo of Ms. Pulitzer on the upstairs wall shows her as a young brunette in a beehive hairdo, wearing a canary yellow shift replicated in miniature on two matching children. They are standing behind the tall cast-iron bars of what I presume was their Palm Beach estate, looking a bit like inmates of a five-star sanitarium. In another photo, she stands in her first shop, where her clothing hangs from modified gilded birdcages.

How does one become as polished, poised, cheerful, and sane-looking as Jackie O, while living a life as bent, backward, and whitewater-intense as hers? How was Jackie able to assemble herself after the assassination of her first husband? How did she carry herself from a White House in mourning to a yacht deck in Greece, and bewitch the man whose indifference killed Maria Callas?

Perhaps chintz pedal-pushers were the key to Jackie's self-possession in a flesh-obsessed, dog-eat-dog world. Or perhaps the answer lies in one of the songs from the musical *Sweeney Todd*, which gives explicit advice on life in a cage:

> *My cage has many rooms*
> *Damask and dark*
> *Nothing there sings*
> *Not even my lark*
> *Larks never will, you know*
> *When they're captive.*
> *Teach me to be more adaptive.*

Apropos of the Demon Barber of Fleet Street, cannibalism made a comeback in Miami, in 2012. The first report was allegedly the result of an improper combination of homeless people and bath salts. The next report I read allegedly happened to someone in a wheelchair sleeping outside an abandoned Hooters.

Given the popularity of flesh-eating zombies and dog-eat-dog finance, cannibalism in Miami seemed to make perfect sense. In Miami, after all, people are mostly nude, which underlines a basic connective truth unifying everyone: the rich, the poor, the crazy. Scarface gangsters and heiresses alike. In Miami, more than anywhere else in America, it is abundantly clear that at the end of the day, all human beings are made of meat.

6

KANSAS / THE GUN BELT

Crow-Eating and Cognitive Dissonance
in the Heartland

━⌇

*Anything that's new takes a while before it gets disseminated
across the country. You get the J. C. Penney versions of fashions
of what the style-leaders are wearing. There's an interesting
premise in all of this, in the youth world. You take the lunatic
fringe, the avant garde, the style leaders, the nuts. And if you
are careful enough to determine what they come up with that's
a legitimate trend, then you'll be able to figure out eventually
what the people in the middle, I don't mean necessarily
geographically but in the case of our country it is pretty much
the middle, will be doing in the next couple of months.*

—AMERICAN BANDSTAND HOST DICK CLARK,
IN AN INTERVIEW WITH LESTER BANGS, 1973

had a few reservations about going to Kansas, at the beginning of 2010.

I was at the tail end of an unhealthy seven-year obsession with politics. In addition to writing about fashion retail for the *New York Times*, I was also writing political articles for a handful of small weekly papers. I was intensely bothered by the widening red state/blue state ideological divide. I was worried that America was cultivating a social apartheid by amplifying cultural differences unto xenophobia and mutual mistrust, and worried that this enmity, exacerbated by the media, was preventing the majority of Americans from realizing shared goals, such as wage increases. The beginning of the Obama administration had been nerve-racking: Republicans had undone women's rights again, explicit racism was making an unwelcome recrudescence into the public dialogue. Groups of "grassroots" Tea Party supporters had begun carrying assault rifles into town hall meetings on health care. Everyone in my circle was terrified for Obama's safety. Society seemed to be going full-steam retrograde, and there didn't seem to be any legitimate adults around to stop it.

The twenty-four-hour news cycle was cultivating an absurd sports-fan-style rivalry between the only two parties in our political system by chasing sex, disasters, shootings, and marital infidelities, and dominating the cultural conversation by re-problematizing divisive civil rights issues like abortion and homosexuality, instead of giving citizens enough real information during wartime to have an informed democracy.

Writing the fashion articles was pure fun for me—a welcome comedy relief from spending the rest of my writing energy banging my head against the Pentagon, trying to make it rounder. To my surprise, it was a fashion article, not a political article, that

plunged me headfirst into the red state vs. blue state ideological ravine.

In August 2009, the *Times* asked me to write an article about the new J. C. Penney flagship that had opened in Herald Square. It was an odd assignment, but I was game.

I figured the fairest thing I could do would be to review the store exactly as I would review Gucci or any other New York retail fashion establishment. I figured it would be rude to pander or talk down to J. C. Penney. I decided to neither protect them nor condemn them more than I would any of the luxury players I usually reviewed, whom I routinely stomped the daylights out of.

I had *no idea* what I was about to stumble into.

When you write for a living, you're basically alone and typing most of the time. There is no water cooler to stand around with other human beings and catch up on Internet memes or last night's TV event or other large public topics. This isolation can result in occupational hazards such as galloping myopia, massive blind spots—and, in my case, a grand-mal episode of whopping stupidity.

I hadn't realized that there had been an ongoing muttering campaign, in most of the country, about the *New York Times* being totally out-of-touch and elitist. I traipsed right into the middle of a culture war I had no idea was already in progress. It was something of a perfect storm, in which I offended roughly a million people.

J. C. Penney has broken free of its suburban parking area to invade Herald Square, and the most frequent question on New York's collective lips seems to be: why?

Why would this perennially square department store bother to reanimate itself in Manhattan—in the sleekest, scariest fashion city in America—during a hair-raising economic downturn, without taking the opportunity to vigorously rebrand itself? Why would this dowdy Middle American entity waddle into Midtown in its big old shorts and flip-flops without even bothering to update its ancient Helvetica Light logo, which for anyone who grew up with the company is encrusted with decades of boring, even traumatically parental, associations?

J. C. Penney has always trafficked in knockoffs that aren't quite up to Canal Street's illegal standards. It was never "get the look for less" so much as "get something vaguely shaped like the designer thing you want, but cut much more conservatively, made in all-petroleum materials, and with a too-similar wannabe logo that announces your inferiority to evil classmates as surely as if you were cursed to be followed around by a tuba section."

But things, perhaps, have changed. The juniors section of the new Manhattan Penney's seems to be trying, in a somewhat timid fashion, to thump with new energy. Mini-sections flirt with Topshop-like knockoffs and Goth-wear lite—not quite a Hot Topic, but nearly lukewarm. It is possible for a raging tween to walk out of Penney's looking mildly subversive in a zebra-print tee, a studded punk (vinyl) belt and black ankle-zip jeans ($42).

Since the 1970s, J. C. Penney, like a retail Island of Dr. Moreau, has been doing a sinister experiment with various designers, turning them into something not quite human. The plot is a fashion democratization known as "masstige," which sounds like something terrible your ob-gyn would tell you after the tests, but is a marketing term created by a fusion of "mass" and "prestige." It refers to a downward brand extension: designers compelled to put their good names on downmarket lines of "affordable luxury." (Read: items in cheaper materials, sold at lower prices.)

Masstige theoretically began with Halston, a top designer of the 1970s, who, after dressing First Ladies and the gilded habitues of Studio 54, created the Halston II line for J. C. Penney. It was an idea ahead of its time, which was devastating for Halston; his reputation was tragically diluted unto total ridiculousness, but Penney's reputation remained imperturbably clunky. (Google Halston II now, and all you'll get are ceiling fans.)

But, after Halston died for the sin of masstige, designers seem to be enjoying a post-shame era. Penney's now carries I ♥ Ronson by Charlotte Ronson, and Fabulosity, an off-the-belly-chain line of clothing and extremely complicated metallic blood-on-the-dance-floor pumps by Kimora Lee Simmons, which look as if they'd emit sounds of heavy panting if you held them to your ear. There are collections by other designers who insist on going by their first names (perhaps because Penney's is a friendly, homey place, like Oprah's couch): Nicole by Nicole Miller, Allen B. by Allen Schwartz (who the heck is Allen Schwartz?), Joe by Joseph Abboud in the men's section, with sweater-vests for Dad, and—drumroll please—Liz & Co., an offshoot of Liz Claiborne, key provider of looks that say, "I have been in a senior management position at this DMV for thirty-four years."

A good 96 percent of the Penney's inventory is made of polyester. The few clothing items that are made of cotton make a sincere point of being cotton and tell you earnestly about their 100-percent cottonness with faux hand-scribbled labels so obviously on the green bandwagon they practically spit pine cones.

It took me a long time to find a size two among the racks. There are, however, abundant size tens, twelves, and sixteens. The dressing rooms are big, clean, and well tended. I tried two fairly cute items: a modified domino-print swing dress with padded shoulders by American Living (a Ralph Lauren line created for Penney's) and a long psychedelic muumuu of a style generally worn by Rachel Zoe. Each was around $80; each fit nicely and looked good. I didn't buy either because I can do better for $80, but if I were a size eighteen, I'd have rejoiced.

And herein lies the genius of J. C. Penney: it has made a point of providing clothing for people of all sizes (a strategy, company officials have said, to snatch business from nearby Macy's in Herald Square)—the middle market. To this end, it has the most obese mannequins I have ever seen. They probably need special insulin-based epoxy injections just to make their limbs stay on. It's like a headless wax museum devoted entirely to the cast of *Roseanne*.

The petites section features a bounty of items for women

nearly as wide as they are tall; the men's big and tall section has shirts that could house two or three Shaquilles. In
the men's big and tall section, even Voltron could find office
casuals.

My escort, Dr. Redacto, bought a T-shirt. He ordinarily
wears a large. I advised him: "Get the medium. I guarantee,
a large is going to be five times larger than any large you've
ever seen." While modeling it for me later, we agreed that
even a Penney's medium is five times larger than any large
T-shirt either of us had ever seen. The sleeves came down
to the elbow, and there was enough room in front for eight
months of unborn twins.

And that will probably make some guy feel pretty svelte.

I knew it was rude, but no ruder than any of my other articles.
It was my way of keeping my laptop a true democracy: I recognized no sacred cows.

When the article hit the newsstands, letters began pouring in
to the *New York Times*. My editor phoned me.

"I want to warn you, they are not nice."

I'd stuck my foot in it before, as a journalist. I girded my loins
to assuage the mild fury of several hundred ticked-off people,
somewhat pissed.

This was different. Blogs began calling it "The Fashion Apocalypse" and/or "JC Penneygate."

I got that people took offense that I was being snarky about
how oversized J. C. Penney's clothing was. I *was* being snarky. I
wasn't thinking about how that fact might be perceived as deeply
and personally inflammatory and painful for some people. I wrote
the article in a state of wide-eyed disbelief because the clothes at
J. C. Penney were *quite frankly and truthfully fucking gigantic compared to clothing in the rest of Manhattan's retail establishments.*

J. C. Penney really knew how to lard subliminal U.S. propaganda onto an otherwise "meh" vintage cowboy shirt (Texas thrift store).

I didn't see it coming that my article would be seen as an attack on Middle America's Place to Shop by a snotty, classist, elitist, skinny New York bitch. Writing about fashion for the Newspaper of Record had somehow given the rest of the world the idea that I had been born rich and educated in a lead-windowed, Ivy League university where I earned prestigious degrees in anorexia and Natalie Portman. It wasn't an impression that I was conscious of avoiding, only because *real* snotty, rich, classist, elitist New York bitches don't consider to me to be one of them, *at all.* Journalists are a tribe roughly on a par with janitors in such high society.

My sisterwomen from the middle of America had lathered up en masse into a collective ecstasy of anonymous trollish gangbanging. The words "bitch" and "cunt" were wall-to-wall in the subject lines of my e-mail inbox. Many women wrote in to tell me that I am incredibly ugly, and that I desperately needed plastic surgery. Several women agreed, on the comments section of my blog, that I had something to do with my ex-boyfriend's accidental death, in 1996. One openly accused me of murdering him.

A self-described "oversize nurse" wrote to me to say that I'd better pray I never ended up on her ward, in her hospital, or she would kill me.

An Internet editor writing to offer his condolences told me that in the case of such uproars in the anonymous blogosphere, female journalists generally get roughly forty times the abuse that male journalists do.

"This is why ERA was never passed, babe," wrote my friend Nancy, lamenting with me over the fact that women are still, invariably, the worst enemies of women. "Despite what anyone says about What a Long Way We've Come, Baby, a profound misogyny is still there. This kind of thing doesn't happen to people with penises."

So despite my absolute terror of Midwestern nurses, I flew to Kansas in early 2010 to be present for the birth of my godson Vale. His mother, my oldest and dearest friend Mitzy, was living and working in a small town near the Kansas–Missouri border, where there are two Kansas Cities right next to each other. I had never been to Kansas before, but my maternal grandparents grew up and were buried there, in a family plot I've still never seen.

Every once in a while a small town will transport you back in time, to the era when its oldest surviving coffee shop was built.

The town Mitzy was living in, Weston, MO (population 1,642 in 2010), is a quaint, eerie, and windy place, full of old white clapboard houses; at one point in America's history it had the distinction of being the westernmost edge of the colonies. Weston is a lot like going back to the administration of one of Kansas City MO's native sons, Harry Truman. Judging from the stores on the main strip, many quilts were made in the vicinity, apparently to be preserved in cedar and mothballs and never to travel beyond the town limits; they seem to be a mysterious pinwheel-block wall of small flowers and tiny stitching, harboring the lingering energies of ghosts from the pioneer era who never made it further than this white-picket gateway to the West. There are also beautiful, rusty old grain silos, and a handful of retail shops selling references to a time when gender divisions of labor made more sense: handmade gingham curtains, rusty farm hardware. Tools exclusive to the construction and distribution of pie.

I got the same feeling in Weston that I did walking down a residential street in Poughkeepsie years ago, when I was stopped in my tracks by the beauty of a backyard clothesline. It was nothing I had ever seen in my lifetime, having always lived in an era of convenient, labor-saving appliances: well-loved, embroidered cotton pillowcases, hand-stitched aprons, appliquéd napkins and tablecloths, secured on a fuzzy white rope with hingeless wooden clothespins, waving in the breeze before a wall of pine trees. It actually brought tears to my eyes; it was like stumbling on a time capsule full of lost femininity—all the stuff that 1970s women's libbers abandoned for being contaminated by patriarchal social engineering.

I didn't want to love it, but there was something so careful, constructive, and deeply *good* about that ravishing laundry. It was a genuine example of *home-making* as a verb—a creative act that reifies the idea of "home." There is a lost paradise evident in these mundane niceties that is very moving to me. The most under-valued thing in this world is the time, attention, concentration, and patient effort of unhurried human beings. There is a distinct improvement in the quality of life when one is in the midst of that uncelebrated cornball magic known as the "female touch": that mythical lattice-crusted pie made with blackberries from the garden, cooling on the windowsill, steam rising and threading through curtains nearly transparent from years of washing and ironing. It's the kind of modest, good-faith creative energy that exists only to dignify and spruce up the immediate vicinity. It is a drive to beautify that never seeks anything so vainglorious as outside affirmation, because it would never put on such ludicrous airs as to call itself "art." These elegant works are merely (*merely!*) well-practiced, gorgeously skillful expressions of *care*.

In the nearby, more populous town of Leavenworth, most of the town's economy operates around the medium-security federal prison. As a result, a lot of the townspeople are either the families of prisoners in the penitentiary, or the families of prison guards, so, for practical reasons, you see a lot of Carhartt jackets. Sometimes these roles can switch—which results in a predictable level of weird social tension in diners.

There are large areas of Kansas that are indistinguishable, in that painfully homogenous way, from too many other flat, strip-mall-and-large-box-store commercial real estate eyesores around other American interstates. Walmart and other ubiquitous beige squares, franchises, and fast food chains have successfully obliterated an enormous percentage of American regional character. Long stretches of Kansas may as well be in northern Virginia, or the Gulf Coast of Florida, or Merced, California.

I found it striking, on my walkabout writing this book, that (aside from neighborhoods that look as if they'd been suddenly air-lifted and dropped in eight-block chunks directly from a foreign

country) the lower-income the retail area in America is, the more the retail products in the chain stores are festooned with aggressive corporate marketing. My friend Mark Johnson coined the term "monopulated" to describe this phenomenon. The more economically depressed the venue and the cheaper, more mass-produced and petroleum-based the retail items become, the larger, louder, brighter, and more aesthetically intrusive the corporate branding is.

Retail stores such as Kohl's and J. C. Penney feature "masstige" collections, third-tier dispersion lines by designers like Vera Wang and Nicole Miller. On a shelf choked with Chinese vinyl handbags, the "Chaps by Ralph Lauren" logo is positively massive—etched on huge brass plaques riveted to the logo-handbag while still sealed in factory plastic. Coercing money out of poor people apparently means cranking up the ad campaign volume to a kind of *Clockwork Orange*, strobe-torture, throbbing scream level—and limiting choice. The poor, it seems, must pay for the sin of economic despair by acting as free billboards. Now, instead of slaves being branded by plantation owners, the poor must pay to brand themselves.

I could not help but wonder, in the couple of days I was loitering in the Kansas hospital, if the insidious power of branding hadn't leaked all the way into the maternity ward. I happened to see a wall of construction-paper hearts bearing the handwritten names of recently born babies, which read like a character list from *Grand Theft Anglo: Game of Thrones:* Addison, Amoire, Alexandyr, Auxane, Brenley, Braylon, Evalina, Fenix, Highland, Kixton, Jaydence, Caleb, Kaleb, Kemper, Kaylee, Kaylie, Caylee, Kayla, Serenity, and Xander.

More X's than a medicine cabinet full of antifungals. Kaylier than thou. This trend seemed to be a quest to bestow regal Saxon ancestry unto the babies of Kansas. I understood this desire to trace my blood origins back to some old druidic stone, being an American mutt myself descended of Kansans, with a spotty genealogy that suggests ancestral horse thieves and other colorful losers on both sides of the Civil War. I pictured this roomful of swaddled newborns with long red braids and chain-mail rompers, growing up in fortified grain silos, protected by a wall of Rottweilers and Sears chainsaws.

In a bizarre coincidence, ten minutes after Vale was born, one of the nurses, in her zeal to clear us out of the delivery room, threw my backpack onto a wheeled cart and ended up dumping my computer on the floor and killing the hard drive.

Call it karma, but a Middle-American nurse done got me in the end.

What suprised the hell out of me, though, was how the heartland, unlike New York, actually has a *heart.* The hospital administrator was so *reasonable* about working it out with me, it was mind-altering. I bought a computer, gave them a receipt, and they *cut me a check.* In New York, I knew I would have been screwed over for months until I was too frustrated to deal with a never-ending battle for reimbusement, but in Kansas, I was actually being treated *fairly*—like a real human being. The hospital was grateful I wasn't trying to gouge them for negligence or seeking morbid overcompensation for pain and suffering or software whiplash.

It was the way human society is technically *supposed* to operate, but so rarely does, since one usually deals with automated customer service representatives who put you on hold for three days and then connect you to technical support specialists deep in a call center mineshaft overseas. Having a nurse crash my hard drive may have been a nasty karmic scissor-kick from the plus-size goddesses, but it ended up being one of the nicer, more life-affirming disasters I've ever had.

Apropos of this regional aesthetic id, baby Vale's first outing in the outside world was a favor to me: we all went to the closest Cabela's, the "world's foremost outfitter" of all clothing and accessories related to hunting, fishing, and obsessively serious and gadgety outdoorsmanship (and, one must presume, a favorite of separatist militias, Unabombers, and other hobbyists whose leisure activities require assault rifles with laser scopes).

I felt like I had been taken to the Holy Grail in terms of fashion op-ed. For me, Cabela's was a brain-blisteringly perfect fashion articulation of the ideological gulf between left-wing coast-dwellers and right-wing heartlanders. It was Everything America Can't Reconcile With Itself boiled down into one big, billowing camouflage poncho.

The Cabela's in Kansas is a truly jaw-dropping spectacle—a kind of retail Disneyland for angry human carnivores. Pilgrimages to Cabela's are made often enough by out-of-town customers—heavyset families with small children, older couples in matching tracksuits—for the store to have its own log cabin–style hotel resort across the parking lot, replete with indoor water slide. Funnel cakes are sold outside the front doors, next to a bronze statue of an elk huge enough to look size-appropriately threatening next to a bronze Stalin.

The store features massive Costco-size lodge walls hung with every form of weaponry deemed necessary (or merely desirable) for the felling of every conceivable earth-beast. There are sumptuous racks upon racks of weapon-snuggling straps, holsters, and death-causing-object-concealing-and-transporting accessories in Kevlar and leather, Gore-Tex and waterproof canvas. Duck blinds sit on stilts about the aisles, looking a bit like the chicken-footed lair of Baba Yaga, if the legendary witch of Russian folklore had done a few tours in Nam.

There are camouflage outfits for virtually every human shape, ritual, and occasion—camo-and-lace onesies for the christening of baby girls, formal murder accoutrements for discriminating Cub Scouts, banquet attire for Moms of Anarchy.

The most astonishing spectacle at Cabela's is its profound wealth of taxidermy, all of which is represented with Grand Guignol theatricality and monumental expense. This dead animal collection rivals that of New York's Natural History Museum. The main difference: at Cabela's, most of the animals are on gigantic, if not life-size, facsimiles of natural settings, and stuffed into surreally ultraviolent attack poses, as if they'd been arranged by Art Basel conceptual pranksters, or a giggling group of seventeen-year-old sociopaths raised in a militant animal-hating cult.

Example: on a very steep artificial mountain approximately three stories high, an entire herd of mule deer are posed crashing downward at perilous speeds, slipping on fragmenting shale, skidding out of control and crash-landing en masse at the bottom of the hill onto their own faces. They are all captured ashamed, and mid-head-fracture.

Overhead, cheetahs chase monkeys through the air (simply because, like Chuck Norris, they *can*).

My favorite display featured a full-size female lion, frozen launched in midair while plunging its teeth into the neck of an agonized zebra. The zebra, however, was at this same moment simultaneously kicking a male lion in the face with both of its back hooves. The male lion, presumably the mate of the female zebra assailant, was fated by his taxidermist to have his face forever contorted into a sideways action wince like one of the more painful still shots from *Raging Bull*.

Next to all the infinite gun-rack and the war-of-all-taxidermy-against-all-taxidermy brought to you by Mutually Assured Destruction's *Wild Kingdom*, there was a tank of mysteriously live albino catfish swimming amid a veritable forest of fishing poles (perhaps they weren't albino, and merely pale from fright).

If you are the kind of person who sees nature as something that needs to be prosecuted relentlessly with an endless, obsessively accessorized campaign of all-out slaughter and turned into cold cuts, Cabela's can and will outfit this quest. It has every object necessary to annihilate the entire food chain, even if you are a 500-pound man who wants to hunt the most dangerous game with a TenPoint Stealth SS Crossbow with ACUdraw™, in size sixteen hip-waders and a ghillie suit. Most mind-blowing, for me—more so than even the rack of BBQ lighters shaped like M16s, or the fact that children are allowed to run around the store shooting one another with artificial guns that resemble nearby actual guns— was an extensive section of the store entirely devoted to professional delicatessen-style meat slicers.

(Incidentally: Cabela's restaurant, despite an overall atmosphere resembling that of a hospital cafeteria, was voted one of the ten best restaurants in the area in 2009.)

If you are looking for world-beating, animal-humiliating family entertainment, shark-killing machetes, bushmeat sausages, Confederate flags, or meat hooks big enough to hang a Panzer tank, Cabela's is your one-stop, ripstop nylon, camouflage paradise.

If you want to dress in garments that don't have kidney warmer slots or Molle webbing to hold your extra cartridges, well, honey . . . that's *your* problem. Good luck surviving the zombie invasion, or the robot apocalypse, or life after the inevitable water wars in 2023. Somebody needs to establish law and order, and make the grown-up decisions. Cabela's provides the fashion statement that says: *Hey, I am going to hit nature* first. *In the event of a societal collapse, I can and will be King.*

What little exposure I'd had to any hunting culture had come from New York retail—the Beretta flagship on Madison Avenue, to be exact—and despite the fact that both establishments are veritable savannahs of taxidermy, the aesthetic differences between Beretta and Cabela's were, for me, one of the most vivid examples of how regional style can fetishize something intrinsically neutral, like the sport of hunting, and bend it into drastically separate cultural universes.

⬥

THE ITALIAN FIRM Fabbrica d'Armi P. Beretta S.p.A has been run by the Beretta family for fifteen generations, ever since Bartolomeo Beretta made handmade muskets for the doge of Venice in the 1500s. Fetishists and Italians alike nurture a cultural tendency to idolize objects by making them ever more baroque. The Beretta store is an ornate, sentimental shrine devoted to the hunting-lodge aesthetic and the sport of shooting things.

His and hers safari khakis and grouse-hunting tweeds reside on the first floor, as do Habsburg linen suits and offerings from the Susanne von Dörmberg Country Classics line of pricey German tweeds (jacket, $975)—very Queen Elizabeth when worn with Wellingtons, an Hermès scarf, and hounds. A hallowed display case contains Ernest Hemingway's actual S03, the rifle he used for Venetian duck hunting and around Finca Vigía, his retreat in Cuba.

Hemingway is clearly Beretta's man-god, the embodiment and apotheosis of the Beretta mystique. In thrall to the image of this hero of letters and adventure, Beretta provides all the equipment a Hemingway wannabe needs. Zebra throw pillows ($350) go with zebra-hide ottomans ($6,500). Horned matter from a variety of beasts decorates pewter beer steins and magnifying glasses ($75). A leather game book records Shoot, Guns, Bag, and Remarks ($185). For the man who hates ostriches, there are wallets, as well as large eggs on ornamental chrome stands ($250).

Perusing the silverware and cocktail tumblers, I asked if Beretta had a bridal registry. The counterwoman was so nonplussed I was tempted to ask where they kept the weapons of feminine protection.

On the second floor there is small gallery of framed, limited edition paintings, such as *Devoted*, a tribute in oils to the dewy-eyed obedience of the noble Labrador retriever ($895). A grouse-hunting scene is also available for your home or hotel wall. The American Waterfowler line on the second floor is distinctly butch: Indiana Jones hats, lots of Gore-Tex and leather straps.

On the third floor: racks of rifles and shotguns (the store does not sell handguns on the premises), alongside black and white photos of handsome markswomen with dead cheetahs, and a photo of George H. W. Bush loading an SO6 EELL (Extra Extra Luxo Luxo) with members of the Masai tribe.

"So, how do I buy a gun?" I asked Beretta's affable master gunsmith, Ed Anderson. I was fantasizing about an Xtrema2, Max-4-camo-print 12-gauge to match my Xtrema Gear Decoy Gloves and Gear Bib with 18-inch overboot cover flange and high-back kidney warmers.

"For a rifle or shotgun, you'd have to go down to Kew Gardens, Queens, and get a permit."

"What about a regular handgun?"

"You'd have to get a permit at One Police Plaza. Do you drive?"

To my dismay, I learned that even with a permit, one can't take one's rifle on the subway.

Mr. Anderson opened a display case and showed me an obscenely terrific $130,000 rifle with enough minute, currency-style engraving to have previously belonged to Sir Walter Raleigh.

Killing clay pigeons with quarter-million-dollar guns is apparently all the rage these days. "All the guys on the front of the business pages are in shotgun clubs that cost $100,000 just to walk in the door," Mr. Anderson explained. Enviable shooting is largely determined by the free time you can afford to devote to it, and customizations like the carving-down of the walnut butt to minimize impact on your face during kickback.

It is a strange romance of conspicuous consumption that Beretta indulges, but rich guys apparently love dressing up like Ernest Hemingway and shooting things just as much as little girls love to wear tutus and dance around like prima ballerinas.

A champion marksman I know said he can shoot just fine with a $1,000 gun, but that's beside the point.

For a gentleman in the big city, your gun isn't your means of protecting or feeding your family or seceding from the Union. It is primarily another way to assert your individual will to power through obscene extravagance.

⊰⊱

NEW YORK IS NOT the rest of America, and rich people are not like us. My people may have been born, lived, and died in Kansas, but I am not like them, either. I just blew through like a tornado.

I am not in Kansas anymore. But then again, I'm not sure I ever really was in Kansas. Given the globalized free market, its pervasive box-store epidemic, and the unchecked brandalizing of America's unprotected regional identities, Kansas probably hasn't been in Kansas for quite a while now. If there is a Kansas still in Kansas, it probably won't be there for much longer.

7

LOS ANGELES / THE STAR BELT

Hollywood and the Uncanny Valley

$\backsim$

French designer Lucien Lelong was once asked by French *Vogue* if he thought that the fashion industry in France was taking its cues from Hollywood. "Hollywood dresses films. *Paris* dresses women," he said.

I would revise this to: Paris dresses women, and Hollywood *undresses* women.

Coco Chanel once said, "Elegance is the absence of vulgarity." Today, she might be moved to say that elegance is the absence of Los Angeles.

I lived in LA for one year, in the mid-nineties. It was all I could take.

LA is a city whose economy centers around the movie business. Fame causes people to spend their lives circling the drain of Los Angeles. Since the entire industry is organized around the pursuit of attention, everyone is terrified of not looking hot enough. As a result, everyday gender performance is so over-the-top as to create

WILEY LA TEEN SCORES PALIN AUTOGRAPH
(AND STILL MANAGES TO BATHE, AFTERWARD)

a kind of wholesale sexual dysphoria, and in most women a constant self-loathing.

An LA fashion statement tends to beg for positive feedback: *How f*ckable do I look?*

No, really, do these size 8–10 children's jeans make my ass look fat? Kill me now.

In the first week I lived in LA, I was taken to hang out in the wee small hours at the Sunset Marquis—a famous, rich, and sleazy VIP bar scene. I had never seen so many terrifyingly perfect young women before. I had suddenly been dunked for the first time into the gene pool's top .01 percent of the type of young, mercenarily beautiful, universally desirable women that the nasty Lotharios refer to as "mattresses" (model/actresses with no actual job or visible means of support).

I became abruptly self-aware that in the context of LA, I looked like a lesbian auto mechanic.

Girls in LA devote their entire closets to a kind of monosexual, full-time femininity that looks as broad as a clown suit: strappy, unlikely clothing, shoes you need three of to balance in, pants that require the help of two friends in order to get the tiny array of hooks in back of their souls fastened.

Girls who live in LA too long, participating in the constant sexual competition of "the industry," become dangerously, erotically jaded: eyes buried in layers of frosty grime, no subcutaneous fat or muscle, lots of cigarettes. They all look recently guilty of crimes against themselves, like they'd just unloaded a staple gun down their inner thighs to quell their anxiety before a meeting with Leonardo di Caprio's development company . . . or worse.

Girls who stay *way* too long in LA try, for way too long, to remain girls. There is no sexual value for women over thirty-five, and this is so dehumanizing that at a certain point, the urgent desire for plastic surgery becomes louder than anything else in an LA woman's mind. On the sidewalks of Beverly Hills, a distinctly surgical *difference* is the dominant first impression many of these women deliver. They have knowingly and enthusiastically plunged themselves into the Uncanny Valley—that territory in robotics or animation when an animated Thing begins to look too realistically human: it invariably ceases to look adorable and begins to look startlingly creepy. The extensive modifications that LA women make to their faces and bodies in their struggle to retain youth tends, at a certain point, to make them look off-puttingly unreal; their disproportionally small noses, huge lips, lineless foreheads, and enormous breasts evoke the same Freudian sense of the uncanny that they would if their bodies were extensive circuitry systems covered in latex. They seem as if they might be able to pack themselves into a shipping crate to a new owner/husband by unscrewing their own wax-polished limbs.

On an LA visit years after my move to New York, I wandered

into a famous Beverly Hills gown store. A stunningly perfect woman in a champagne-flute corset-dress was about two inches away from her reflection in a floor-to-ceiling mirror and shouting, "Fuck! FUCK!"—at herself.

I suddenly realized I knew her. She was a talented actress who had been in one of my plays several years earlier. I had always liked her and recognized her star power. Since I'd met her, she had risen from New York obscurity to the Hollywood red carpet, and was enjoying what anyone on the rest of planet Earth would consider an enviable stretch of success, landing various roles in films and TV. I delightedly called her name—I wanted to tell her how proud I was. When she spun around, I realized from the whirling axes in her eyes that this was *not the time*—she was in the grip of a demon I'd seen before. She was having a full-bore, LA-specific, self-hating meltdown. Her lovely, vaguely ethnic nose, I saw, had been recently surgically reshaped. She appeared to have had a recent eye job to repair bags she was never old enough to have. She was photo-perfect—an exquisite princess, in the mirror—but her fists were clenched and she was hunched furiously over herself and barking at her reflection like it was trying to kill her. It was becoming a death match. One of them had to go.

Nonetheless, shopping in LA can be a wonderful experience (if you're the daughter of someone like Alec Baldwin). Even if you have no spending power but are a fashion enthusiast, there are still quite a few LA shopping destinations that you must make a pilgrimage to just for your own sartorial education and visual pleasure—to bask in an expansive articulation of an incredibly advanced style code.

I am anything but original in declaring that my favorite store in Los Angeles for this kind of adventure is Maxfield, on Melrose.

I know that when I'm shopping for clothes, I'm not truly happy unless the decor involves taxidermy chickens dressed in Edwardian formalwear. Maxfield provides these, a virtual library of first edition and/or out of print art books, stunning examples of vintage modern furniture (a compulsion so addictive that Maxfield recently opened a furniture annex across the street), and two other elements that have come to symbolize the mark of true retail sophistication for me: sex toys and human remains.

Maxfield represents decades of a rare and decadent style with enough means behind it to express itself fearlessly and unrestrainedly. Tommy Perse, Maxfield's creator, is the father of James Perse (the expensive T-shirt baron), and has long been a legend among the wealthy intelligentsia for his daredevil design eye. He was the first Angeleno retailer to embrace black garments and cutting-edge looks from Yohji Yamamoto and Comme des Garçons, back in the earliest 1980s, when most humans found the creations so jarringly weird as to be unthinkable as clothing.

Nearly everything at Maxfield is black on black on black on black. Despite the prohibitive price points, I feel very much at home there.

Mr. Perse's eye for treasure has been encouraged to indulge and pervert itself in every way conceivable. Just stumbling around inside the store is a master class in aesthetic decadence, and this is why you go (because, unless you're an Olsen twin, the price tags will feel like open-palmed blows to the face).

It's a huge black space with everything uniquely and impossibly wantable inside: stuffed white peacocks standing on Ed Ruscha photo books. Black Japanese golf bags covered with skulls, for the Connecticut chapter of the Hell's Angels. You can buy a Prada motorcycle helmet made of zebra hide, if you have $1,635.

Among Maxfield's offerings are pre-owned luxury goods— collected, I learned, via Perse's acquaintance with old European families. Vintage medical vitrines are full of old Rolexes and Cartier baubles; tall glass cases are packed with old Hermès desk sets, thermoses, bottle openers, horse brushes, and other instruments of aristocratic equipage. A moth-eaten Gucci suitcase made of genuine zebra hide will set you back $21,500 (but it just *screams* old money).

The brands on the racks represent a flirty tussle between posh and punk. I lusted over a rack of one of my favorite Japanese brands, LGB (Le Grand Bleu), which has mastered a look that fetishizes sexy fictions about the aesthetic of the old American West and expresses these through a new Japanese fashion sensibility. There are long, skinny, distressed plaid cowboy shirts, some with zippers. Generally speaking, they are clothes that Sam Shepard should wear to be hogtied and dragged three miles behind a 1959 Chevy Apache.*

Balmain, at the moment, might be the luxury brand that both attracts and repels me the most. Balmain brings a mind-bending new unattainability to your wardrobe with motocross-style jeans weighing in at an unforgivable $2,915. For jeans. Made of denim. No Kevlar, no sheared ibex, no major electronic, automotive, or weapons capabilities whatsoever. Just motorcycle pants that cost a full 300 percent more than my second motorcycle. But if you are so obnoxiously well-off that you're willing to drop the equivalent of a schoolteacher's monthly salary on your day look, then you're probably married to someone like Scarface or Hank Paulson (and you are going directly to hell.)

There is, as there should be, a dedicated erotica case. Maxfield's, discreetly placed at the back of the store, holds scrimshaw and quartz crystal phalluses, silver slave collars, real horsetail whips, and $3,950 handcuffs designed by the sex scholar, author, and bondage expert Betony Vernon.

---

* I saw Sam Shepard once, leaning against the mantel at a little cocktail soiree at Francis Ford Coppola's apartment in the Sherry Netherland. True to his code of rodeo cowboy realness, he was wearing dark, starchy, uncreased new Wranglers.

HOLLYWOOD has NOTHING on IOWA when it comes to producing Ridiculously Gorgeous SUPER-BLONDES! Eat your hearts out, Mouseketeers: these tow-headed Marilyn Monroes contain 0% bleach! Behold the radiant results of sunshine, clean-living, and genetics that would win blue ribbons anywhere on earth.

I have always wanted to see a real shrunken head, and Maxfield granted this wish. I could have bought one, if I'd had $37,500. Next to it was a Dayak human trophy skull, also for sale—his tag described him as having a "very well handled patina." Near him was perhaps the most frightening objet d'art I've ever seen: another real human skull with huge ram horns knotted onto it with rattan, decorated with a knot of shredded floral fabric. It strongly suggested that someone's bird-watching aunt toddled way, way too far into the heart of darkness ($39,000).

The first outfit I tried on: the Balmain motorcycle pants (just to feel the ungodly spleen), a long tank top by LGB ($185), and a reversible plaid shirt by Serenade ($1,275). I realized two things once this outfit was on.

1. If I ran out onto Melrose right then and was involuntarily manslaughtered by a car, my life would be worth approximately twice as much as it had been previous to my entering the dressing room in the eyes of the insurance adjuster evaluating what sum to award my family.

2. The outfit was staggeringly similar in numerous ways— shape, mood, distress—to outfits I'd liberated from dumpsters as a punk rock teenager.

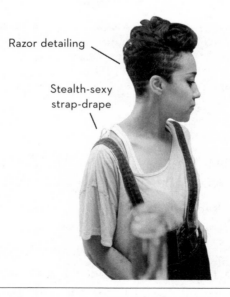

Razor detailing

Stealth-sexy
strap-drape

THE ELEGANT BARISTA

The Young Ladies of Seattle, WA, have their own subtle techniques for looking comely, without jumping the sartorial shark into the overt sluthood that tends to infect most coastal feminine attire. Sleekness in Seattle.

The soundtrack, ironically, pumping through the dressing room speakers was the eighties' ABC song "How to Be a Millionaire":

I've seen the future
I can't afford it

Tommy Perse will never move anywhere near the volume of merchandise as his T-shirt mogul son—but quality, not quantity, is the goal. The intelligence and kicky transgression of Maxfield is evident in every object selected. It is a thrillingly chic, grown-up inventory, which is in itself a high-level conversation about art, culture, modernism, morality, and footwear.

What you're really getting, shopping (or sightseeing) at Maxfield, is a rich subtext—a mind-expanding introduction to loads of secret, wonderful things you may never have heard of . . . because you don't have the money to find out. There is something that feels sincerely radical about $3,000 jeans, rare art books, sex tools, the viscount's old luggage, Le Corbusier patio chairs, and human skulls all being sold in the same room.

It does beg the question: Is Maxfield avant-garde art? Or is it sexily complicit, capitalist luxury kitsch?

Only Mr. Perse's hairdresser knows for sure. And you can bet your Balmain boots he always looks flawless, and probably does the cut in some whacked-out new way, blaring Wagner with two buck knives under a fan that was once a jet engine.

⌐⌐

I SHOULD HAVE BEEN ABLE to obtain, if not an unaffordable purchase in a shopping bag, at least a similar intellectual rapture at another famous Beverly Hills boutique. LILY et Cie, a Los Angeles institution for more than thirty years, is famous for being a veritable museum collection of (the owner claims) more than half a million pieces of rare, top-shelf vintage fashion.

I visited the boutique in 2011 as an emissary of the *New York Times*. But even a passive vintage aesthetic education proved to be too much ask from LILY et Cie, which may be one of the world's most jealously protected shrines to vintage fashion, vanity, and vexation of the spirit on earth.

One must roll hard to survive Los Angeles during the tense times preceding an awards season.

Driving there, I saw a black-windowed, black Escalade with chrome spoke rims blast across four lanes of traffic, past the iconic Beverly Hills sign and straight up the tree-lined hill to that forbidden paradise on tree-lined North Sierra. On Burton Way, I was driving behind a black-on-black Bentley with the license plate "HUSTLR."

As luxury seeks to redefine itself in the wake of the global pandemic of conglomerate brand takeovers, there has been, in certain (very rich and trendy) circles, an increased demand for swanky vintage couture. It is, in a way, insurance against a photograph of you on the red carpet next to another starlet in the exact same dress. The rarity of vintage essentially guarantees that when you sashay down the red carpet, there is no way in tarnation you'll be wearing the same dress as a Kardashian.

Rita Watnick, the owner and self-described "curator" of LILY et Cie, is notoriously prickly to people who don't happen to be famous fashionisti like André Leon Talley, or A-list actresses like Mary-Kate Olsen or Renée Zellweger (both of whom have graced red carpets in treasures from Ms. Watnik's zealously guarded vintage stash). The store boasts an impressive record of such high-profile victories. Penélope Cruz wore a 1950s white strapless (and somewhat bridal-looking) Balmain from LILY et

Cie to the Oscar ceremonies in 2009. There have surely been others, since.

A young salesman rushed to intercept me the moment I walked in the door, before I could touch anything. He was quite friendly, but had obviously been instructed to lay down a frightfully extensive list of airtight ground rules before I was allowed to move any further toward the clothing.

"Please move the clothing by the hanger," he said, physically demonstrating this motion in space, like a flight attendant. "If you want to see something more closely, take it *off* the rack to inspect it." (He said this while actually taking a garment gingerly off of the rack, just in case I had never used a closet bar before.)

I felt a bit like I was shopping for Gutenberg Bibles. I was actually surprised he didn't hand me white gloves and a particle mask, or offer me an antibacterial Silkwood shower.

The boutique, for having such uptight, helicopter-proprietor vibrations, is no great thrill to the eye in terms of retail decor. In fact, it's pretty nutty-looking, like one of those overcrowded, overpriced junk shops where the owner gets such severe attachment to the inventory that he can't sell it. The clothes I had been instructed so severely to protect were cram-packed and squished onto the racks so tightly that looking at any individual piece would be virtually impossible without removing it from the rack completely.

There was a work table behind a partition, where, I was told, alterations were done and original pieces were made. The back of the store, I was informed, was reserved for "special clients."

The pervasive aura of neurotic terror aside, LILY et Cie possesses an inarguably thrilling abundance of rare and wonderful vintage apparel. I had never before seen anything by Edith Small, a popular but largely forgotten designer from the late 1940s (a competitor, I was told, of the better-known Adrian, who I'd also never heard of). There was an entire rack of her bewitching handmade dresses—exhaustively structured pieces in black silk, most priced at around $1,300. One sleeve had delicate ruching that resembled wood grain. I wanted to ogle these dresses more closely, but they seemed to emit a threatening aura evocative of the high-voltage Taser jolt one might receive while trying to steal Dorothy's ruby slippers. Touch anything made of chiffon, and you can practically smell your own hair burning.

A tiger rug from the thirties was draped over a ledge on the back wall. "It was a gift, given to the owner," said Mr. Woods, the kindly salesman, with an apologetic lilt in his voice I didn't understand. "She's a strict vegetarian, but it's *so* beautiful."

It was a shame, I thought, that Ms. Watnick felt obliged to *eat* the rug—because it was truly fabulous, with its glass eyes and lead-and-clay-fortified tongue.

There were some knockout coats on the floor, with equally cold-cocking price tags. I gurgled over a bright pink Yves Saint-Laurent overcoat ($10,500) and a heavy black pony-skin Hermès ($6,500), from the 2007–08 season.

Ms. Watnick had been lurking and fussing in the background while I browsed, just beyond my eyeshot, but I felt aware of her tracking my every move—her laser gaze might as well have been the red dot from a sniper-scope. I was finally emboldened to come face-to-face with her when I got carried away by a spectacular wool trench, ideal for both flashing and espionage.

"She'd like to try this on," Mr. Woods pleaded on my behalf. It sounded as if he was asking if I could use the patients in her intensive care unit to practice my Rolfing technique.

"Well, *all right*," Ms. Watnick moaned with an audible eye roll. Subtext: *It's your lucky day, little Miss So-Not-On-My-Radar.*

Since I was just throwing on a coat, I suggested that I didn't really need a dressing room. (Or a delousing, for that matter.) "Daniel Hechter?" I asked the tracksuited Watnick, reading the coat's unfamiliar label. I pronounced the name "Hector."

I immediately felt aware that I was too stupid to insult this coat by putting my unworthy body in it.

"It's Daniel *Hesh-TAY*, darling," Ms. Watnick clarified, as if to say: "You don't know your French designers from the early seventies? Is this the first time you've worn shoes since leaving the Ozarks?"

The cut of the trench was a poem. The lining, however, was rotten and discolored all the way through—the previous owner seemed to have perspired something akin to battery acid. I thought the price, $795, was a bit stiff, considering the extensive damage. Ordinarily, I'd have started bargaining for the piece like a Berber—but I was too scared. I knew it would be a pointlessly nerve-jangling and possibly even traumatic endeavor.

I listened fretfully as Ms. Watnick gave instructions to Mr. Wood about a tiny, black, horizontally striped, mesh-velvet-spandex Giorgio Sant'Angelo creation—a pure hoochie-mama tube dress of the *Glitter*-era Mariah Carey variety.

"Take it off the floor," she snapped, hooking the little hooker dress onto a wheeled rack to roll it into the back. "People will trash it. They'll think they can get into it, and they just *can't*."

I shuddered. This was the level of concern Ms. Watnick felt about a dress that was perhaps *90 percent spandex*.

Even for a Teflon robo-cobra like me, who has spent enough time in snotty high-end establishments to have retail nerves like bridge cables, it was getting very hard to breathe in LILY et Cie. I ended up escaping before I terrorized Ms. Watnick any further with my beastly and unwanted patronage.

It struck me, later, *why* LILY et Cie has half a million pieces of vintage clothing: Ms. Watnick isn't *selling* her formidable collection so much as she is *hoarding* it.

Each piece in Ms. Watnick's mountain of untouchable fashion is an integral pixel; all of them are deemed necessary to maintain her Ring of Power in the flea circus that is Los Angeles. Most of the creations she has, hidden in airtight warehouses somewhere in the Valley, perhaps, or several stories underground—will probably remain invisible, concealed from the world for their own protection, until Ms. Watnick is pushed into a volcano.

⊰⊱

THE EXPERIENCE WAS SO UNSETTLING, I did something I never do if I can help it: I went to the Galleria—a big stupid mall in West Hollywood—just because I knew I'd be able to *touch the fucking clothes if I wanted to.*

I was so rattled I ended up buying something utterly ridiculous, just because I *could*—a silk military shirt in the exact pink-orange neon coral that made me painfully aware, while I was in Miami, that I suffered from terminal Goth-damage. I even took the tags off the shirt so I wouldn't be allowed to return it. I was going to wear that loud-ass shirt, by God, because I was never going to let my character shrivel into something ungenerous, hyper-vigilant, neurotic, overwrought, and gloomy. I was determined to bash myself into that color for my own good.

I was never able to. The shirt mocked me from my closet daily. I couldn't get rid of it fast enough. Within a month, I had sold it on eBay at a 70 percent loss.

I felt like a failure. Colors, after all, are emotion. I felt like my black-on-blackness, while hip and urbane and easy, represented some blind spot on my psychic mapping—an emotional obstacle holding me back from finding more sunshine in my life.

Finally, I got creative and began mixing Rit household fabric dyes in a big pot on my stove. After a series of messy experiments, I finally succeeded in integrating two actual colors into my otherwise monochromatic wardrobe: a dark greyish purple I call "Bruise" or "Burnt Prune," and a brackish-looking battleship teal I've dubbed "Old Prison Tattoo."

As colors go, they are drab and sludgy and gulag-esque. They surely ain't no electric mango, but they are colors, dammit. I may never look right in Florida.

I can live with this.

Coming from a wardrobe that has gone from black to blacker to *even blacker* for years, even "Bruise" felt like real progress. A prisoner in solitary confinement can't just traipse out into the yard at noon, once his door slides open. The light can be wounding.

Like any internal change, wardrobe color adjustments are infuriatingly slow, gradual processes. Like the speed of light, emotion really can't be forced to go any faster or slower than it wants to. The heart will arrive at its destination only when it is already there.

In the interest of being a reliable narrator, I should reveal a slice of my own psychological fashion history.

In 1994, the year I lived in LA, my fashion sense inexorably drifted toward a more LA-centric representation of femininity. It happened slowly; it seeped into my closet from the outside, on the totally subconscious level of frog-boiling.

I had no idea how far off the deep end LA dragged my style until a year later, when I moved to New York.

When I first arrived in New York, I was introduced to a very, very cool, attractive woman a few years older than me. I very much wanted to impress her—she worked in theater, we knew some of the same people in the music business, and—most badass of all—when she was in her early twenties, she'd had a fling with Muhammad Ali. She invited me to come out with her to a bar to see some of her friends play in a band.

The year I was in LA, I was living with a rock musician. Since I was going to rock shows all the time, this was an evening ensemble I felt confident I could assemble, so I whupped out some of my better "dressing to see a band" drag.

The minute I showed up at my new friend's door, I saw that she was wearing black jeans, boots, a leather jacket, and a black T-shirt. My new friend's face literally washed over with pure mortification at the sight of me. Her eyes scanned me up and down, her mouth was open but involuntarily turned down at the sides—before she caught herself.

"Wow. You really dressed up," she said, with a weak smile.

"Oh God," I said. "I called this one wrong, didn't I?"

"Well, it's too late now!" she said cheerfully. "We gotta go!"

She was pretending that she still liked me and wanted to be my friend, but I knew that any possible alliance we might have made had cratered in her doorway the moment she saw my outfit. I knew in the cab uptown that despite her chitchat, she was trying to figure out ways to roll me out and into a steaming manhole before she had to introduce me to anyone.

The bar was an uptown Irish bar. The band: a middle-aged, intellectual, Pogues-type outfit called Black '49. Everyone there was cool, in their thirties, intellectual, and dressed entirely in black. I will never forget the deep shame of having arrived in this insular scene wearing a white vinyl jacket, a sleeveless, light blue, plastic Barbarella minidress with white vinyl, over-the-knee, multiply buckled fetish platform boots.

In LA, I would have been more or less invisible. In that bar, my outfit was a billboard, screeching in an adult baby-voice, *Hi, therious bethpectacled New Yorkerth! I'm an intergalactic blonde thyber-whore! I was just banished here from the future becauth I'm too thtupid to be utheful as a thex thlave.* My friend bravely attempted to introduce me to a few of her tribespeople, but the writing was on all of their eyebrows—it was really no use.

We never spoke afterward, we never hung out again. I didn't blame her.

I don't think I've worn anything but black ever since.

8

THE 137TH KENTUCKY DERBY /
THE BOURBON BELT

Lifestyles of the Rich and Plastered

～

The Kentucky Derby is decadent and depraved.

—DR. HUNTER S. THOMPSON

Four days before the 137th Kentucky Derby, I packed up my 22-inch hatbox—the size of a bass drum box—and shipped it to my Louisville hotel via UPS. I had no faith whatsoever in Delta Airlines, or their ability to successfully navigate such an object onto my connection flight in Detroit.

The Louisville flight, however, was full of crispy chattering blondes with pinched eye jobs, who confidently stuffed their huge hatboxes in the overhead compartments of the small plane; they apparently were intimately familiar with the storage dimensions of Boeing 737s in their heads, and chose their hats according to the largest possible box dimension. Accompanying these women were their male analogs: blue-eyed, bourbon-flushed captains of industry in navy blazers, happily group-drinking in the early afternoon.

In the back of the plane, excitable gamblers in black windbreakers were pulling out their wallets and comparing OTB cards. I am pretty sure I was the only person on the flight reading Marxist political philosophy by Slavoj Žižek.

This was my second trip to in Louisville's Churchill Downs for the annual Kentucky Derby, widely referred to as "the most exciting two minutes in sports." On this trip, I had more specific goals. I was codebreaking: looking for the interpretive style drift, inspecting women's hats for deeper symbolic meanings and vital clues toward the understanding the code of Kentucky's regional fashion dialect.

In the Kentucky airport restroom, I noticed a red plastic bio-hazard container absolutely brimming with diabetic syringes, right as a robotic female voice announced the terrorist alert level: high.

The Derby itself is a strange, overblown, and somewhat tawdry affair—basically a massive, drunk adult prom with a lusty extra oomph provided by the presence of million-dollar racehorses and high-stakes gambling, a touch of high-end vice that permits other-wise reserved society wives and debutantes to leap up and down, screech epithets, pound wooden railings with $40,000 charm- and tennis-bracelet-jangling fists, and generally act like a flock of escaped cockatiels that have found their way to an outdoor bour-bon bath. Because the Derby is such an airtight regional phenome-non—which has been going on for nearly 140 years—its fashion is wholly specific and peculiar to itself. It is a very advanced, looped-out, self-referential style that has been gradually exploding into ever more freaked-out, bizarre, and fabulous variations of itself since the inception of the event in 1875.

Like a wedding dress, a prison jumpsuit, or a black latex zipper hood, a proper Kentucky Derby outfit would look violently wrong anywhere outside of its intended social context.

Kentucky was, after all, always the most Southern of the

Union states. The white Kentucky establishment were unapologetically pro-slavery Lincoln-haters. Slaves tended the bluegrass for the horse farms that migrated over from Virginia. Physically small slaves were occasionally able to win their freedom as the first jockeys, in silks that were a throwback to races hosted by Charles II.

Kentucky's slaves weren't free until the ratification of the Thirteenth Amendment, and Kentucky didn't officially support the amendment until 1976.

The sexual economy, too, has also been handed down from Southern aristocrats, their nineteenth-century aristocratic colonial pretensions, their emphasis on social life, leisure, and fine clothes, and their nostalgic pride in such Southern traditions as preferring liquor to psychotherapy, cigars to celery sticks, and cast-iron jockey sculptures to actual black people.

The sartorial code for the Kentucky Derby, in my opinion, is *Back to the Plantation*.

When everyone in the stands rises to sing "My Old Kentucky Home," there is a palpable yearning for that lost paradise of cotton, magnolias, and human trafficking.

Southern ladies seem, in large part, to be big-hipped, small-nosed blondes with huge white teeth—essentially the Ur-text of the hyperconservative, Lady Bird Johnson–like dress codes of Washington DC's women. Many Southern ladies compulsively stand in third position when you photograph them (a clear sign of early beauty pageant abuse).

The first time I was at the Derby, I was the guest of a couple—a Southern gentleman and his girlfriend. The gentleman was embroiled in a brutal divorce and had, through this process, developed an interesting theory about the life cycle of the Southern female, which he narratively broke down into bloody Lego components for me.

Southern ladies, he said, are first constructed by elite all-girl Catholic elementary and high schools. They attend social dancing lessons to learn how to be charming, graceful, and desirable. They go to cotillion and are introduced into society as debutantes. They join sororities at prestigious universities, where they are expected, by themselves, their peers, and their families, to get husbands and enviable academic degrees—in that order.

(I later read that while there is a lot of chaste sister-love encouraged within the halls of Southern higher education, surprisingly few actual lesbians came out of them. Whatever existed of a "lesbian community" was apparently so slim or so marginalized as to be virtually invisible. This, it was theorized, is because the Southern gentry still clung to traditional views of honor and manhood. Educated Southern women don't traditionally work for a living; I read that there was never enough of an evident economy to support two unmarried women for enough lesbians to make any serious claim on a Southern neighborhood.)

Once married and university-degreed, my host continued, Southern ladies tended to devote their lives to remodeling their husbands' homes until they got pregnant. Once their children were old enough to speak English and stop wetting the bed, they were shipped off to boarding schools. This was the point at which life got tricky: with the children out of the house, the wife, suddenly a decade or two older than the bride she had been and bereft of activity, began to examine her marriage more closely than ever before, only to discover that her long sexually neglected Southern husband had invariably been cheating on her. This effected a major evolutionary change in a Southern woman's life—the shattering of all of her myths, as it were. In her mid- to late thirties, predictably bitter and resentful, she then routinely accused the husband she had expertly landed like a giant sea bass of "depriving her of a professional life," even though this was the primary goal of her higher education in the first place. (The "MRS degree" is a hoary old nickname for Southern women's university diplomas, still in parlance.)

At this juncture (the Kentucky gentleman embroiled in hellish divorce proceedings continued), the jilted ex-debutantes, who had always had fine heads on their shoulders under all that tortured hair, reembraced academia with new passion. A goodly percentage, he said, went to law school—specifically to devote all their rage and long-untapped creative energies toward seeking righteous and outrageously costly revenges on their soon to be ex-husbands. Divorce proceedings in the South tended to become the main focus of these women's post-childbirth lives, taking on the pole position that the Dream Wedding once had in terms of planning and obsessive production value. The ex-bride and proud leading lady, once she had traumatically realized that she had been recast in the movie she thought was her life, transformed into her ex– true love's most lethal legal nemesis. Southern divorce proceedings are famously acrimonious, and many go on longer than the marriages themselves.

The Churchill Downs venue itself is architecturally arranged in the same kind of hierarchical structure that aristocratic Southern society itself thrives on. The ladies' hats, amazingly enough, seemed to reflect this.

Beyond the gates of the stadium, there are a few concentric rings of excluded locals, with no hats whatsoever, save an occasional trucker cap. Along the roadsides, weatherbeaten people resembling sharecroppers wave cardboard signs offering $20 parking spots on their own lawns. Hopeful participants (or more likely scalpers) wave signs with peel-off vinyl lettering reading "NEED TICKETS" (intentionally devoid of punctuation, I guessed, to promote plausible deniability, if busted).

Hellfire-and-brimstone Christian families—parents with stair-step collections of miserable-faced children—often grimly inhabit corners sitting on portable deck chairs, wearing disposable rain ponchos. Their selfless, thankless daylong mission is to save the souls of Derby participants, a feat they accomplish by holding up cardboard signs with hand-painted red block letters (in that all-cap font I like to call Schizophrenia) reminding gamblers: REPENT BELIEVE GOSPEL, and THE ONLY WAY TO HEAVEN IS JESUS.

Churchill Downs' cheapest seats are in the infield. The crowd in the center of the track resembles that in a stadium parking lot at a NASCAR race or a Slayer concert—young people in bikini tops and black T-shirts are already wearing Mardi Gras beads and staggering drunk on plastic cups of Bud Light by 11 a.m.

As a rule, I noted that the lower the level of the stands (i.e., the cheaper the seats), the more oversexed women's fashions became: the tighter the strapless, shiny spandex sausage of an elasticated minidress; the higher the shiny nude knockoff Christian Louboutins (which the girls have visible trouble walking in, particularly after their sixth or seventh mint julep). Cosmetics, too, are heavily amplified in the lower stands. Spray tans are much darker; breast implants a great deal larger.

Paradoxically, those women seated in the lowest tiers, who have devoted so much attention to amplifying their femininity in every other sartorial and/or cosmetic way—biggest breasts, shortest skirts, highest shoes, tallest hair—have the smallest hats. Their hat of choice is a tiny satin "Fascinator" attached to the head with bobby pins or a tiny elastic strap, decorated with a teensy spit of tulle or mini-rosette spot-glued on one side. (Perhaps, because they are so small, these tiny chapeaux are capable of enjoying useful lives beyond the Derby. They may serve as uncomfortable head-decor for Pomeranians, or lend a festive touch to the rear-view mirror.)

The higher one rides up the Churchill Downs escalators, the

more expensive the seating becomes, and the richer the clientele. The hats, I noticed, grew incrementally larger on every floor. By the time my research assistant, Dr. Amanda Parkes, and I were able to schmooze our way up to the private dining and viewing areas on Millionaires' Row on the sixth floor, the custom millinery extravaganzi favored by the ladies were Marie Antoinette–worthy feats of circumference and gravitational defiance nearly the size of bed canopies or outdoor café coach umbrellas.

When I covered the Kentucky Derby in the late nineties, female fashions seemed primarily bent around competitive conspicuous consumption. Women wore loud signifiers of social prestige and wealth, like tribal warlords. Many accessories were worn mainly to inspire peer jealousy and/or imitation: sunglasses with large gold Chanel logo medallions; gold Fendi medallion earrings, gold YSL jacket buttons, pants with gold Versace medallions. These were the trophies conferring the status of top-shelf male pampering (the attainment of which, for Southern women, is a fiercely competitive bloodsport comparable to Rollerball).

On my second trip, the primary rule governing wealthy Derby women's fashion seemed to have reprioritized into the proud outspending of one another, as demonstrated by enormous, one-of-a-kind, custom-made hats (and they are delighted to give credit to the exclusive milliner whom they commissioned to design them). Orders are placed months in advance, at presumably gruesome expense. Each belle has her well-rehearsed, obligatory hat-obtaining horror anecdote—an adorable litany of fret and alarm. Oversize grosgrain ribbons didn't arrive in time from Paris. Systems of mesh loops resembling fuchsia Hot Wheels tracks couldn't be assembled for love nor money! And yet, by some Christian miracle, all hats, like brave lost pets having survived insurmountable obstacles, found their ways home to their intended mistresses.

It was probably because I was obsessed with Slavoj Žižek at the

time, but I couldn't stop smirking into my long black glove thinking about the similarity of the largest and most exquisite hats at
the derby to flamenco skirts (the back ruffles of which can have
the effect of making a woman's backside resemble that of a baboon
in estrus) and imagining what Žižek's post-Freudian view of them
might be. There was something distinctly, intensely, unavoidably
labial about these enormous floppy hats, laden with silk flowers and
filled with hair. I kept remembering a Žižek quote from the docu-
mentary *The Pervert's Guide to Cinema*. Žižek is filmed watering flowers in his garden, and he suddenly goes off on a rant against tulips.

"Just imagine," he says, with palpable mock disgust. "Aren't
these some kind of—how do you call it—vagina dentatae? Dental
vaginas threatening to swallow you? . . . Are people aware what
a horrible thing these flowers are? I mean, basically, it's an open
invitation to all insects and bees! 'Come and screw me!' I think
that flowers should be forbidden to children."

Southern white men at the Derby are largely oblivious to such
psychological nuance. The bulk of them tend, even the ones in
their early thirties, to be thick-necked, small-eyed, and prematurely jowly from the privilege of having consumed entire pastures
of T-bone and lakes of bourbon. The middle-aged men often still
have thick and abundant hair, but their skulls seem to taper in a bit
too much around the eyes—the unfortunate markings of a person whose apex of physical attractiveness peaked in his teen years,
or, perhaps, of the inbreeding of earlier generations. Their looks
tend toward one of two sides of the GOP White Male collection:
a beefy, scotch-flushed, Rush Limbaugh–type physicality, or an
overcompensating look of the John Boehner variety: overbleached
blue-white teeth set into a burnt sienna head, overtinted with
accumulated applications of a gradual bronzer.

Out of context, anywhere else on earth, Kentucky Derby
men's fashion would read as rompingly, screamingly, pouncingly

OH THE CLOTHES SHINE BRI-I-GHT . . .

. . . On this Totally Dapper Southern Gent at the Kentucky Derby. This is no OTB outfit, Baby Gurl. Huh-Uhn. This look is decidedly ON-Track.

gay—even in Miami, Washington DC, the Hamptons, or on a Hawaiian golf course. The older gentlemen loiter together in whispery pastels like shelves full of Hummel figurines, the younger in flashy greens, pinks, lavenders, and bright yellows like chocolate Easter bunnies.

In the press box, we met Mr. Steve Eubanks, a Fox sports reporter, who took one look at my truck tire–sized black hat and informed me that I looked like I was "dressed for a New Orleans funeral." I noted that Mr. Eubanks was wearing a cloisonné pin on his lapel that read "Mucho Macho Man," and asked if this was the name of his favorite horse or merely a shallow sexual boast.

Mr. Eubanks described men's Derby fashion as "Early American Pimp." Dr. Parkes and I had, indeed, witnessed examples of this.

There was a gauche young white guy in his late twenties, hanging for balance on the bar on the fifth floor, whose occupation, he said, was "retired." He was wearing a bespoke three-piece suit, which was, in my opinion, not so much an outfit as a harrowing object lesson. His suit was, in itself, a completely articulated argument for why feckless young men should never be given large sums of money (and, following that, why they should never, ever be allowed to tell a professional tailor how to do his job). The suit was, in effect, a garish, badly yet expensively built mega-mansion: an oversize black chalk-stripe gangster suit, built with such ridiculously overwrought pretensions of a nonexistent street credibility that it managed to fail in both all conceivable penthouses and all conceivable ghettos, equally. The tailoring evoked that of the suits young hip-hop bands wore in the early nineties, before they were successful enough to have stylists. It was essentially a zoot suit that looked like it had been measured on a vertical washer-dryer set: huge, long, boxy vest, oversize, droopy, baggy pants, way too long jacket, all intentionally designed to fit this way, unintentionally resembling some kind of finery improvised by a member of the Little Rascals for a formal dog-chasing event. His friend/lackey— an entourage member obviously on his payroll—pulled up a photo on his phone of the custom SUV this young tycoon had designed for himself. The car, too, was a boxy and oversize mess of an over-chromed Escalade that also misappropriated and abused "street" ostentation. I asked the young zillionaire if his car had gun turrets. No, a member of his entourage answered for him—but it did pull a really large boat.

I bolted before his lackey could pull up the boat photo from his phone.

⚔

DR. PARKES AND I spent two days at the races interviewing people in the stands with exceptional dress style. We had a lengthy conversation with a guy in a pink-silver sharkskin suit from Lexington, after we complimented his shiny chrome Dolce and Gabbana eyeglasses. We had hopefully assumed from his garish metallic ensemble that he was gay, but he quickly announced that he was a gynecologist and that when we photographed him, we had to make sure each photo properly displayed his newish dental veneers.

During this conversation, I complimented a dapper African American gentleman who walked by in a pair of turquoise argyle Harlequin slacks.

"I could tell just by looking that you like black guys," the gynecologist snorted, reaching into his suit pocket to retrieve his iPhone. "I gotta lock this thing or those people will take it and *do* shit with it."

This comment, apart from the fact of my liking black guys, didn't really make sense, even as casual obnoxiousness. The Kentucky Derby looked like it had suffered an ethnic cleansing during the apartheid era. There was only a scant handful of African Americans at the races who weren't working service positions, and they all looked considerably more together than the gynecologist. A couple of smart, haute-casual Kanye West types were causing an understated sensation on the fourth floor, swanning around in white jeans with cashmere sweaters tied around their shoulders. One spectacular gentleman, a true fashion star, was rocking a Billy Dee Williams marcel-wave and a baby-pink zoot suit—perfectly.

The overt racism in Southern states is so stark, brutal, and totally unlike anything that ever came out of the mouths of the adults I grew up with in my integrated-à-la-*Sesame Street* coastal cities, that hearing such statements makes me feel as queasy and violated as I did years ago in Mexico City, when an anonymous, well-dressed man in a restaurant suddenly grabbed an aggressive handful of my ass (assuming, perhaps, that any young blonde in a sleeveless dress, in that context, was a submissive prostitute, openly advertising my professional interest in receiving rare and specialized forms of advanced sexual abuse).

Near the end of the day, a pithy Turk and I were thrown together quite spontaneously while trying to watch the eleventh race. The Southern couple standing in front of us was quite drunk—the woman, wearing a transparent ivory dress that looked as if it was made of embroidered Cheerios, was awkwardly clambering over a line of security tape in order to stand directly in front of us, obscuring our view of the racetrack. Her husband turned around and asked, by way of unspoken apology, "How long have you two been married?"

"Thirty years," I said, too quickly for rebuttal.

The Turk looked at me and drew hard on his cigar, stone-faced.

"He kidnapped me when I was a child while my family was vacationing in Istanbul."

The Southerner's eyes widened.

"He raped me repeatedly for the first ten years—then I grew to love him."

"I hear that happens," said the Southerner, turning forward to watch his wife lift a nude-pumped foot and tilt hazardously over the balcony railing.

"I still love her," said the Turk, gamely putting a hand on my shoulder with a straight face. "I'm finally getting a vasectomy next week."

I naturally ended up hanging on the arm of this cigar-chomping Turk for the better part of the evening. He was not a tall man, but he was impeccably dressed in a very well-tailored blue pin-stripe suit in exquisite three-season Italian wool, a custom white shirt of exceptional starchiness and thread count, and a lurid pink silk tie. He was a "businessman" of some unspecific variety; his card bore a nondescript three-letter name such as those preferred by sinister umbrella corporations. The Turk was visiting the Derby with his business partner, a vulpine young Russian, whose professional talents, guessing from his attire (running shoes, jeans, two-tone windbreaker) were somewhere on the spectrum between designing computer viruses and pistol-whipping. The Russian, wall-eyed drunk, was singing rowdily and pouring champagne on himself; he had won $87,000 in the eleventh race. The Turk smiled calmly. A moment later, when the gloating Russian walked off the deck to get more bottles from the bar, the Turk broke out giggling and launched into a bouncing, euphoric little dance. "He's going to be so angry!" he whispered to me. "I just won so much more than he did!"

Things got weirder, as they inevitably do at the Kentucky Derby—particularly around big winners. Champagne suddenly began flying around; unknown sources repeatedly sloshed refills into our flutes.

⚜

A CURIOUS FASHION RITUAL TAKES place in the parking lot purgatory after the races—it is the moment that the women have been waiting for all day. Hundreds of them suddenly crouch in the parking lot, remove their five-inch torture-pumps, and collectively expose half a stadium's worth of carnage: mangled, blistered, bandaged (but recently pedicured) toes. As if on cue, the women then produce ballet flats or flip-flops from their shoulder tote bags and lay them on the asphalt. Using one another's shoulders for balance, the entire female population suddenly shrinks by four to six inches, and breathes a hearty collective sigh of relief.

Dr. Parkes and I managed to pull the Turk away from his friends and out of the parking area, which was increasingly resembling a Monsanto feedlot-cum-concentration camp—an endless maze of chain-link fences guiding an ever-increasing horde of limping, wilting women and their sunburned mates into shuttles and interminable taxi lines.

I walked into the middle of the street to flag down a lovely young civilian female in a late-model Buick sedan. I offered her $100 (from the Turk's softball-sized wad) to take the three of us approximately four miles to Parkstown Road.

We stopped briefly at a famous post-Derby hotspot called Jeff Ruby's, but we were almost simultaneously thrown out for attempting to videotape a potbellied jackass in a woman's hat who had decided to stand up in his booth and dance with his shirt unbuttoned to the house band's horrible rendition of "Fire Down Below."

IF YOU WEREN'T BEING EXPLOITED FOR SURPLUS VALUE,
YOU COULD LOOK THIS FABULOUS EVERY SINGLE DAY

Bachelor party Rat Pack enjoying pre-Derby juleps in Lexington, KY.

Very important people were here, I was informed by the maître d'. People whose careers would not benefit from being videotaped semi-topless in women's hats, singing "Fire Down Below."

We followed the Turk to a much richer, much trendier event at an Art Basel–style gallery/hotel/restaurant. In the ladies' room, I was delighted to witness two enormously drunk, stumbling hookerish blondes in Swarovski-spangled pink taffeta minidresses. One yelled unrestrainedly at the other over the top of the stalls: "Gurl, I am not TRAHYIN' to hurt yer feelings. I am just trahyin' to tell you the TREWTH. You need to give it up—he just DOESN'T LIKE YEW!"

Southern sisterhood, in all its glory.

While I was loitering in the lobby and admiring the general spectacle, Martha Stewart stomped through, looking deeply aggrieved and very alone. She was dressed down with no lipstick, carrying a beachy tote bag at midnight and looking through narrow, stabby eyes at the world. I had always been impressed that she was able, while in prison, to knit an iconic poncho that made her audience trust her again. But I was frightened by what I perceived to be Martha Stewart's impenetrable loneliness— she seemed to gravitate around an internationally fabulous fun event-orbit while encased in an invisible shock-fence of solitary confinement. I felt for Martha; at that moment, I realized that I, too, was beginning to look like I could turn everyone in Kentucky into pillars of salt.

The owners of the winning horse of the day, which had made so much money for the Turk and his partner, were sitting in the back of the restaurant eating and drinking fatly and handsomely with their hyper-styled wives. Their hats were the most spectacular millinery achievements I'd witnessed all day—enormous off-white custom extravaganzae, like Frank Gehry wedding cakes—cream-colored grosgrain ribbons seven inches wide, draped like cake batter pouring from a great height over the brims. I recognized them as Philip Treacy creations. (All the more impressive given that this event occurred some two years before the Royal Wedding that made Treacy's hats an international sensation.)

The drunk Russian and a conservative middle-aged couple who were introduced as "business clients" joined us for dinner in this poshly rowdy hotspot. The Turk introduced me to the nonplussed couple as his future ex-wife. Both of them looked at their shoes and grimaced while giving me limp handshakes.

"They're scowling at you because they know I am married," whispered the Turk.

"Oh, don't worry," I assured the fist-faced woman. "I absolutely *adore* his wife."

❧

I FLED FROM THE TURK after dinner when he started ordering double martinis, his stories started conflicting, and the waitress chastised him for being "too grabby." I pulled a "French exit"—I suddenly picked up my purse and bolted without explanation.

Rain was driving in heavy sheets outside. To my bewilderment, a policewoman was stationed directly outside the door with two tattooed male bouncers. She looked me directly in the eye.

"Ma'am, are you all right? Is someone bothering you? Are you with someone?"

This was, I later realized, an actual *protocol.* There had apparently been enough bad episodes during such post-Derby nights that at some point in time it had been deemed *necessary* for the law to protect Southern women (who were almost unanimously crippled, sunstroked, overserved, and wobbling like sick colts after twelve-plus hours yelling at horses in their billowing vagina hats and foot-slashing pumps). History has apparently proven that on such evenings, Southern men, many of whom seemed to be in collectively cordoned, voracious, rip-snorting blackouts, tend to come on a bit *rapey*.

"Well, I'm not being *oppressed* or anything," I explained, not entirely sure as to what was happening. "I was with someone, but I'm not anymore."

I was just exhausted; I needed to go back to my hotel. Like most of the other surviving females, my feet were literally bloody after two days running around the races in stilettos and micro-fishnets, and I was also 68 percent drunk.

The next morning, Dr. Parkes, who had remained at the bar, informed me that the Turk had chased me to the door, but bouncers had physically prevented him from walking outside to speak to me by threatening him with jail time. They'd apparently seen him grab my arm and try to stop me from leaving—a fact I hadn't even noticed, let alone thought significant. I had been oblivious to this dramatic red flag, even as it triggered the enforcement of what was, for all intents and purposes, a spontaneous restraining order by Louisville's finest.

The Turk phoned me on his way to the airport the next day to rant about the police event. He and the Russian had apparently not slept, and had been drinking nonstop since my departure from the bar. They were both so walleyed and morose they were slurring vulgarities in hip-hop slang.

"Shiiih. Tell me to stay, I'll turn the cab around. I fuckin' LOVE you, you crazy beeyotch," yowled the Turk, in a way I knew he'd never remember.

He and the Russian collectively offered me $100,000 if I sent them a photo of myself wearing my Derby hat, my pumps, and nothing else.

I told them I'd do it when the money hit my Paypal account.

I am still waiting. And I am getting really cold.

9
THE IOWA STATE FAIR /
THE BUTTER BELT

The Culture in Agriculture

⌇

As early as the stopover in Detroit, it was clear that the Midwest and New York were going to be two entirely different balls of wax, style-wise. The fashion codes were already becoming inscrutable. I knew I was dealing with a new gravitational style-orbit when I saw women in the airport with stretch pants, lunar-white tennis shoes, and extremely high-maintenance salon hairdos—the upkeep of which would consistently outspend the body, including the feet (unlike New York, where shoes are usually the most expensive object on a body, because they double as transportation).

Body types were markedly different from those of people in New York, it occurred to me, while witnessing an older lady on a people-mover with upper arms the size of pumpkins. It made me wonder, in a real (read: un-snarky) way, if human bodies tend to emulate their environments. Have New Yorkers, through some unconscious process of internal mimicry, become comparatively scrawny people because their bodies were somehow imprinted to grow in imitation of the tall, narrow, shoulder-to-shoulder, multistory brownstones that the Dutch built to get around their real estate lot laws? Midwestern bodies seemed to be reflective of what is never seen, and therefore not reflected by bodies, in New York—a rural abundance of lateral space.

(Note to those sensitive about weight issues: this insight is *not* intended to be fat-bashing. It is plausible that all New Yorkers might just be caffeine-swilling, nerve-shrunken, yoga-abusing stress-monsters subsisting primarily on wine, Adderall, and cigarettes, like myself. But I have found other theoretical sources supporting the feasibility of this body-emulating-environment notion.)

Since Iowa is in the Corn Belt, I wanted to see as many tractors, towheads, farm animals, and 4H Club agricultural *objets* as possible. The Iowa State Fair has been happening for over 100 years, replete with a traditional cow carved annually out of butter ("100 years of the Butter Cow!" shout the pamplets).

The fair is also famous for stands upon stands selling the most brazen, defiantly health-killing, whompingly caloric, heart-attack-in-a-plastic-dish edibles. Greasy joke food is almost a sport for Iowans: the whole state seems to revel in competing in a hilarious frat house "I Dare You to Eat That!" contest. E.g.: red velvet cake apparently isn't decadent enough until it is run through a funnel and deep-fried into a scribbly mass of what looks like a disemboweled churro that leaves a dark oil slick under the paper plate. Iowans are also amused by culinary gambits that conflate meat and dessert—for example, the All-Beef Sundae.

One of the major attractions of the State Fair is Iowa's talent for taking foods already possessed of bad reputations for their dietary indulgence factors, deep-frying them, and then putting them on sticks. Deep-fried bacon on a stick is only where the fun *begins*. Twinkies. Snicker's bars. Pork chops. The new item this year that had the crowds aflutter: sticks of butter, deep fried . . . on sticks.

It's joke food, to be sure; but if you're a real Iowan, actually *eating* these ever more absurd culinary atrocities is almost ritualistic—an annual pagan team-building exercise, like snake-handling or walking on coals, designed to inspire and display superhuman gastrointestinal fortitude and health-flouting.

My research on this day was focused on the most casual Iowa fashions. Most of the Iowa fair attendees were dressed down in appropriate carnival attire to have fun on this day—in sweatshirts, T-shirts, cut-off jean shorts, and other clothing they could cover with petting-zoo hair, baby saliva, and butterscotch all day and then put directly in the wash once they got home.

For many fairgoers, the fashion accessory of choice was a Rascal—those little electric supermarket go-carts for the infirm. Rascals are in fact the preferred mode of transportation at the Iowa State fair; there are stands set up in multiple locations where you can rent a personal scooter for the day (good news for your shoes when making that long beeline to the deep-fried Ho-Ho stand).

I figured a lot of Iowa gentlemen worked many a day on agricultural machines, or at least drivable lawnmowers; they were accustomed to covering a lot of territory in the course of a day, because in Iowa, there *is* a huge, whomping amount of territory. Expansive areas are arguably the main point of Iowa; machines with wheels are practically an extension of any Iowa body that isn't already on a horse.

There's a pervasive kindness and wholesomeness to Iowans that makes it difficult to take a picture of a couple or a family and have it not look like a Norman Rockwell painting or a corporate stock photo. In the broadest and most general strokes, Iowa citizens tend to bedeck themselves in crisp, clean, wrinkle-free American rural wear accentuated with classic Western details such as bandannas, bolo ties, and pearlescent shirt-snaps. I was delighted by the sight of numerous senior couples: men in trucker hats and suspenders over short-sleeved button-up shirts, women with salon-curled hair and cotton print blouses. Virtually all of the older couples with whom I spoke had been married more than forty years—and (at least it seemed from the outside) *happily.* I felt they took pride in their lasting love; it seemed to have a great and obvious value to them, judging from their hilarious mutual sentence-finishing rapports and touchingly respectful duets of body language. Their relationships had been honed over decades into harmonies I have rarely witnessed in my urban life.

"If your whole livelihood is dependent on the soil and whether it rains or not, pretty soon you figure out that you're not in control

GOLDEN ANNIVERSARIANS

Having fought the long, good fight, they seem remarkably capable of enjoying each other.

of everything, so you'd better figure out how to be a good person and make a few friends," one gentleman told me, when I asked him to help me understand Iowa's ineluctable charms.

Iowa is full of gorgeous young people full of humility and fine manners, responsible God-loving teens who seemed to spring right out of some Western idyll from 1940s ad illustrations: sun-splashed, hardworking, athletic, sweet-faced young ladies with backlit baby-blue eyes and long blonde braids in 4H sweatshirts or starchy western-shirts; heartbreakingly polite, cocky young cow-boys, wearing their dusty boots, their favorite oval belt buckle, and the hat that was made for them. Sure, it's an agricultural ste-reotype—but these cowboys and cowgirls seemed especially gor-geous because they were stone *legit*.

My friend Toby was raised in Iowa, and happened to be in town visiting the fair the same time I was. "For guys here, it's all about the jeans, see," he explained. "Levi's are for pussies. Wranglers are for *real men*. Tight Wranglers are cut to really hug a man's ass for that gay rodeo look."

Clothing-wise, Iowans, I thought, were a modest, fancy-averse people, not unlike Canadians. Clothing is often representative of a service to land and beasts of the field, and punctuated by cow-boy accoutrements. There are, however, many group activities and contests where an Iowan may splash out into clothing items of rodeo-flavored spectacular—some of which, to my overwhelming delight, involved wildly pimped-out horses, giant flags, and young girls in deliriously spangled outfits including cowboy hats with *built-in tiaras*.

I had to stop a ravishing couple in their late thirties—a gor-geous blonde woman and her black-mustachioed, Platonic ideal of a cowboy husband—in order to gush how perfect they looked. Both were wearing flawlessly pressed Western apparel with mag-nificent piping and tapestry-level embroidery, and top-end, silver-

YOU CAN SEE BY HIS OUTFIT THAT HE IS A COWBOY

A fearless young Iowan, instantly ready to tackle the job of the moment, whether it involves spurs, a shovel, or enough natural glamor to stare down the barrel of a New York camera with no hesitation whatsoever. All Boy and No Bull.

and-leather belts, hand-tooled into dizzying rococo patterns that I had never seen before outside of Las Vegas mall boutiques.

"Oh God, thank you for saying that," said the blonde, pressing my arm sincerely. "He left his good shirt in the bedroom," she whispered, "and he's been kicking himself *all day.*"

Since it would have been physically impossible for her husband's "good shirt" to be an aesthetic improvement on the one he was wearing, I deduced that it must have been possessed of unusual powers—perhaps its searing beauty could cure the blind.

I saw zero punk rockers, but punks and rednecks, like enemy desert tribes or estranged twins, while totally unalike, are almost exactly the same: broken teeth, broken boots, crude tattoos, profane belt buckles, interchangeable T-shirts. They'd beat the crap out of each other in any parking lot on earth, but it's the fashion equivalent of when Pat Buchanan argues with Rachel Maddow—they agree on every bullet point for an entire argument, then right when you think the snake is going to swallow its own tail, they draw completely opposite conclusions.

There was also a surly multitude of women around thirty who, it seemed to me, had been savaged by love earlier in their lives and had taken to expressing their rage through softball, dark hair dye, and multiple tattoos. But even these chicks got friendly after singing a pro-redneck, Josh Thompson karaoke anthem or two:

> *Our houses are protected by the good Lord and a gun*
> *And you might meet 'em both if you show up here not welcome son*
> *Our necks are burnt, our roads are dirt and our trucks ain't clean*
> *The dogs run loose, we smoke, we chew and fry everything . . .*

> *We won't take a dime if we ain't earned it*
> *When it comes to weight brother we pull our own*
> *If it's our backwoods way of livin' you're concerned with*
> *You can leave us alone*
> *We're about John Wayne, Johnny Cash and John Deere*
> *Way out here*

⁍⁌

I BOUGHT MY TICKETS TO the Iowa State Fair without knowing that my personal whipping-Republican, Sarah Palin, was going to be at the fair on the exact same day.

From the moment she was trotted out into the public arena, the Voluptuous Horror of Sarah Palin has commandeered my

This retired Staff Sergeant sports a look that perfectly complements his beautiful machine: proud, relaxed, care-worn, spanking clean; perfectly customized to his peripatetic lifestyle on the road, and fearlessly personal. This perfect gentleman made me more grateful for all veterans (and especially grateful for his own service as a fashion veteran when he gave me a super-cool T-shirt from a local Iowa hot-rod show).

unwilling attention. I feel a fiery mix of emotions for her: outrage and fury at her political betrayal of my gender, begrudging admiration for the advanced lethality of her military-grade tractor-beam powers of seduction. She fills me with shock, awe, prurient fascination, irrational rage, sexual dismay, and existential nausea.

So naturally I was super-excited.

In the middle of the day, Sarah Palin was suddenly There, making her cameo appearance, ostensibly to upstage the Republican straw poll that was in progress.

You had to hand it to her, as a spectacle—she was a very strange and compelling sight. Through some kind of advanced, alien, beauty-pageant technology, she was pulling off wearing a white T-shirt with her usual high-maintenance, vertical, brunette, ziggurat-Bumpit hairstyle. To walk among the common people, Ms. Palin was surrounded by a literal phalanx—a human shield of media and security agents six to eight people deep, all shuffling around her in a strangely noiseless way, occasionally letting a fan squeak through their shoulders for an autograph. I got the feeling that although she was still an active political animal, the crowd thronging around her was interested only in her as a celebrity—several people shuffling alongside her scrum were wearing Ron Paul T-shirts. Toby's daughter Charlotte used her roller derby skills to mosh her way into the center of it all and managed to get Ms. Palin to sign her forearm.

Iowans seem to have no particular animosity toward those

WINNER: BEST USE OF MUD-BESPECKLED-JEEP-AS-FASHION-ACCESSORY

While parking in Perry, Iowa, a vehicle screeched into the spot next to me that looked like it had just been violently subdued with chocolate firehoses by rodeo riot-cops. The driver, upon hearing that I was on my way to the State Fair, observed that I wore no hat—and in a fearless display of gentlemanliness, removed this one from his own head, and insisted that I take it. I wore it proudly. There is no style so becoming to a guy as raw chivalry. (But added to a soul-patch, swagger, cowboy-kickers, and the world's filthiest Jeep?) Props to your Mom, Mr. 100% American Honcho.

they might describe as "fancy people," just a kind of vague, age-old mistrust—something like the Catholics seem to reserve for the Methodists, or vice versa. Charlotte's grandmother, a lifelong Iowa resident, was Not Having the Palin circus. "You should have seen her Humvee," she said, rolling her eyes. "It's bigger than any other Humvee I've ever seen, and it was parked right in front of the Applebee's with pictures of her painted all over it. So I walked in and said [in an innocent old lady voice]: 'Excuse me, but are the Beverly Hillbillies here?'"

In trying to boil down Iowa fashion to codes and micro-encapsulations, it struck me that the older people really articulated it best: they seemed to favor bright, crispy-clean, poly blend western garments, with sharp permanent creases. It mirrors their rude health and clear-eyed sanity, and gives them a kind of preturnatural shine, a superhero-as-humble-Clark Kent look. This struck me as being reflective of the astringently clean-cut crop fields. Iowans seem to like their natural fibers seasoned with a bit more pesticide than we do on the coasts—but then, they're the ones actually *growing food* from the earth, and raising *actual animals as food*. It is what *works*.

And sometimes they raise these animals to the level of Gods.

The livestock was really breathtaking. One tent contained what must have been essentially the Westminster Dog Show for exotic, blow-dried sheep. I was stopped in my tracks by a prize-winning white bull in his pen. He was exquisite—stone gorgeous and gigantic—a colossus of animal muscle densely packed into marble-white fur, roughly the size of two Lincoln Town Cars stacked vertically—and this when he was *lying down*. His perfect long horns seemed to be the size of mastodon tusks; his hubcap-sized eyes were glistening, thickly lashed, and soulful. He was so content, so radiantly luxuriating in his prize stud-self, that I almost understood, for a microsecond, how minotaurs happen.

CUTIES SHRED FASHION LANDSCAPE AT IOWA STATE FAIR

AYE, Mateys: It takes a coordinated effort to pull together matching twin beach-party cowgirl ensembles . . . BUT 'TIS CLEAR the feathery buccaneer hat throws their look overboard into A VICTORY FOR STYLE PIRATES EVERYWHERE.

I was charmed by what was, for me, the totally foreign agricultural awesomeness of the State Fair—but I really fell in love with Iowa a couple of nights later, driving back to my hotel in Perry from a hot rod show in Jefferson. The moon was rising like a colossal butter pat melting over the edge of the flat earth stretched out endlessly in all directions. I had never in my life seen this much space before, and it was dizzying; cicadas were buzzing in synchronous throbs and the sun was slanting in backlit oranges and blues over the screaming green cornfields.

The landscape suddenly had a weird and profound impact on me. I was forced, in an almost physical sense, to surrender to it.

I suddenly felt aware that I'd given myself a kind of slow-drip, accumulative heavy metal poisoning by pulling too much of my energy from shiny black pants and concrete skyscrapers. The land suddenly rolled up a steel garage door in my soul and threw a beauty bomb into me. It was like an inward-moving tsunami that smashed noiselessly through my skin and owned me in such a way that I felt the shimmering green of the cornfields inside my chest. It was weird and transformative; Iowa was cheerfully absorbing my neurotic urban toxins and giving me a spontaneous color transfusion. It was so *generous*—this earth, this ravishing abundance of beauty, feeding us, embracing us—that it made me cry like a child.

The enormity of this weird revelation really brought home for me the pointlessness of all the vanities and vexations that take on such ridiculous importance in an urban life. I started seeing all

Young Iowa troublemakers still enjoying the party they started in the early 1950s.

Yes, these are his work clothes.

my sufferings as symptomatic of the sin of forgetting, or never knowing, what it is like to have every part of your vision filled with a wild expanse of growing, green life—and how rhapsodic it feels to be inextricably connected to all that lives and breathes in nature.

They say a tree grows in Brooklyn. After visiting Iowa, I am determined to find it.

Mother Earth—our post-industrial Eden—is looking a bit rough these days. She's overheating and has some nasty scars. The pork has not been kind to her. She has suffered abuse, neglect, and exploitation, and has been the victim of many bad perms and unfortunate tattoos. But she's still under there. If we demonstrated a little more appreciation, I think she'd soften up again. If we could get her to stop overplucking her eyebrows, wipe off that trashy makeup, and shuck off that drip-dry petroleum minidress, she'd still be the mother of all beauties.

It was difficult to articulate what I felt the bottom-line Iowa fashion statement was, but in the end, I arrived at *Already Redeemed/ Yet to Be Redeemed*. They're both the same thing, ultimately, in the midst of Iowa's infinite, paradox-dissolving cornfields. Whatever you're putting on to cover your nudity, you've either already arrived at an acceptance of your own intrinsic virtue, a conviction that crystallizes upon your body in crisp true-blue Wranglers and unblemishable Western plaids, or you're just taking your time getting around to it, enjoying the evolutionary square dance while breaking your glorious boots in. However many off-road detours you take to romp in the splendid, life-giving mud, however many butter-sticks on sticks must be consumed on your journey, the green world will rotate and the sun will surely rise, every morning. Eventually, you are bound to shine back.

Can't look at hobbles and I can't stand fences
Don't fence me in

10

THE BELLE JAR / THE BIBLE BELT

Scarlett Wears Her Corset on the Inside

*As God as my witness they're not going to lick me. I'm going
to live through this and when it's all over, I'll never be hungry
again. No, nor any of my folk. I will lie, steal, cheat, or kill.
As God is my witness, I'll never be hungry again.*

— SCARLETT O'HARA, IN *GONE WITH THE WIND*

Nothing has been more complicated or difficult for me to wrap
my head around and write about than the sartorial codes of
the Southern belle.

I grew up in the Bay Area, brain-laundered by feminism. My
mother always called excessively feminine women "Uncle Toms."
I grew up snickering at French manicures and *Cosmopolitan* magazine; I thought they represented the kind of training that advanced
risible sluts gave to up-and-coming risible sluts.

On some level, I thought, there was a fundamental *same-
ness* between boys and girls. But this has led me to a world of

dashed hopes and bruised expectations, because it is basically wrong.

Southern women have never suffered from these coastal delusions. They have always known that men are Not Like Women. They don't treat men like equals; they treat men like *men*. They know they're not interacting as one human mind to another, but assembling, in each conversation, a ballet of gesticulations, a music of pleasant speech—a web of evolutionary biology–savvy, subconscious trigger points designed to charm, delight, amuse, and ensnare.

I always thought such blatantly deployed feminine finesse was . . . *lying,* essentially. I thought manipulating people to get what you wanted was *evil*. I always thought that excessively performative femininity was a kind of *black magic*.

Since Miami, I had become self-conscious about my own fashion handicaps. After several years as a fashion critic, I firmly believed that the best clothing inspires fear. I had succumbed to a regrettable affection for shiny black things with superfluous zippers. After growing up an uncouth, anti-establishment person informed by punk rock and drag queens, I had let these tendencies ferment in New York unto the point where I was dressing like I just got deported from the sadomasochistic Death Star.

Before departing for points even deeper South, I was beginning to realize, having been pulling forty for some time, that I had never been taught—and in fact had deliberately avoided learning—all those subtle arts and maneuvers of feminine charm, finesse, and tact.

Lately, when reflecting upon my abysmal romantic track record, I had been questioning the intelligence of avoiding these skills that might make me a more viable female. I felt I was being perceived as fairly frightening to all but the most adventurous and vainglorious (read: sociopathic) males. Architecturally, fashion had become a moat that was keeping most people at a distance from me, and I was feeling like I didn't know how to lower the drawbridge anymore, even if I wanted to. I wanted to learn how to have the *option* of being softer—if this was possible.

I hoped that being around Southern women might inspire me into undergoing some kind of Eliza Doolittle–style transformation. I have always thought of Southern belles as a super-elite task force of lethally disciplined femininity—like the Spartans. In my experience, they were wicked-smart academics who also amplified and honed their natural beauty, grace, and charm until they, too, were advanced weaponry. I recognized them as being exceptionally well-versed in all of the codebreaking and covert psychological operations necessary for competitive, ruthless, and dead-serious sexual combat.

I figured I could probably use their help.

Across the aisle on my plane to Birmingham (my first trip to Alabama) was an ageless woman, hovering in a time lock somewhere between fifty-eight and seventy-eight. Her curls might have been carved from cinnabar. Full face of precisely applied "natural" makeup, bright gems, gold jewelry, spangled zebra-print shirt.

I leaned over. "Ma'am, I am a fashion writer, and I must ask: how does someone become as lovely as you are?"

She lit up like a Christmas window. "Thank kyew!" she twinkled, with the graciously tilted eyes and beauty-pageant smile of a woman who has heard that compliment her entire life. "Well, my grandmother is turning a hundred this week. She was raised that way, and she raised my mother that way, and my mother raised me."

Her warm, trilling voice, tuberose perfume, and swirling diamonds all harmonized into a beguiling, welcoming spectacle, like a hazy waterfall soundtracked by Mantovani's Cascading Strings. Her style-text spoke to me of a wholly absorbing domestic life.

LOVELY LADIES OF THE GALLANT SOUTH

Unlike the blonde girls hanging around Oxford Square after the first Ole Miss game, these young women seemed to be having a good time in each other's company, and not so morbidly obsessed with husband-snaring . . .

The gumball-sized grey pearl, I guessed, was her silver anniversary present from her husband. Her imperturbable hair gave me visions of the right napkin rings and monogrammed towel sets. It occurred to me that she wasn't just wearing her house—she *was* her house. Just as her mother had once lived inside her grandmother/house, she had lived inside her mother/house—a generational chain of nesting wooden dolls.

If her hands were her living room, her expert charm was the ultimate set of blackout drapes. I had no idea, while she spoke, if she was actually being sweet to me. She giggled so wickedly with her companion a minute later, I had to wonder.

"FINESSE. THIS IS THE word you need to meditate on. Finesse is the thing you need to cultivate," advised my longtime friend Dirty Bobby as we dined in Birmingham's Chez Fon Fon, a chic eatery full of overweight white men in flat-front khakis and button-up blue checked shirts on dates with hyper-fit, significantly younger women with abundant hair, over-perfect posture, and important handbags. Dirty Bobby had lived around the West Coast for years before finally returning to his roots in Alabama to become, like his daddy, a Southern patriarch. Dirty Bobby was extremely worried that I would offend his Southern people by being my usual brash and tactless self (urbane, ADHD types like myself having the unfortunate social handicap of saying exactly what we mean).

"We got a good thing going on here. Have you ever heard the term 'laughing like a loon'? I hang out with surgeons on lakes that have actual loons laughing. If you fuck it up for me, I'll have to come to New York and break your kneecaps."

"Seriously," he said. "The South is *very* conservative. Let's put it this way—we still talk about the Civil War." (Subtext: we may have been friends for half our lives, but here you keep your Yankee shit off my porch.)

I summarized, for Dirty Bobby, the narrative I'd been told about Southern women at the Kentucky Derby. To wit: Southern belles get top-shelf educations, mainly in pursuit of a MRS degree"—land a husband, redecorate, and have kids. When the husband cheats, they get law degrees, then expertly gouge their husbands in legendarily brutal divorces.

"Yes, but women all over do *that*," said Dirty Bobby.

Actually, no.

I had never known a single woman in LA, SF, or NYC who had openly aspired to a life of motherly leisure. The women I

NOBODY DOES "TRAD" BETTER THAN A REAL SOUTHERN GENTLEMAN

From his silver-tipped walking-stick to his cool glasses and waxed mustache, this style-conquering hero from Tuscaloosa, Alabama, I met in Oxford after the Ole Miss game inspires deep sartorial delight. His flair is such a natural emanation of his character, so pronounced yet restrained, he deserves to have his own set of cheerleaders and a marching band following him around, all the time. BRAVO, SIR!

knew who got sterling degrees from pedigreed universities did it because they wanted real careers. Children were a brief hiatus in their otherwise unrelenting attack on the professional world. Divorces were usually resolved as early and as amicably as possible. Men, especially ex-husbands, rarely occupied the lion's share of their attention.

The sexual politics of the South—as manifest in the way the ladies still dress (and the way they non-ironically call themselves "ladies")—all seemed to fall voluntarily into submission to the aristocratic patriarchy, the old one belonging to the myth of an antebellum Eden from which Southerners were so rudely expelled. The feminist theorist Judith Butler described Southern belles as participating in a "regulatory fiction" of gender performance, which upholds the social status quo. Southern social codes are heavily colored by the Old Southern tradition of hospitality. The noble lady is the beautiful home; the chaste daughter is its vulnerability; the honorable father is their protector. The beautiful, well-bred, educated Southern belle, corseted by diets and hobbled by heels, pollenates with alluring cues of frailty, that she may be answered by the gallant ministrations of a Southern gentleman.

"There's a delicate ballet that happens here," my new BFF Dr.

DR. JULIE STEWARD needs you to know that TEXAS GIRLS are NOT SOUTHERN GIRLS. Pictured here modeling a light-green polka-dot ballgown liberated from a Texas Salvation Army, Dr. Steward says: "Although my mother does her hair every day with the help of Lord Jesus, Texas is technically NOT in the Bible Belt. Texas is its OWN BELT."

Julie Steward explained over cocktails at my hotel bar, the next night. Dr. Steward, a gorgeous blonde with big nerdy glasses, is a literary theory professor and former Future Farmers of America beauty queen whom I was fortunate to connect with through mutual friends. She had grown up in rural Texas and relocated to Alabama—not as easy a transition as one might think. She had endured no small dose of culture shock. "Texans are *not* Southerners," she clarified. "It took me a year to figure out that men *always* open the door for you. Any door. Men you don't know. A man *needs* to open that door for you."

Southern belles, Julie explained, had a different approach to feminine power: "Ixnay on eminist-fay. That's the f-word," she continued. "If women like us aren't using our femininity strategically [Belles think], we just aren't even being *smart*. Southern women are not going to have power in the overt ways—they have it in covert ways. It's not like they reject the idea of female accomplishment; *it's that they've seen feminism in a utilitarian way, as not being a productive means of getting what they want.*

"Why do you and I reject that?" she asked, quite seriously.

We looked at each other in silence. I was asking myself the same question.

The next day, looking at clothes in a quaint row of retail shops, I stopped in front of a window display of a little boutique that seemed fashion-forward for the South—I was charmed by a cheerleader dress that someone had made out of butcher paper. That was how I met the owner, Brittany Hartwell, the Southern belle who, in my opinion, came to represent the best balance of all possible feminine worlds in that fretful fashion region: she is a sassy, funny, cool, self-actualized chick who also happens to have been raised to be a real, honest-to-Christmas Southern belle.

In grammar school, Brittany told me over cocktails with Dr. Steward, she had been taught etiquette, charm, and how to give a camera the best possible smile by a glamorous Sunday school teacher. In high school, she was chosen to be a Hoover Belle, which is a serious honor in Alabama; girls selected for their loveliness and gracious behavior are allowed to stand prettily around public and civic events in hoop skirts and sun hats.

Southern belles, I commented, all seemed to want to find their Rhett Butler.

"The girls around here all want to marry their high school sweetheart and move to Mountain Brook," Brittany agreed.

THE LOVELY BRITTANY HARTWELL, RECOVERED SOUTHERN BELLE SAVING THE
PLANET, ONE DRESS AT A TIME

Although she can still bust out a beauty-queen smile and make pageant-ready "pretty geet," Ms. Hartwell has established a life well beyond the usual domestic Thunderdome of the South, as the proprietress of Molly Green, Birmingham, AL's first eco-responsible, sustainable fashion boutique.

Mountain Brook—locally known as the Tiny Kingdom—is Birmingham's wealthiest enclave. (It is perhaps best known for being the home of Natalee Holloway, a teenage blonde who was murdered in Aruba by a privileged young European man named Joran van der Sloot.)

What had changed the trajectory of Brittany's life, I learned, was that she had survived the ultimate ego-death of a Southern belle—a broken engagement to her high-school sweetheart. The devastating impact of this, in the South, really can't be overstated.

Every American parent I know of a toddler-age girl child has had to fret over what is casually known as "the Disney princess thing." There is a social and consumer conditioning that is Trojan-horsed into girl children through the princess—the spangly pink dress is a gateway dress that leads to Barbie clothes. Barbie begets prom dresses, then harder stuff, especially in the South: cotillion formals or beauty pageant gowns. But encoded in every party dress (and it's really all the same dress) is the same unspoken goal: marriage to the handsome prince, living happily ever after in the castle on the hill, in the Tiny Kingdom.

Down South, you are supposed to marry your high school boyfriend. That is the proper narrative. If your life doesn't work out that way, you are essentially exiled from the herd.

Brittany, thus ostracized, was forced to evolve. She went to a different school, where she found two real and sustainable passions: her husband, Brandon—an exceptionally smart, good-looking guy—and the inspiration for her boutique: eco-fashion.

Ms. Hartwell had opened Molly Green to introduce the ladies of Birmingham to clothes manufactured in local and/or otherwise sustainable ways. Molly Green, Brittany said, was an act of love: she wanted to share her hard-won joys and discoveries with her Southern sisters, and open up a whole new direction for Southern femininity. However, she was struggling to find her audience, due to the strict conformity of local ladies and the rules of their sartorial tribe.

"It's hard for Southern women to change styles," Brittany sighed. "People just aren't malleable in the South."

Dr. Julie Steward assessed local women's clothing in the area as being highly based on SEC football. Brittany emphatically agreed. "The boutiques I connect with on Facebook are all asking, 'Do you have your game-day outfit?' "

"Game-day outfits" are, in fact, so incredibly important to the Southern female wardrobe that I was compelled to drive with a photographer friend Brinky to Oxford, Mississippi, to girl-watch after the first home game at Ole Miss, "the Harvard of the South."

THIS YOUNG DANDY . . .

. . . Was by far and away the Best Dressed in Oxford Square after the game at Ole Miss. (The other young men dress like RETIRED southern lawyers.)

Hugh Hefner has proclaimed that there are more beautiful girls on the Ole Miss campus than anywhere else. There did seem to be a glut of that particular type of beauty—Gattaca-level triumphs of all-American eugenics: button-nose blondes with long butterscotch legs, waist-length ironed Barbie hair, guileless baby-blue eyes. Most were wearing mini sundresses in Easter egg colors, with pearls. A few were, indeed, wearing padded shoulder minidress versions of the team football jersey.

I pointed out a particularly riveting specimen of blonde to a young guy in a red Ole Miss alumni polo, who happened to be smoking on a bench next to me. "Dime a dozen," he spat. "I went to Ole Miss. I used to sit next to one of *those*. She'd be next to me in class, all falling out of her shirt. I asked her, 'What are you here for, anyway?' And she told me right out, 'I'm here to be a trophy wife.' I told her, 'You're disgusting.' Money and marriage, that's all they want," he sneered. (He was parking cars for one of the local restaurants.)

A group of handsome young men emerged from the pizza restaurant, dressed in the uniform of the Southern patriarchy. Brinky and I begged them to reveal their secrets of sartorial success.

"You have to dress like this to get your foot in the door with the girls," explained John Wolfe, indicating his madras shorts and polo shirt. Mr. Wolfe, despite his movie star looks, had required a full closet overhaul upon arriving in Oxford. Urban metrosexual looks (such as the army-jacket-and-jeans coastal uniform my associate Brinky was sporting) would get no suction with belles, who, the men explained, exclusively lavished their attention on boys in old-money drag: Ralph Lauren button-up shirts, khakis, tasseled topsiders. "Once you get a girl really into you, then you can relax your style," added his friend, a public policy major with frosted Justin Bieber hair.

(Brinky asked where his alternative, straight, skater-guy style might go over in Oxford. The boys, eager to be bro-helpful, gently broke it to him that his look designated him as someone who might prefer the action at the local "alternative" bar. A few minutes later, they confided to Brinky that "alternative" was their region's polite synonym for gay.)

I had a drink in one of the local sport bars while Brinky dealt with some telephone business. The various college football games of the day were being played on numerous TVs. It was strange, having thought all day about Southern eugenics, to realize that this game day—around which the entire area's whitest and brightest rotated in their seersuckers and miniskirt number jerseys—was a game played by football players who unanimously appeared to be so jet-black—glossy, *panther-black*, I thought, watching them run—as to all have been recruited from remote sub-Saharan regions. Were the players, I wondered, selected partially on the basis of this particular, distinctly undiluted African skin tone? Were Southern athletes also prized according to the purity of their bloodlines, like Southern wives or Derby horses? (And, if so: how was this unrelated to a cultural history based on slavery?)

The next morning was Sunday, so I went to a small Catholic church that looked like a little gothic barn in Tupelo, Mississippi, the birthplace of Elvis Presley, to see if I could witness any church hats. Tupelo was no place for frivolous Southern church fashion; it was a somber, dead-serious crowd. There were entire families of women in tank tops, jeans, and plastic hair clips, white-knuck-ling the pews in fervent prayer for serious problems. Quiet, glum children with wet-combed hair sat stock still with their hands in their laps, staring at their sneakers. Men were noticeably miss-ing from these families. They were in the wars, maybe. But this absence of men, I felt, was where these women's troubles prob-ably began.

⌖

IF BRITTANY WAS BIRMINGHAM'S Scarlett O'Hara—the self-sufficient woman—Amy Bailey is its Melanie Wilkes.

Miss Mellie in *Gone with the Wind* is everything a Southern belle is supposed to be: so excruciatingly well-bred that there is no ugliness in her to be found, in any corner of her home or her psyche. She is the loving ideal—grace, elegance, kindness, chastity, selflessness. She performs herself with effortless, ceaseless prettiness, and no hellfire. All is softness and hospitality—and a certain learned helplessness and amplified frailty which forces men to carry her luggage. Miss Mellie never wags anything but a smiling, loving, maternal finger at men, as if their transgressions were some adorably precocious thing done by her own toddler son.

Back in Birmingham, a hurricane was raging; water killed all the electricity in the hotel, and turned the commercial streets into little brown rivers. I brought Brinky along to meet Amy Bailey—a society It Girl around Atlanta and Birmingham who runs an influential fashion blog. She was adorable, scampering in from the rain in her high-heeled boots. She peeled off a white trench coat to reveal little jean shorts and a flesh-colored silk blouse with a navy blue bra underneath. She was clearly proud of her décolletage—quite ample for such a slim young lady. I detected vocal coaching in the musicality of her laugh; she confessed she'd had training for both singing and television. She had participated in "beauty walks," and she could sing. She was in all ways a perfect feminine ornament, designed to be loved, cherished, and admired.

Some women get whatever they want all the time, and know how to get away with it.

In an open-handed demonstration of feminine wiles, in *Gone with the Wind*, Scarlett smirks to herself before putting the new hat Rhett Butler has brought her from Paris on backward, in order to let Rhett show her how to wear it—she allows herself to be scolded by him as he ties the satin bow under her chin. It makes Rhett feel capable, necessary.

I never thought that kind of shit would actually work with real men, which was why I was agog when Amy delicately leaned against Brinky's shoulder and asked him how to use some function of her own iPhone (and perhaps give him a better view of her lovely blouse).

Right, I sat there thinking. *Like he's going to believe that this smart girl, who runs her own fashion website, doesn't know how to use her own phone.*

I almost laughed out loud, until I saw that it was *working.* Brinky couldn't help himself. He'd taken the bait, hook, line, and sinker, and was compulsively jabbering instructions at her like an Apple Store Genius. Amy had handily tied him up in a big pink ribbon and had him chuckering like a turtledove against her shoulder within three minutes of arrival. It was formidable.

God, I realized (for the eighty-zillionth time in my life). Playing dumb swans right past men's conscious/intellectual defenses, as lethally as psychological depth-marketing. Amy had tipped Brinky's hat brim down and made all the marbles roll out of his brain and down the front of her blouse, just like that. What may look like the most artless connivance to other women sure as shit wraps men around a girl's finger. It's awful to watch; the men look so dumb when they fall for it, but God—*they always fall for it.*

There is a point at which you realize, with enormous dismay, that men do not respect your femininity unless you are manipulating them with it.

A few rounds of drinks happened, like they do in the South. Amy, being very sweetly candid, showed me a picture of her handsome husband, confiding (with laudable candor and real vulnerability) that they had recently separated. He was dressed just like the Ole Miss wolves in their Harvard sheepskin, preppy camouflage.

She related an anecdote about her toddler-age little girl. They had been at a wishing well, and Amy had taught her daughter to throw a coin in and make a wish. She asked her daughter what she had wished for.

"And she said, 'Mommy, I want to find my prince!' and I said, 'Oh, honey . . .'" Amy's eyes welled with real tears. "'I hope you can think of other wishes besides *that*.'"

The hurricane was still raging outside when we finally left the restaurant. She invited Brinky and me to her apartment for a nightcap, which we declined. It was late, and I couldn't drink anymore. The photographer and I unchivalrously watched lovely Amy toddle home to her toddler alone after midnight, in the rain, under emergency streetlights, in her high, high heels, while I punched him in the arm and teased him for going Full Dunce around a pretty girl (which, like any red-blooded American male, he naturally and vehemently denied).

⌗

EARLIER, AS WE STOOD in the rain to sneak a cigarette together, I had begged Amy for constructive criticism.

This was really quite hard for her to do; she was far too polite to criticize me. It ran against all her pleasantness training; I thought it might cause her physical pain. But she was so bent on pleasing me, and I was so adamant, that she eventually obliged me (which I considered to be a genuine act of Southern hospitality).

"Well," she said, most delicately and reluctantly. "There is something to be said for looking . . . *approachable*."

Touché, sisterwoman.

I might also wear lower-cut shirts. I have great cleavage, she said, why wouldn't I flaunt it? And why don't I wear my hair down?

Amy's advice on how to soften my affect and increase my approachability was top-notch. It was exactly the advice I had come to the South in search of. But I knew I wouldn't, or couldn't, follow through with it.

As much as I genuinely admire the art and artifice of Southern femininity, I can't escape a queasy feeling that these choreographies are really quite dangerous. Like wearing four-inch stilettos in the rain, or competitive cheerleading: they may result in injuries far more serious than the spectacle might suggest.

Cinderella myths crash hard, and I've seen the burning pumpkins next to the freeway. Lost glass slippers sometimes still contain a human foot.

Coincidentally, while I was in Alabama, Joran van der Sloot was sentenced to twenty-eight years in prison. Not for the murder of Natalee Holloway, the Barbie princess from the Little Kingdom, but for murdering another young woman in Peru, five years later.

Wasn't there just a little bit of Joran van der Sloot/Stanley Kowalski in all the boys? Who, while irresistibly attracted to the manipulations of femininity, were equally enraged, disgusted, and moved to violence by them? Who really wanted, in their deepest, most forbidden, unspoken, reptilian, caveman-survival-level recesses of primitive desire, to humiliate, rape, and kill us?

A paradigm of feigning weakness can settle on a lady like Spanish moss after a while.

Chivalry and God will be long gone, but Sweet Charlotte, that shrieky old woman in the moth-eaten pink prom gown, will wait forever, playing her harpsichord, raving batshit, keeping the crumbling myth alive, waiting for the men who loved her to return from the dead to her rotting house full of creaky baby carriages, dry rot, and dolls with crazy hair. A shattered Blanche DuBois is reduced to finding Southern Comfort at the Tarantula Arms, in the arms of tarantulas.

Say what you will about Scarlett O'Hara, but for all her scandalous maneuverings, she survived when the Old South burned down around her. She birthed babies, contended with carpetbaggers, shot invaders and buried their bodies herself. Scarlett at least had the sense to have her heart broken for good and all while she was still young and strong. She found in herself a lone, competent strength, among sick women, children, and males too wounded, enfeebled, or uninterested to assist.

But I am thinking about growing my hair out again.

11

BROOKLYN / THE FUTILITY BELT

The False Patina of Poverty Drag

⌿

Brooklyn, which was long considered by Manhattanites to be as unthinkable a destination for shopping or dinner parties as Perth Amboy or Newark, got "hot" in the last fifteen years. Real estate brokers make a killing juicing up Brooklyn's reputation for being a hotbed of artistic creativity and a hub for creative jobs (which is ironic, since the artists and writers responsible for Brooklyn's new cachet are now being forced out by the skyrocketing rents the mystique of their "creative capital" created).

The influx of artists, and students, and independent art galleries in once-cheap and now-unaffordable areas like Williamsburg and DUMBO eroded what once was urban and scary and made it cool. The fear factor attending the industrial blight in neighborhoods like Greenpoint wore off quickly once it was juxtaposed with fearless young white women wearing kooky eyeglasses and sarcastic vintage pantsuits, riding bicycles at night. Once the bohemians began to get comfortable, the developers naturally rolled in, and an epidemic of high-rise condominiums transformed several Brooklyn neighborhoods from neglected areas where cabs wouldn't take you into dirty-posh, commissioned-graffiti-art-decorated bedroom communities for young, hip, and well-heeled breeders.

William Faulkner once said, "The aim of every artist is to arrest motion, which is life, by artificial means and hold it fixed so that a hundred years later, when a stranger looks at it, it moves again, since it is life."

The role of the avant-garde, generally speaking, is to push cultural boundaries and oppose market forces dictated by the dominant mainstream culture. Art-in-itself is a thing that has traditionally been outside the prescriptions of the status quo; for a long time it enjoyed its own role in the world as something with a metaphysical, rather than an explicitly economic, value. But ineffable qualities such as "resolved tensions" or "enlightenment" have now been replaced by an exchange (read: $$$) value. The art market, these days, is a microcosm of the stock market. Culture critics like Theodor Adorno have railed at length against the culture industries changing and corrupting the character of art; when art becomes a commodity, it loses its "field" of autonomy and ceases to function as art. The creative motivations of art, if they are to serve the purpose of art, are not supposed to be fettered by the desire to sell. Art's main purpose is to be functionless, to exist as an autonomous world beyond the marketplace.

Nowadays, sales figures have replaced all other metrics for determining artistic merit and success, and the omnipresent id of the marketplace has literally broken down the DNA of art.

Since the culture industries—movies, music, visual art, literature, etc.—are now pure commodities, art is beginning to be regarded—like yachting or luxury shopping—as a playground for the rich, to the extent that actual artists are being pushed off the playing field because they aren't commercially motivated enough.

The art world, now, is best represented by the international

Art Basel/Venice Biennale crowd, which follows itself to its own parties all over the world. Their fashion is post-nervous and post-trying-too-hard louche; they like deconstructed play clothes and expensive versions of the Ghetto Fabulous.

While Williamsburg and DUMBO were becoming the new SoHos, and celebrity parents began naming their children Brooklyn, certain avant-garde retail establishments in lower Manhattan began indulging style directions that seemed to directly address the daring fashion needs of the hip, artistic pioneers civilizing the

**A LONE KNIGHT IN ANCHORAGE, AK, DEMONSTRATING
THAT "GAMER CHIC" IS ITSELF AN ACT OF VALOR**

Dressing full-time in the tribal regalia of your online gaming avatar is a commanding fashion statement unconfinable by state lines. One dare not call such style mere "cosplay" when this is what you wear to visit the ATM machine at 2 p.m. The self-customized denim trousers are capable of concealing a broadsword, a mace, a crossbow . . . (perhaps even an occasional Elf maiden . . .?) +50 STYLE!

wilderness across the East River. Brooklyn's city limits, or at least its fashion-forward sensibilities, seemed to bleed out into a number of retail establishments below 14th Street.

Ironically, in hipper-than-thou, art-infested Brooklyn, while the rest of the creative arts were falling like limping gazelles under the claws of predatory capitalism, fashion was the lone field of creativity that seemed to be embracing a previously unseen avant-garde functionlessness—even while it was deliberately designed to be super-expensive. Sometimes with old, eccentric artists and designers, there is a fine line where self-permission gets pushed to excess. Sometimes they let go of the rope completely and allow their whims to wander totally off the reservation. This can make for compelling art, a powerfully dissonant psychological clang, or both: a vertiginous feeling of being divorced from context.

Clothes in more experimental boutiques may be virtually unwearable, in the way that the food of ingenious chefs can become perversely inedible: fiendish experiments wrought in strawberry-dill fish foam and raw poultry.

Many items in New York's more avant-garde boutiques have entirely relinquished any pretense of being viable clothing. Maybe they are art. Maybe they are just intended to make their intended audience feel frustrated, helpless, or perhaps even violent. Many times in my career as a fashion critic, I have suspected that this was exactly the case.

Some clothing just doesn't seem to want to be clothing anymore. It refuses to conform to clothing stereotypes. The meanings of many garments may become seriously destabilized. Are these clothes posing a theoretical antithesis of clothing? Are they attacking my sartorial prejudices and forcing me to problematize human body measurements, in order to see them as a form of subtle yet all-pervasive oppression?

Or are they just really expensive yet exasperatingly malfunctional, shit garments?

"*That's* not a dress," my mother says about garments she considers too complicated. "That's a contraption."

The mind unspools.

The first Marni dress I ever saw was at a Brooklyn boutique, and it scared the shit out of me. It was a voluminous gray mass of cotton sheet material with crooked stitching that resembled a valiant Cub Scout attempt at a cat parachute ($1,215).

Marni's look is post-sexy and senile-fabulous: sporty, loud, intentionally clashing, and slightly clownish. Much of it can and should be accessorized with white golf shoes and a Phyllis Diller wig. Marni's 2009 fall collection, designed by Ms. Consuelo Castiglioni, seemed to be reveling in the weird glitz-modern of early 1970s square almost to the point of all-out, anti-sex hostility: wonky plaids in lurid, oversaturated green; strange neck-concealing dickeys.

My first thought: First Lady Jan Brady. My second thought: If Jackie Chan was in a screwball fight sequence that took place in a wealthy retirement community and he jumped down a Salvation Army donation chute, this was the stuff he would fly out wearing.

What I like about Marni is that it gives a fashionable girl a creative direction if men finally dismay her past the point of no return. It provides a high-fashion women's shelter for those too scorched and shell-shocked by the battle of the sexes to return to the field. When you've really had it up to your push-up bra with the unfair sex, there may come a day when you stop waxing your legs and start hand-painting your car, brewing your own tattoo inks, and converting your dining room into a shelter for abandoned pets— and Marni will be there for you. Marni embodies both permission and direction by saying: *Unchain yourself from that patriarchal old stump and frolic, sister. Whup out the gin and Chex party mix and*

cavort in the Technicolor playgrounds of unhinged eccentricity—albeit in a polished, together kind of way.

Marni's inventory, however, was practically Agent Provocateur–level whorish compared to the items in a SoHo boutique called Creatures of Comfort, which carried offerings by Belgian designer Christian Wijnants. On the rack: a batch of blazingly warm, painted desert colors in regal fabrics: burnt sienna, sunrise peach, sandstone orange—and all the pieces were hu-u-u-uge.

Not NBA huge—like, Mothra huge.

An ocher velvet toga seemed to be formalwear for an inflatable Macy's parade version of Barney Rubble ($785). A jumbo bathrobe sweater ($775) had enough volume to house a sumo wrestler and the back end of a pantomime horse. I dubbed the collection "Gargantua and Pantaloons," because, like Rabelais, I respected it but couldn't get into it.

Then I had the aha! moment. I realized that the selections at Creatures of Comfort weren't designed for me . . . but for actual *creatures.*

Suddenly, the more bewildering items, like a $665 Margiela jacket I thought looked like something the Nazis might have done to Cookie Monster, began to make sense.

The loungewear basics weren't there to gratify my imperial, humancentric expectations—they were made for differently-shaped beings with tapering limbs such as tentacles or pogo hooks.

I tried to stop identifying the sweaters according to culturally hegemonic stereotypes, and see them for the infinitude of things they had the potential to become: radiator cozies. Octo-snoods. Prius merkin-shrugs. Something for the schoolteacher with a stomach-foot who really makes a difference in the lives of young snails.

I thought I was inured to such sartorial abominations by the time I visited OAK, an industrial-style boutique in Nolita. It was

so fashion-forward, it wasn't even backward. It was perhaps mul-
tidirectional, or maybe completely still. All I knew was that wherever it was, my comfort zone wasn't on the same globe. I was OK
with this.

OAK, I allowed, was successfully *problematizing* fashion, by
asking difficult questions, such as: Why should windbreakers submit to the dominant paradigm of human torsos? Do pants actually
need to conform to traditional stereotypes of genital covering?
And: Why should I assume that new things should be *clean*?

OAK's recklessly edgy couture, in broad strokes, was fearfully
top-of-the-line casualwear that looked like it was designed exclusively by winos, for winos (but hip, East Berlin, tortured genius
winos—the A-list under-the-freeway set). These items were made
by rebellious design spirits too creative for conventional tailoring. Soaring into bold new directions, they discarded everything
bourgeois, domesticated, predictable, and inessential . . . such as
comfort, style, function, and affordability. OAK's sartorial com-
positions had stepped through the veil of fire and were now . . .
batshit crazy, by most standards.

Right as I walked into the bare concrete alley of a retail space,
my path was blocked by a sinister geodesic igloo in black tar paper
and plywood.

"Is that a giant armored slug?" I asked one of OAK's
whippet-thin, pale, androgynous salespeople (all dead ringers for
the teenage runaways who came to NYC in the eighties to bar-back
for CBGB's: pegged cigarette jeans, stretched-out grey T-shirts,
vertical New Wave raccoon hair, runny noses, hacking tubercular
coughs).

"That's exactly the look we were going for [hack, hack]," he
said, dripping with so much cheerful drollery and virus I thought
I'd need an emergency poncho.

Fortunately, emergency poncho-like garments—such as one

slick, black Hefty bag apparatus by Chimpala ($345)—were on the racks in abundance. These ponchos, despite their intriguing FEMA-realness, couldn't actually be worn in a monsoon, however; most required dry cleaning.

I launched into the women's clothing—or, more precisely, what I *presumed* to be women's clothing. In retrospect, it was probably inspired by an idea of what the coat-check room looked like during the original *Star Wars* bar scene.

A garment by Bless #32 was an oatmeal-colored sheet-cape attached to a pair of pleated linen shorts by exactly one half—the back half—of a grey cotton tank top ($568). If Heather Locklear had a parasitic twin emerging from her sternum who happened to be a nun, this would be something they'd both agree they could wear to Starbucks.

One armless black bat-cape of a T-shirt with front pockets on both the front and the back would be ideal resort-wear if you were an incarnation of Vishnu and fourteen sleeves were just too bunchy for the beach.

DOWN, PERHAPS, BUT BY NO MEANS OUT

I liked this guy's style. He was selling a homeless newspaper in Dallas, but rocking a sweet look: Red Bandanna under leather-brimmed, Ralph Lauren, golf-bastard hat. Subversive swank! LOOKING SHARP Against All Odds.

The Mario label featured an oversize, grey-on-grey bumble-bee-striped elastic bubble-shroud, which might have been ideal if you happened to be an eight-foot earthworm working the Soccer Yob of Turin look.

"How do you like this dress?" asked the coughing salesman, handing me a tie-dye sackcloth tank-smock by Clu ($242). I thought it would have evoked pity even in a Walker Evans photograph.

"I hate it," I confessed. "These clothes make me feel old and confused."

The salesperson laughed. "Ha," he said comfortingly. "I think we *all* feel that way."

"But you're only *nine*," I observed.

"You don't have any pants on!" I shrieked at a petite salesgirl, who, by way of response, flipped up the front of her large, belted man's plaid shirt to show me the micro-shorts hidden underneath.

These clothes were mocking me. A certain Mario cardigan was really starting to piss me off.

OAK had a small sitting area, which created the mood of a store that had been living at the Salvation Army for a while but was finally getting its life back on track. There was pair of filthy, white, vulcanized rubber club chairs from, I assumed, Mothra's Chew-Toy home collection. A large, crudely constructed particle board bookshelf contained a large mason jar showcasing a gay magazine called *BUTT*.

The Mario cardigan ($682) was asking for it.

It looked a bit like a Muppet restraint harness. The arms seems to disappear and reappear somewhere else. There were, at my first count, two neck holes, but that was mainly because I couldn't figure out which way was north on it. It was a bronco I was determined to break.

I removed my jewelry, spit on my palms. The salesman coached me by pointing out the garment's weaknesses.

"You can wrap it around your waist and kind of make a tank out of it," he suggested.

"Does it come with an instruction manual?" I asked.

He became visibly excited.

"Oh! We actually do have a dress with an instruction manual! Let me see if I can find it!" He scampered off.

I felt very much alone.

When I saw the dressing area, fear shot through me. Little black rooms down a dark concrete hallway. It wasn't so much the lint-infested black shag carpeting, or even the flat black-grey walls that inspired distress once I was behind the curtain. Most menacing was the fact that there was no light whatsoever.

Actually, it was worse than no light: OAK seemed to want to humiliate its customers by intentionally *denying them* light.

The tomblike dressing rooms had elegant, tall, backlit mirrors . . . but what little light there was exclusively illuminated only the sides of the mirrors, for a solar-eclipse effect which makes the mirror seem to hover before the shopper in a retrograde Satanic ecstasy. It watched as I struggled blindly with the openly hostile, mutant-octopus cardigan, which suddenly had 117 sleeves, no neck holes whatsoever, and no capacity for mercy.

I felt lucky to get out of that cardigan alive.

As I stumbled out of the dressing room, clammy, gasping, and disoriented, the salesperson reappeared.

"We unfortuntely sold out of the dress with the instruction manual," he shrugged. "You had to wrap it around yourself three times!"

I pushed past him and fled into the street. I wanted a Karen Silkwood decontamination shower and antibacterial flea-dipping.

This may have been a coincidence, but it struck me as cosmically uncanny: thirty seconds after my escape from OAK, right next to the entrance to my subway, I saw a Hare Krishna struggling to get off his bicycle.

For nearly half a century, the Hare Krishna signature look—shaved-head-with-ponytail hairdo, gauzy orange robes, wooden prayer beads, bongo drum—has horrified Western parents with nearly the same visceral dismay as a large neck tattoo or giant plug holes in the face (Hindu-style enlightenment, in Western society, being essentially synonymous with lifelong unemployment and evangelical panhandling).

This Hare Krishna was trapped; his big gauze diaper-dress had become entirely tangled in his bicycle chain.

I wanted to clutch his wooden beads, weeping. I wanted to confess to him. *I failed, Brother . . . I don't have the training. My mind refuses to open past its hinges. But you . . . there is HOPE for a fashion warrior like you!*

<hr />

I'VE ALWAYS ADMIRED THE astringent fashion rules of my childhood friend, Lord Relentless Ha. Discriminating San Francisco hoodlums favored a certain heavy twill, bomber-cut jacket by Derby of San Francisco, a favorite local brand of industrial workwear. Mr. Ha thought that the crisp industrial angles of a new Derby jacket were gauche, so before presenting one as a gift, he put it through a rigorous set of tortures, which, I believe, began with dragging it behind his mufflerless ("loud 'n' proud") late-model Cadillac. "Then I marinated it in the bathtub in beer and cigarette butts," he said. "Then I tied it up in rope and let the ocean chew on it for a while." A proper Derby, Mr. Ha maintained, required a certain history of abuse.

In Brooklyn, during my research, I discovered that one may pay more for such stylish abuse, in a way not dissimilar to how the staff of Wilkes Bashford would once break in your shoes for you.

At Eva Gentry, one of Brooklyn's more wonderful clothing boutiques, I espied a dapper Japanese gentleman with striped lavender socks in the small shoe section, helping his daughter select a pair of handmade Guidi shoes.

Guidi shoes fall into what I call the "stealth wealth" category. They have the tragic look of something you would find in the net of a police boat, until you look closely. Then your eyes bug out, because they cost around $1,400. While your jaw is dangling, it dawns on you that it is difficult to quantify the luxury of an *actual* luxury brand, like Guidi—seven centuries of Tuscan leather-tanning, 113 years of family shoemaking. These are handmade, private, not mass-produced, non-conglomerate luxuries.

There has been this prevailing look going around Brooklyn since about 2010: designer pieces I'd describe as "deceptive day-time casual," or maybe "haute liberal arts dormitory." To wit: *Oh, this silly old thing I tie plastic bags on and wear to the dog park? It's Prada.*

It's an I-don't-give-a-damn, soft-baked casual look, preferred

Let's face it, this guy is seriously ROCKING Panhandler Chic with a whimsical new mash-up of athletic and industrial men's sportswear with simple, flattering accessories. And: . . . AN ACTUAL PAN!

by youngish persons of inherited wealth and wives of hedge-funders. In short: extremely expensive clothing items with artificial histories of the type of stresses that come from actually difficult activities (like *poverty*).

The rich young stay-at-home yoga moms who wear this look travel in packs of two and three, pushing five-digit-sticker-price strollers full of two-foot martinets with names like Lucien and Saskia. They are jobless, but as a friend once described it, "anti-gravity"—i.e., no visible means of support but flying anyway, with limitless discretionary funds and rare-bloodline pugs. These girls like to dress way, way down, in a way that still enables them to look down on everyone else. Brooklyn shops fall all over themselves to cater to them.

It's a unisexy, faded appearance. New things look as if they were worn by Dust Bowl sharecroppers. Thin cotton sackcloth dresses with button-up Sunday-school collars in neutered retro-plaids with unfinished edges seem to say, "You come into my yard and bust up this chifforobe." Thick oversize sweaters. Leggings in wool, denim, or leather, and damaged-yet-durable plaids.

In my favorite book, *À Rebours* by Joris-Karl Huysmans, the protagonist, a decadent and contrary aristocrat, spends enormous amounts of money commissioning his home decor to be made out of the finest available materials, but deliberately crafted to look cheap and low-rent. I thought one boutique in Manhattan's meatpacking district was a particularly eloquent demonstration of this Brooklynesque fashion perversion.

Thierry Gillier, the founder of Zadig & Voltaire (and a Frenchman of fine fashion pedigree: his father was a founder of Lacoste)—a meatpacking district boutique featuring faux-patinated hippie-luxe—established his line with the explicit purpose of creating items that, according to its website, "look like street fashion at first glance." T-shirts, skinny jeans, long ultrathin sweaters, made only

THERE IS NOTHING ARTIFICIAL ABOUT the PATINA of LABOR on this ALASKA FISHERMAN. He EARNED it. With WORK. (But on the event horizon of Luxe, you pay extra for fake dark matter on your pants. . . .)

of luxury fabrics: silk, cashmere, and a specially developed cotton jersey. The cashmeres are slouchy, petulant, and rebellious; a purple sweater-vest has a marijuana leaf outlined on the back in what looks like malachite studs ($265). If hemp isn't your issue, there is a sweater bearing the peace logo ($220). The staff was blissfully relaxed, in a pleasant and civilized manner, and took no notice of my eccentricities as I stood around obsessively scrutinizing and jotting down notes on the highly specific, high-maintenance wash instruction tags on their pre-mangled jeans. These jeans had very fussy suggestions for upkeep and seemed to prefer that I never wash them, lest I fade their artistically pre-faded denim to a more amateurish color level.

The cashmeres demanded prima donna–level attentions: "Cashmere yarn is fragile (little goat hair)," explained the wash tag. "Air it out to remove smells and let this natural living fiber rest."

"Maybe you guys should wash these slightly less beforehand, so they can withstand use," I offered. The staff laughed.

Many garments bore words vital to self-determination: a cotton T-dress identified the wearer as a HIPPIE ($185). ELVIS, declared the studs on a viscose sweater-vest ($190). MICK, said another wispy cashmere. One $75 T-shirt bore the word ARTIST across the chest in a bold glitter font.

Now, any artist I know who's worth his salt would print the shirt himself if it cost more than $14—and it would never say ART-IST. It might say JANITOR, or IDIOT, or possibly HOOKER. But wearing a $75 T-shirt that says ARTIST suggests that the most artistic thing about the wearer is the T-shirt itself, much as you know that anyone who actually uses the word "classy" probably isn't. Even if they could afford it, real artists wouldn't wear such redundancies, any more than raccoons would buy themselves $75 T-shirts that say RACCOON.

"I was looking for the KEITH sweaters, but I guess they're in the hospital," I announced to a salesman, who burst into giggles. He sounded like he was stoned.

The wash tags, the more I looked, got ever more difficult and inscrutable. They were fraught with high-strung, ruling-class anxieties, delivered in increasingly neurotic broken English: "Please wear it with maximum care and wash it under 30 degrees Celsius warm water with soft detergent. Tap it first with a towel then lay it flat to dry."

I had questions. Soft detergent? Tapping? Does it come with a Fahrenheit/Celsius conversion chart I can keep near my laundress?

Such are the perils of stealth-wealth. Kleenex-thin cashmere and pre-aged "street clothes" are extremely sensitive to ungentle treatment; they require truly capable servants. "Hand wash: do not wringe [*sic*] to remove water. Place it first in a sponge towel and then dry flat. Soft cool ironing on inside out garment. Avoid low cost dry cleaning services that would not guarantee optimum results."

Portrait of the ARTIST, frantically relaxed, placing her HIP-PIE dress inside a rare sponge towel and beating her maid for her inability to find the "soft cool" setting on the iron.

Are the little *quelquechoses* of Zadig & Voltaire designed exclusively for the rich? Or, as they claim, do they support revolutionary ideals of *égalité*? Only their uptown dry cleaner knows for sure, *mes amis*. (But I know which store I will visit first when eBay delivers my guillotine.)

⊰⊱

When entering Bird, a similarly haute-casual boutique in the formerly grotty Brooklyn zone of Williamsburg, one is practically knocked backward by a refreshing gust of cedar. It is an aggressively relaxing surplus of softly lit space, filled with mellow acoustic indie rock. It is like being suddenly hit in the neck with a Klonopin dart and transported to Wellfleet in late June.

I characterized the Bird shopper as a Bennington graduate whose quiet weekends upstate have evolved into a full-time escape from Manhattan for the explicit purpose of writing divorce poetry. It's a thoughtful, slouchy, Disillusioned Preppy Unisex look, still accustomed to intense, status-minded fashion scrutiny, but overcoated by a spa-like, destressed and soul-seeky note I'll call "Reprioritized Values" or "the Benefits of Acupuncture."

The colors are muted and nostalgic; diaper-soft cotton button-down shirts by Steven Alan ($170) are wrinkled and sun-bleached, as if wadded straight from Grandma's clothesline. The jeans, like the Current/Elliott "boyfriend" cut favored by starlets caught Starbucking in daylight ($210), have been expertly ravaged to appear as if they have endured many train-hoppings and boating accidents but are now safe at the family vacation home, tanned and comfy, reading Doris Lessing and responsibly refusing their third glass of wine.

Much of the clothing at Bird appears to be recovering from a too-adventurous life. To live vicariously through the scars on one's casualwear is an interesting kind of psychic trompe l'oeil, suggesting that one has been more kinetically active than one really has. It seems a bit perversely bourgeois to demand a patina of robust character from our clothes in an economy in which garments bearing the marks of age are not an elective style choice for many. But if your leisure is too demanding for you to damage your play clothes through the rigors of actual motion, Bird poses an interesting conundrum. It is possible to view these pre-trashed jeans as more than just a look that sedentary poseurs borrow to mimic outdoorsy virility. They may be seen as a declaration of taste, to wit: *I may not have had to fight feral, screwdriver-wielding nine-year-olds in the Outback, but I am wise enough to appreciate the pants of those who have.*

When something looks so utilitarian but costs so much, there are bound to be issues once the tags come off. Can you really pack that sweater and wear it upstate in your survivalist Victory garden to fondle soiled turnips and tear feathers out of the chicken you ironically named Tina Turner?

⚜

A BARNEYS CO-OP CHAIN OPENED on Brooklyn's Atlantic Avenue in 2011. When I reviewed it, it seemed to have one driving sartorial message, which was recited like a mantra on virtually every rack: Lock 'n' load!

The men's section may as well have been titled "Remembrance of Police Actions Past." It was all *very* ready-to-rumble: crusty World War II–style motorcycle leathers, leather-brimmed Harris tweed Confederate army caps, overcoats in thick duck and boiled wool, for the haute nightwatchman along the Western Front.

Something was rubbing me the wrong way, but I couldn't quite put my finger on it.

Then I put my finger on it: a prewadded NSF shirt, a garment affecting all the "realness" of a Vietnam veteran camouflage jacket, replete with a living-under-a-freeway patina ($195). On the next rack, there was another retro-camouflage jungle-jacket (Rag & Bone, $475). Among the handbags was a brass-studded Desert Storm sand-tone canvas field pack ($295). A fur-lined sleeveless army parka in olive drab was $2,300.

Heavily distressed pants were suffering from severe army fatigue and post-traumatic stress. A warped leather kit belt looked as if it had washed up on the beach at Iwo Jima; bleach-worried cargo pants appeared to have been found in the sand years after the crash of an F-4 Phantom outside Pochentong. I gave them a moment of silence.

I like a faded military look, from a purely aesthetic perspective, so I am part of the problem. But I felt queasy seeing so many luxe faux-military fatigues in Brooklyn's fanciest new retail establishment. It felt a little too disconnected from the fact that we still have actual wars going on to be surrounded by rich Brooklyn moms with a quarter-million-dollar set of in-vitro twins, chatting on new God-phones and fondling $965 Helmut Lang leggings while dressed like extras from *Apocalypse Now*.

Barneys isn't the problem. Like the Pendleton mill, it simply read the tea leaves and delivered the trends its audience wanted to buy. I was just getting concerned that fashion in general seemed to be directly reflecting a distinct cultural schizophrenia. I mean, OK, hippies also wore combat fatigues and Native American love beads, as a means of expressing solidarity with peoples oppressed by the American empire. But I am not sure it counts as sociopolitical consciousness to pay too much for workless work shirts (for all the ditches we won't be digging) or warless war shirts, for all the fights we keep conveniently forgetting are still happening over there. Can luxury combat-rock chic fatigues really camouflage the fact that the falcon cannot hear the falconer? What rough boot slouches toward $2,000, waiting to be born?

Such is the danger of great luxury—at a certain point, the snake swallows its own tail. When societies become too rich and civilized, they decline and dissipate around the edges, and finally, like all things, they begin to adopt signifiers normally associated with the peasantry, or the criminal class, as new and luxe. The very rich become afflicted with *nostalgie de la boue*, after a while— they want stuff that looks like it has the dignity of entropy after a few decades of everything looking too shiny and clean. Even Marie Antoinette built her *Hameau de la reine* because she needed to dress like a dirty little milkmaid once in a while.

When Lord Ha gave you a jacket, there was real sweat equity in it. Its wear and tear had been *earned,* however artificially. To legitimize the fictional distress of designer jeans is to step through the dressing room looking glass and leave one's brain behind. Destruction is sometimes described as a creative act—but if you've ever watched a library burn down, you know that concept is a very specious and slippery slope.

I figured out what was really bothering me, finally, in a sea of $188 T-shirts. I felt something vital to mankind was being violently ignored to death. The commodity that is currently the most undervalued thing on earth is the attention, care, and labor of individual human beings.

When you devalue actual labor—when you falsify and

fetishize a look of artificial work and legitimate heavy use in a garment—how does this corrupt our ability to recognize and value *actual work*? The dignified patina earned by objects of actual use and usefulness? To say nothing of *actual combat,* and looks created by *actual death*?

⚜

SOMETIMES, LIKE A REAL patina, actual art is earned, rather than bought.

Sometimes all you need to do to acquire an artistic fashion treasure is to twist the dial on your outlook a little, have a broad sense of humor, and see things in a new way. The most unexpectedly far-out discount merchandise can be recontextualized into amazing style finds, or at least fabulous gift items.

The Flatbush section of Brooklyn is a warm and vibrant community—a fertile mix of Caribbean families, art-school hipsters, neighborhood discount stores, and specialty shops crammed to the ceiling with exotic imports you don't see every day.

I got a kooky magazine assignment to try to buy holiday gifts for famous people for under $20, so I went to Flatbush with two of the smartest fashion experts I knew: the wonderful designer Gary Graham, and his friend, artist Charles Beyer. We agreed that when shopping on a tight budget for Brad Pitt and Angelina Jolie, the goal was to find unexpected items that would underline qualities we liked about them, and speak to what we felt were their particular needs.

"I think Brad would appreciate something that helps him control his children," I offered. "I mean, he has *so many* of them. We need to find him a six-headed lollipop, or something else that can keep them consolidated in space for a few minutes, so he can rest."

In a Flatbush clothing store, we found a gift that with just a little bit of creative doctoring would do the trick: an XXXL T-shirt featuring a hand-airbrushed portrait of the late hip-hop artist Tupac Shakur. "We could cut five more neck holes in this Tupac and call it a six-pac!" said Charlie, with dazzling imagination. This masterpiece of modern babysitting cost us only $8.99.

Charlie found the real money item of the trip. "Check this out," said Charlie. "it's a camouflage duffel bag featuring a FAKE McDonald's logo!"

I agreed with Charlie that anyplace on earth where a manufacturer would go to the pain of concocting a knockoff version of the golden arches logo as a fashionable status symbol had to be one of the most exotic locales known to man. Like . . . Saturn.

Even more beguiling, however, was a secret pocket outside the bag, the fabric of which was printed with the image of a cheerful, anthropomorphic French fry. It was one of the best handbags I had ever seen.

The price: $4.

12

THE UNDERWORLD /
THE GARTER BELT

Appropriations and Inappropriations

After traveling around parts of America I'd never been to before, I was reasonably certain that if I had lived the last fifteen years in Salt Lake City or Savannah or Anchorage, instead of New York City, my underpants would be markedly different from the tangle of black thongs inhabiting my top drawer today.

One of the more interesting retail lessons of this ongoing economic depression was the discovery that sexy underwear, like manicures, is an indulgence women across the economic spectrum refuse to live without, even when times are tough.

For years, it seemed that only Victoria was privy to this Secret.

Victoria's Secret began as a niche business in 1977 when a Mr. Roy Raymond came to the conclusion that men were very much in need of a retail environment where they could buy lingerie for their wives without being terribly embarrassed (one can only imagine the unspeakable mortifications he must have suffered at the claws of severe, bra-measuring department store matrons that made him devote his professional life to this solution). At that time, there really was no obvious middle ground in the world of lingerie: women's unmentionables were either sturdy, utilitarian solutions to the problem of nudity, or the kind of hypererotic, crotchless marabou extravaganzas sent in an unmarked brown paper package from the illicit Frederick's of Hollywood. In 1982, Leslie Wexner of The Limited Stores Inc. paid Mr. Raymond $4 million for his three thriving Victoria's Secret boutiques; within five years, Victoria had opened her pink velour doors at 346 new locations.

If Siegfried and Roy ever wanted to start a Nevada chicken ranch-cum-amusement park—a stretch-lace and animal-print McDonaldland of acceptable corporate erotica for the family casino crowd—Victoria's Secret would be the ideal jumping-off point.

Like a porn star with too many memoirs, Victoria is overexposed these days; her secrets are common knowledge. "Let me let you in on a little something, girls," says Victoria, her voice raspy from the wear of nearly four decades of champagne bubble baths. "You want sex? *Hit the guy real hard with blunt sex objects.*"

Voilà: Eros demythologized. All double entendres reduced to one big fat entendre.

Subtleties of eroticism can turn the banal into the fantastic, but Victoria has not made her money by playing hard to get. Her apparent secret formula for mass-marketing fantasies is to turn the erotic into the banal. Victoria, after all, can't be bothered with nuance; she's got thousands of seductions to perform today in malls all over America.

The week before Valentine's Day is a veritable nonstop Black Friday for this chain—it is essentially Christmas for underwear, and Victoria's Secret is the Toys"R"Us: your one stop for totally unimaginative erotica shopping. There are no psychological role reversals or complex slave-master power dynamics in Victoria's bedroom. Girls are always young, svelte, and submissive.

Judging by their names, the pastel-colored body lotions, on white shelves against a perfectly innocent, nursery-colored wall, seemed to be hoping a nice boy will ask them to dance at the church mixer: Love Spell, Romantic Wish, Endless Love. The candy-fruity-floral smells of these hormone-sick unguents are, without exception, both sanitary and cloying, and remarkably like those cardboard deodorizers that Brooklyn livery service drivers hang from their rearview mirrors. Dream Angels, according to Victoria's propaganda, enjoyed pole position as America's number one fragrance, which makes sense in a nation struggling with obesity—it smells like an alcoholic Twinkie.

A sticker on the Sexy Little Things Body Mist begs, "Pick Me Up . . . I Purr!" ($20). Sure enough, when I lifted this bottle off the shelf, it propositioned me. I set it down quickly and wiped my hand on my pants.

A section of novelties is seasonally devoted to the martyrdom of St. Valentine: gifts that a young man may buy his girl in order to do all the bedroom begging for him. Boxer shorts get straight to the point, silkscreened with slogans like "Love Me." Powdery sugar hearts printed with PG-13 content ("Beg Me," "Dare Me") are packed into a plastic tube the size of a didgeridoo.

For lovers aspiring to cannibalism, there is Very Sexy Edible Body Icing for $19.50. I figured a tubful of Duncan Hines wrapped in a note that says "Remove Your Clothes" would get you the same wallop, for $11 less (but then, Victoria's packaging was pink and decidedly not letting anyone eat cake).

The nail polish seemed slightly more mature: it was distinctly more flirty in its pursuit of puppy love, with names like I Won't Bite, Nibble, Skinny Dip . . . and Pet. (Come hither, Gloria Steinem, and bring your flamethrower.)

Victoria gets considerably more forward the further you move down the makeup aisle. The lipstick colors were brazenly uninhibited: Satin Sheets, Beg Me, Don't Stop, Sex Kitten, Sensual . . . but the lip stain was basically just an all-out, no-frills, escort service drive-thru menu: Quickie, Nubile, Proposition, Unzipped. "Very Sexy," shouted the rhinestones of a velvet makeup bag, just to hammer the point into a wet pink pulp.

Manhattan's Herald Square Victoria's Secret has an upstairs, where a jailbait orgy is in full swing at the "Royal Academy of Pink." This section is ostensibly devoted to teen and preteen girls looking for loungewear to spice up their pillowfights. "PINK" squeal the derrières on an entire wing of underpants, sweatpants, and slumberwear.

If I had a teenage daughter, I would not support the idea of her smelling like a bundt cake while scampering around in a pair of terrycloth short-shorts with the word "PINK" splashed across her buttocks, unless she was vying for the position of sorority handjob chairman. As Chris Rock once remarked, one of the primary goals of parenthood is to keep your daughter "off the pole." Higher

INKED-UP IN SEATTLE

education at the "Royal Academy of Pink" does not seem to be an effective deterrent to such choices.

There is a certain charm in directness. I am concerned, however, that Victoria is acting out feelings of low self-esteem through indiscriminate promiscuity. I was rattled by what I felt was a deeper, more twisted message hidden in the mounds of bra-padding and candy-pandering: an underlying message that girls should think of themselves as *confections*. It's a short game one plays in stretch lace short-shorts—confections, after all, are guilty little treats, meant to be casually devoured. Once you've eaten your girl, simply wad up her disposable pink wrappings and throw her away.

⊰⧓⊱

IT WAS TRULY REVELATORY to witness how many new high-end lingerie shops confidently opened around Manhattan between 2007 and 2010. I supposed it had something to do with a general mainstreaming and normalization of pornography, given the relatively recent advent of ubiquitous free smut on the Internet. Perhaps it was also due to the fact that many ladies were too broke to go out, and were therefore finding new ways to entertain their dates at home. Or maybe the market crash forced droves of Manhattan women to become prostitutes.

In any case: three chic new haut-bourgeois smut stores opened in SoHo alone: Kiki de Montparnasse, Agent Provocateur, and Coco la Mer. All three boutiques trafficked in high-end lingerie, "cosplay" outfits (e.g., gingham cowgirl bikinis, rubberized nurse costumes), high-end sex toys (18-karat tongue vibrators, gold-plated slave collars, fur-lined handcuffs), literary and/or artsy erotica, and naughty things like tuberose-scented candles in a votive with a spout, for dripping wax on your mate. What these businesses mainly sold, it seemed to me, was brand-specific *moods for seduction,* which was to be interpreted as *permission*: it was a new decadent vibe, designed to be alluring to the rich, uptight, and squeamish who, in the past, might have shied away from garter belts and sex toys because they were too garish and sleazy. Kiki de Montparnasse, by virtue of its inventory's expense, makes these things comfortably *exclusive,* and therefore permissible—even (gasp) *sophisticated.*

Victoria's Secret had cornered the greasy-kid lingerie market, but these $400 bra sets and gold-plated slave collars were for real women of Experience.

The high-end sex store with the highest end (at least at the time of this writing) was Kiki de Montparnasse, named for photographer Man Ray's notorious muse. It has a quiet, sleek, and expensively scented interior with lighting dim and indirect enough to flatter even the most aggressive facelift; black and white nude photographs of the Ellen von Unwerth, black-stockinged vintage nymph variety; and a well-stocked library of highbrow filth. The soundtrack was slow, moany stuf: French lounge pop and Portishead.

In the entranceway, a heavy black Jacobean table with spiral legs was set with a plunge-necked silk corset from the Parisian house Cadolle, copies of *X: The Erotic Treasury* by the literary sex goddess Susie Bright, and a mirrored tray with handcuffs and a matching half-mask. Vitrines and glass cases throughout the store hold a royal dungeon's worth of silk ropes, leather whips, and pearly restraints.

The superbly made (and astronomically priced) fetish accoutrements (silk blindfolds, soft leather wrist cuffs) are so luxurious as to look almost *respectable* and necessary—like something Benedict Cumberbatch might use to break a dangerous ingenue in a Masterpiece Cinemax costume drama.

I was curious about two medium-gumball-sized silver ball

bearings. "Are those Ben Wa balls?" I asked the saleswoman, a Library Spice type with cat-eye glasses in a low-cut silk boudoir top. "I thought they were supposed to be attached to a rope."

"These are the more traditional Ben Wa, like the geishas used," she informed me warmly, taking them out of the vitrine and placing them in the palm of my hand, where they jingled in a suggestive fashion. "These are *advanced*," she said in response to the confusion in my eyes. "We also have a practice version, for beginners." She guided me to a much darker corner of the store and produced what I supposed was the Fisher-Price version: larger gumballs in light marble colors with a white rubber ring like a silicone six-pack holder attaching them.

Apparently Ben Wa balls are marvelous for exercising your pubococcygeus muscles. At least you can lord *that* over your Pilates instructor.

The SoHo Agent Provocateur opened only a few blocks away from Kiki de Montparnasse, but the Agent is considerably closer in spirit to dirty old 42nd Street (before *The Lion King* raped it). The lights are brighter, the music is dumber and louder. It is, in essence, a vamped-up version of Victoria's Secret by way of Johnny Rockets, the old retro diner chain. Many items default into a black and pink, rockabilly hot rod style. The vibe is more user-friendly for embarrassed dudes shopping by themselves, and packs of loudly giggling teenage girls. The haute factor is played down everywhere but in the price tags (purple silk garter, $100; matching bra, $150; matching thong, $70).

The saleswomen at Agent Provocateur do not resemble the Anaïs Nin, lipstick feminist, sexual adventuress working-on-a-PhD-in-women's-studies types at Kiki de Montparnasse. Agent Provocateur saleswomen are inked up, Amy Winehouse (RIP) Jezebels with black liquid eyeliner and a uniform: button-bursting clinical pink shirtdresses worn with dark stockings and gold sti-

COCO and BREEZY, Ladies and Gentlemen. Two most excellent examples of the power of Fashion Determinism. I met these stunners at the LaGuardia airport. I didn't get to hear their full story, but they overcame great obstacles with little but their own personal fabulousness and are now successful eyewear designers.

letto mules: equal parts sexy nurse, roller-skating waitress, and lab assistant. It's a look conveying the message, *We're licensed underwear technicians (giggle) here to aid your "scientific research" (in finger quotes).*

The cosplay underthings hit certain nails so directly on their heads as to resemble high-quality, goofy-kinky Halloween costumes: Minnie Mouse polka-dot bra and panty sets; a mini-and-midriff candy striper uniform, a knit Dallas Cowgirl cheerleader leotard ($990).

I guessed that a rack of short see-through plastic raincoats were designed for something akin to intimate pudding wrestling. Then I realized they probably were really designed for . . . I can't remember what, because when I got home, I snorted Clorox and bleached the thought right out of my mind.

Agent Provocateur introduced a "demi-couture" line called Soirée, for those who wish to pay more for what the Agent puts out. A handmade studded bra top with a Peter Pan collar and capped leather sleeves: $1,590. I admired the studded and structured Heloise corset—it had three-inch metal spikes protruding from each hip and resembled an amorous blowfish ($4,900).

It really surprised me when an Agent Provocateur "arrived" uptown, in arriviste fashion, ready to underclothe the NC-17 fantasies of a whole new class of shopper on Madison Avenue. I really didn't think the coddled ladies who lunch were quite ready for it yet. In fact, I didn't think they'd ever be quite ready for it. I pretty much thought it would be one of their worst nightmares realized.

The Madison Avenue Agent Provocateur is a more upscale than its SoHo counterpart—i.e., more like Kiki de Montparnasse. The interior is black and classy. Sumptuous dressing rooms have billowing silk curtains and cherry blossoms crawling up the walls. A sitting room is furnished with vampire-luxe Victorian club chairs. Murals sweep up the staircase: Aubrey Beardsley meets Edward Gorey in an evil garden full of nude Vargas pinups.

The Madison Avenue inventory seems geared to undress women in a particular *Mad Men* fantasy: classic 1950s *Playboy* pinup stuff that appeals to the stag-film-and-martini-marinated male. To wit: marabou peep-toe slippers, lace merry widows in ivory and red. No black leather, no latex. It's stuff that evokes one particular cliché: these are the fantasy feathers that a wealthy businessman buys the chorus girl with whom he is cheating on his proud Madison Avenue wife.

Who, then (besides sex workers, for whom such dainties are a professional expense), has the courage to buy these tricked-out, candy-apple-shellacked, outlandishly expensive yet cartoonishly wanton "Love for Sale" indicators, on Madison Avenue? The women I saw timidly creeping around the store seemed to want nothing more than to throw beige cashmere cardigans over these rococo body-webs. The inventory was uncomfortably *exposing* shoppers brave enough to enter; it forced them to reveal their exact sexual comfort level when it came to bedroom adventure and exhibitionism. Many seemed to regard the store as a deadly new front opening in the ongoing war on aging women's self-esteem.

"I didn't look good enough in these to pay that for them," a fortyish woman exiting a dressing room said, with a joyless giggle. "But I'll be back!"

I didn't believe she'd be back. I doubt the saleslady believed it. She sounded as if she had seen her own shadow in that dressing room.

The main problem of the Madison Avenue Agent Provocateur: it's on Madison Avenue, a shopping area for ladies-who-lunch of a certain age. I'm guessing that porn gear isn't at the top of their shopping lists. It's probably not even in the middle of their lists— and those are very long lists. In fact, chafing dishes, dog jewelry, and decorative pine cones would probably appear on most of their lists before pink leather spanking paddles.

While I was trying to solve the labyrinthine conundrum of tiny straps on a red lace "playsuit" ($370), a dapper couple in their fifties walked in, all matching glen plaid and hornrims. "Look, $280—for just the bra!" the woman squealed, a little nervously.

Her companion overcompensated by trying to act devil-may-care. The Russian beauty working the floor explained that the loftier Soirée collection was on the second floor (e.g., French lace nightie, $1,990).

"Oh, so you work your way up to the luxury line?" he asked, a little too loudly, using the bra as a prop. "I guess that's when you rip this one apart!"

It was an uncomfortable moment—his cool was already blown, and so quickly. The saleswoman gave him a polite golf-chuckle.

⚎

IN *STYLE WARS*, LEGENDARY U.K. fashion journalist Peter York wrote about the palpable collective excitement felt when punk exploded onto a music scene that had been waiting in the doldrums for a decade for something to happen. "The OK subjects [for songs] now certainly weren't sex or love, for that was tedious and middlebrow, but the dole queue, boredom, urban violence, and perversity . . . It was Jean Genet and J. G. Ballard all in one," he wrote. Soon enough, big record labels were able to depoliticize and dilute the meanings introduced by seminal bands like the Clash and the Sex Pistols into slicker bands with lesser messages employing the same palsied jackhammer beat—music York described as "Pepsi-punk."

Bondage fashion, now, has become so absurdly mainstream as to be "Pepsi-sex."

So many shiny, corsety, strappy, trussed-up, enmeshed, and PVC shrink-wrapped selections were bitchy-bouncing down runways in 2011, it inspired public and critical dismay; designers, once again, were called onto the carpet for girl-hating. (It happens fairly regularly—every time an anorexic model dies of starvation on the catwalk, for example.)

Bondage-wear seems to have been virtually unavoidable in high fashion since Riccardo Tisci's hit 2008 "Western Bondage" collection for Givenchy. Once the chaps came out, Pandora's box blacked out the whole runway in every manner of slaps, straps, and leather daddy BDSM.

Marc Jacobs went straight for the darkest vein with his epony-mous line, introducing his explicit "Fetish" collection. He seemed to be intentionally punishing customers who fetishize his Louis Vuitton creations by squishing them into shiny black bustiers and *Eyes Wide Shut* wife-swapping masks. Jacobs articulated similar sen-timents, that season, with sky-high rubber Wellingtons for Louis Vuitton—which are no doubt hazardous in actual rain, and seem to only serve the function of inspiring visions of model-torture to dance in our heads (naked black girls in white boots turning a firehose on naked white girls in black boots . . . falalalala). No line was too classy to join the orgy: Karlie Kloss opened the Hermès spring 2011 show in a black leather bustier, over-the-elbow leather gloves, a ringed equestrian harness around her neck, and a riding crop, looking like she was about to be heel-kicked by Zorro until she stopped moving.

Suzy Menkes was moved to criticize Sarah Burton's new incar-nation of Alexander McQueen, in the *New York Times*, for being too closely in sync with the darker aspects of the late designer's brand: "it was dispiriting to see a female designer (and on the centennial International Women's Day) following the McQueen misogyny by strapping her models into harnesses. Take them off and there were lovely dresses . . ."

The trend begged the question: what exactly was motivating designers to want to stuff women into in constricting, hobbling, shackled looks that are hardwired into our collective consciousness as symbols of sexual torture? Sure, the theater of sexual cruelty has been responsible for a lot of better outerwear (to say nothing of the entire *Matrix* trilogy), but—right now—does it still have any vestigial remains of an actual *critical function*?

When bondage arose in the "legitimate" fashion world (runways and catwalks, as opposed to, say, magazines with Bettie Page), it was the costume of the punk subculture, as imagined by Malcolm

Ladies of Iowa, pray tell, which of these fine young gentlemen's boldly direct fashion statements spoke directly to the pants of your heart? How is any mortal female supposed to choose between "Mr. All-Night" and "Mr. Fuck-Buckle"? Cruel Cupid is all a twitter at the Iowa State Fair.

McLaren and executed by Vivienne Westwood for their infamous King's Road clothing store, SEX. Bondage fashion, through punk, was a subversion built to critique the hypocrisies upon which the ruling class maintained its status quo. Utilizing looks ordinarily ascribed to outlaw bikers, fetishists, and prostitutes, McLaren and Westwood created a critical, ferociously decadent, *épater les bourgeois,* anti-establishment fashion movement. "I was messianic about punk," Westwood is quoted as saying, "seeing if one could put a spoke in the system in some way."

The misspent youths who defaced themselves in service to punk in effect became a living eyesore: walking protest graffiti directly intended to spray-paint a big dick in the mouth on the billboard advertising England's green and pleasant land. McLaren and Westwood had unearthed something giddy and powerful: the catalyzing of protest fashion inspired by a teeming underclass that the whole myth of Empire conspired to repress and ignore for being shameful, dirty, vulgar, low, and embarrassing.

But the recent glut of bondage on the runway subverted that subversion, again.

Q: What does it *mean* when designers like Gaultier send Dita von Teese bare-bottomed down the runway, looking like Liberace restrained her with his belt collection?

A: Absolutely nothing.

(And it means even less when you can buy tween-size knock-offs at Walmart.)

The fetish look has been stripped of its political content, and reduced to amusing (albeit very expensive) kitsch for the well-to-do.

Are we supposed to be toppling empires with these looks, or are designers merely trying to bring women to their knees by turning them into dolls and sexual playthings again?

Bondage actually makes sense as a socioeconomic fashion critique; fashion always reflects the zeitgeist. Economic constrictions are social constrictions. As a mirror of culture, fashion naturally reflects the global depression that has been depressing us since 2007. Bondage could be regarded as reflecting this economic suffocation and restriction of movement, but instead, it is now translated as merely a kicky fashion *choice*. You wear the corset because it is a *corset*, not because it is a subversive comment on insider trading, cronyism, and corrupt monarchies. (Even if *you can't breathe now*.)

There was something much more sinister and unsettling about this phenomenon, to my mind . . . because I am absolutely horrified by the thought that there might never be another zoot suit war.

⊰⊱

HISTORICALLY SPEAKING, IT IS de rigueur for a complicit mainstream press to undermine protest movements by waggling its fingers at particularly hazardous examples of counterculture fashion. The zoot suit became symbolic of the "undesirable element" during World War II—the flashy, extravagant hep-cat style involving an overlong, baggy suit with pegged trousers, brimmed hats, and pocket chains was how black and Hispanic youths distanced themselves from the status quo (which was convenient for white soldiers looking to rumble during R & R). The look was framed by the media as being "unpatriotic." "Dirty long-haired hippies" became the Pachucos of the next war; fashion became the way the establishment besmirched the character of young Vietnam War protesters in the late 1960s and early 1970s.

In his book *Subculture*, Dick Hebdige describes subculture fashion as "a symbolic violation of social order." Excluded cultures reject mainstream fashions and carve out their own subculture style codes to empower themselves, in order to reject being judged by the yardstick of wealth. But when all dress becomes permissible, it is essentially a declaration of total control; fashion has been deemed too unimportant and irrelevant to the social conversation to be considered socially informative or dangerous. The *meaning* of subculture is quashed; the fashions are effectively gagged of all symbolic content, because conversations about what they represent are no longer had.

If there are no fashion rules, then it's impossible to break them. How do you subvert a paradigm when the paradigm has no *there*, there?

"It's hard to be in the avant-garde," sighed Harold Koda, curator in charge of the Costume Institute at the Metropolitan Museum of Art, when I interviewed him with his fellow curator

Andrew Bolton in the Met's gracious meeting room overlooking Central Park, shortly before the premiere of their "Punk in Couture" show. "There *is* no avant-garde."

Fashion, after all, like most businesses or media, is a handmaiden of imperialism. Imperialism has always been given to the vanquishing and subsequent erasure of cultures; but it had been occurring to me more and more that one of the most insidious acts of symbolic violence is when marginalized and/or vanquished cultures (and/or subcultures) get trivialized, cutified, and converted into fashionable kitsch.

A wildly offensive print ad in a fashion magazine articulated this perfectly for me: it was an oversize Hermès silk scarf-shawl, with the kind of noble savage, Native American design you'd find on a T-shirt in a Scottsdale truck stop. It suggested to me that Native American culture had been relegated to a luxury joke for bourgeois housewives, to wit: *Look at my incredibly tacky $3,600 scarf! Aren't I bad?*

(Aunt Jemima rolls over in the cookie jar where her cremains are fetishized.)

What begins, style-wise, as a declaration of symbolic class warfare—a gob in the establishment's eye from the sticky mouth of disaffected youth—gets trendy, coopted, and mass-produced. In an environment with no active or relevant subcultures—where all style has been deemed commercially viable—wealth essentially defines *everything*.

Usually, the second time a fashion look comes around—e.g., the 1970s' revival of the 1930s, or the 1980s' restructuring of the shoulder-padded 1940s—it is neutered of all rebellion and/or symbolic meaning. The second or third iteration of a subculture's dress code asks no pressing questions and poses no problems. If all style is acceptable, no style contains a subtext powerful enough even to question the prevailing ideologies of the status quo, let alone pose a threat to them.

The radical hippie looks of the sixties, popularized by Kate Moss in the late 1990s as boho chic, were brought back to the racks completely devoid of the antiwar sentiment that originally created them. The Krush Groove/urban New Wave, ripped-up eighties T-shirt and pink hair looks being sold at new stores like Topshop weren't resurrecting the actual breakdancing subculture that inspired them; they were throwbacks to movies and videos made in Hollywood by white guys in the eighties looking to *cash in* on breakdancing culture by softening it up and making it less scary (and hence more accessible) to other white people.

Another example: the mythological 1950s in the TV show *Happy Days* (which was in itself a neutered version of the movie *American Graffiti*). This fictional fifties was a fun diner full of juke-boxes, poodle skirts, and hot rods, with all the Cold War tension, McCarthyism, and blatant social engineering replaced by cute greasers and Hello Kitty beatniks. The Fonz was a character ostensibly intended to represent the leather-jacketed outlaw archetype that Marlon Brando played in *The Wild One*, but Fonzie was decriminalized for our protection: a biker without rebellion, violence, or anarchy. He was an ethical knight—a magico-realistic, shark-jumping Jesus—like Snoopy in sunglasses, or a Kokopelli coffee mug.

⇥⇤

THERE'S AN EVEN SUBTLER version of what is essentially the same cultural proxy war that unfolds endlessly on our bodies and those of our friends, neighbors, and countrymen. The battlefield is symbolism and the weapons are prints.

My first inkling of the importance of imagery in textiles was as a small child in the late 1970s. I was at a play date at the home of affluent friends when I was suddenly seized with an absorbing interest in their bold, op art designer bath towels. I was so impressed that I lorded their label over my rube mother and her inferior linens. "Their towels," I informed her poshly, "are by Yes Saint Lorrent."

"Ha! It's pronounced 'Eve,' not 'Yes,'" she chortled.

(Mispronouncing the name of the designer—obviously a genius of the bath set—was a stinging shame that I bore for years. I became obnoxiously competent at French pronunciation, if not comprehension. I finally tasted sweet revenge only recently, when *ma mère* botched "Ghesquière," to my riotous derision.)

But the important thing was the print on that YSL towel set: rearranged bull's eyes, not unlike Jasper Johns's *Target with Plaster Casts*—but cut up, like a William S. Burroughs novel, and wrought in Egyptian cotton in that season's fashionable turquoise and fuchsia.

It took those bull's eyes twenty years to travel from the avant-garde art gallery to the bourgeois guest bathroom—a journey which completely exhausted the imagery of the shock it once inspired. The trickle-down theory may be a risible economic model, but it's a safe bet that whatever cutting-edge styles and shapes the avant-garde curators are fetishizing now will end up a nine-piece sheet set, 30 percent off at a mid-range white sale somewhere in the not-too-distant future.

Prints undergo many changes during their journey from the canvases of the hip and profligate to the laundry baskets of the Connecticut matron, as any look into a 1970s suburban mail order catalog will reveal. One must bear in mind that the mutton-chopped man in yellow plaid pants wasn't always a punchline—he was *hip,* once. He was the wife-stealing Casanova of the country club before mass production stole his flair, turned it out viral in Dacron, and rendered him the type of guy who sells wholesale waterbeds. His pants were originally intended to *épater les bourgeois*, not add a pop of color to your drapes.

Take the recent recrudescence of the bejeweled caftan, a style which began amid the *haute volée*—tax exiles and jet-setters—hanging around in Tangier after Morocco declared independence in 1956. Artists, writers, and drug fiends of all sexual proclivities followed: Paul Bowles, William S. Burroughs, Jack Kerouac, Allan Ginsberg, the Rolling Stones. The spirit of 1960s Marrakesh was epitomized by a Patrick Litchfield shot of Talitha Getty, diaphanous and déshabillé on her roof deck among the domes. The caftan declared allegiance to an artistic, kif-smoking, lotus-eating, louche, and sexually adventurous set of beautiful people and heavy thinkers, who were getting high among the tiles and returning to Swinging London spangled like gypsy Christmas trees in cheap silver tribal jewelry, beads, Berber rugs, and enough sheepskin *objets* to re-create an opium den back in Thurloe Square.

Today, no more decadence remains in the caftan; the Tunisians have been tweezed out of the Tory Burch tunic. The kicky Moorish influences occasionally found in the offerings of today's young professional hipster furniture showrooms—leather poufs, geometric light shades—were once inspired by Islamic tiles, but the designs have been politely de-Islamated for your protection, and now are 50 percent less Moorish—sending a Demi-Moorish signal, if you will—a de-opinionated opium den look for the aspirational loft-dwelling crowd.

The symbols of social transgression inevitably become the hand towels of colonialism. Patterns may endure, but their original meaning and significance is destabilized at strobe speed unto a pixellated blur. The patterns roll through time, losing a bit of their original suction every year, and ultimately succeed most in the marketplace when they finally mean nothing at all.

Even the durable Goth style has been defanged; it has lost its daemon and original death-drive. When Paris designers began dishing out black-buckled patent leather hip-waders of a variety

once worn exclusively by bloodthirsty counterculture sex workers, there was certainly still *sex* in them—they still *winked* like
naughty fetish boots—but in amplifying the cost and quality of
them, luxury removed all threat of *danger*. It was the footwear of
the *demimondaine* without the edgy aftertaste, tragic consequences,
permanent ink, or even that dirty feeling when the dawn creeps
in through the foiled-over windows. Even the skull and bones
beloved by pirates and Hell's Angels are Alexander McQueen–
knockoff pashminas and fodder for toddler bibs, today.

(Help us, shark-jumping Fonzie Jesus.)

13

NEW YORK (HIGH) NEW YORK (LOW) / THE MONEY BELT

The Rich Get Richer, the Poor Get Poorer; They Both Wear Turquoise Fur

~

Society cannot share a common communication system so long as it is split into warring classes.

—BERTOLD BRECHT,

"A SHORT ORGANUM FOR THE THEATER"

I like white in winter because it proves you don't have to deal with the elements.

—MICHAEL KORS

Paul Fussell, in his book *Class: A Guide Through the American Status System*, names two socioeconomic extremes in the American class structure: the "top out-of-sights," people so rich that they are essentially invisible, and the "bottom out-of-sights," people so poor that they are essentially invisible. "It's here," Fussell writes, "that we begin to perceive one of the most wonderful things about the American class system. The curious similarity, if not actual brotherhood, of the top and bottom out-of-sights . . . a remarkable example of the time-proven principle that Extremes Meet."

In New York City, these extremes met, at least once, in 1911, in the aftermath of the Triangle Shirtwaist Factory fire, the worst workplace tragedy to hit Manhattan before 9/11. The factory, on Washington Place just half a block east of Washington Square Park, was a classic sweatshop. One hundred and forty-five garment workers, most of them young immigrant girls from Eastern Europe, were killed on the upper floors when the building went ablaze, because the management had locked the doors from the outside to prevent the girls from taking unauthorized breaks.

The death toll so outraged a group of rich society ladies from uptown that they rallied to support workplace safety laws, supporting and legitimizing the garment workers' labor movement. These ladies, nicknamed the Mink Brigade, were ridiculed by the press, but their diamonds and furs inarguably helped on the picket lines. Industrial strikers in those days were often beaten, jailed, or shot—but even a really doltish cop knew it was probably a bad idea to batter Alva Vanderbilt Belmont. Mink was arguably the best armor for that particular battlefield—and for a while, it helped the labor movement. The rise of unionism enabled skilled garment workers to earn livable wages with proper benefits; they were able to save money and send their children to universities, where they became upper-middle-class professionals such as doctors and lawyers. The American promise of upward mobility was actually true, for a little while, for the "garmentos" of Seventh Avenue and their families, and this was due in part to intervention on their behalf by the most privileged women of New York society.

After the Triangle Shirtwaist strike, it is unclear whether or not the invisible polar extremes of the economic spectrum in New

York ever fully "met" in person again. (The Mink Brigade may have objected to burning factory girls to death, but they were decidedly *not* in solidarity with the unions.)

The Upper East Side, once known as the Silk Stocking District, is New York's only neighborhood with a high concentration of Republicans. Madison Avenue between 57th Street and 85th Street, once identified as "the fashionable road," houses the highest-end luxury shopping in Manhattan. The inventories of Madison Avenue boutiques—gilded old luxury brands like Valentino, Oscar de la Renta, Yves Saint-Laurent, and Chanel—tend to reconfirm the established fashion tendencies of the main shoppers of the area: rich ladies-who-lunch, of a certain age, with tight shiny skin, huge sunglasses, and buttery leather jackets with fur trim during cold weather. There are often tiny dogs and spoiled daughters involved.

Exactly 10.57 miles east of the Hermès store on Madison Avenue, there is Jamaica Avenue: an 8.6-mile shopping district stretching through several predominantly African American, Hispanic, and Caribbean neighborhoods in Jamaica, Queens. Even before recorded history, the strip of land under Jamaica Avenue was a shopping destination for Native Americans from as far west as the Great Lakes, who came to trade pelts and furs for whelk and quahog shells with the bands of Lenape who lived there.

After World War II, African American servicemen came home with money from the Servicemen's Readjustment Act of 1944 (a.k.a. the GI Bill) and wanted to buy real estate—preferably someplace relatively inexpensive, whence they might commute to jobs in Manhattan. The threat of integration threw Jamaica's mostly white, Irish residents into a proto-Archie Bunker-style, *there goes the neighborhood* panic. White residents sold off their homes en masse at great losses, snookered by xenophobic fear-stoking real estate agencies, who found that exploiting racial tension was a terrifically easy way to engage in the shady practice of "blockbusting": buying up entire neighborhoods from terrified bigots at heavily depreciated prices, then marking them back up and reselling the homes to aspirant African American homeowners.

By the 1950s, Jamaica was in a tailspin of "white flight." Chain department stores and movie theaters abandoned the neighborhood, development stopped, and the neighborhood and its residents were left to drift into urban blight, a problem greatly exacerbated by the influx of crack cocaine in the 1980s.

Madison Avenue does not change very much—there is a permaclass of rich people who are untouched by economic calamity. Jamaica Avenue is similarly stabilized during recessions and depressions; its businesses—small Mom-and-Pop 99-cent variety stores, hair-braiding and nail salons, wig stores, and discount clothing stores—have always catered to the lowest-income customers. There is a handful of businesses that are known to survive regardless of the health of the larger economy. It's a relatively well-known phenomenon that manicurists, hair salons, and psychic readers generally report no noticeable loss of business during grave economic dips. Sacrifices may be bravely made in terms of food, heat, and fuel—but ladies who flirt with their hands will only give up manicures when you pry their cold, dead hands off them. Below the poverty line, just as in the .01 percent, there is no noticeable economic fluctuation. The extremes are immune to the big fluxes in the economy felt primarily by the middle class.

The inventories of New York's richest and poorest shopping zones reveal that these tribes share remarkably similar style tastes. In both neighborhoods, the highest-end menswear is tailored for living irrationally large. In general, the menswear inventories appear to exude a certain carnivorous, capitalist ruthlessness, attainable exclusively by CFOs, private equity sultans, NBA superstars, dictators, or those who just want to look like them.

These are clothes that pour gasoline on incendiary power fantasies of world domination, or merely the domination of the weaker sex. Both the highest- and lowest-income gentlemen of New York seem to dress in anticipation of gunfights on the dance floor. It is a look for fresh kills and new exploitations that says: *On your knees, bitches: Daddy's hungry.*

Only on Jamaica Avenue and Madison Avenue can men purchase such dictatorial finery as hooded fur coats, three-piece zoot suits in apricot plaid, and footwear such as lemon-yellow crocodile loafers, zebra-striped oxfords, or super-pointy oxblood eelskin "roach killers." Unlike any other shopping district in New York City, both Madison and Jamaica Avenues sell purple bowler hats.

Women in Jamaica and the Upper East Side are both able to shop for fancy ball gowns of the prom variety (sometimes paired, on mannequins on both avenues, with an appropriate parka), and both realms of shoppers are inclined to adorn themselves with pavé diamonds—whether they be on a Panthère de Cartier pendant, or merely a pavé diamond pendant shaped like a panther.

At the Giorgio Armani boutique on Madison, today's discerning American gigolo might pick up a snakeskin cashmere cardigan for $2,175 (which I presumed, from the price, had been knitted by actual snakes), a long mauve shearling Superfly coat lined in a lavender, chinchillified rabbit fur, or a jacket made of genuine perforated alligator for $50,000.

"What kind of guy buys this jacket?" I asked the Manhattan Armani salesman, genuinely perplexed. "Jamie Foxx? Crocodile Dundee?" Both, I reasoned, would have to be bare-chested underneath and holding a buck knife to really pull it off. "We have a customer who gets one every season," the salesperson replied. "But," he whispered, off the record, *"they're not really my cuppa."*

Dolce and Gabbana's menswear also appears to haberdash

directly toward the ethically askew: gilded mafiosi, sociopathic hedge-funders, wannabe plutocrats. Who else could get away with buttercup-yellow lambskin motocross jackets with laser-cut wing-tip zipper booties?

When I was there, the central casting gods placed a vintage drug lord before me in the stairwell: five foot three, white suit, black shirt, gold teeth, nicotine fog, oversize fawning yes-man.

"Tony Montana!" I growled in fluent Pacino. "Everybody take a look at the bad guy!"

The bodyguard didn't even choke me out; the two men just started giggling. They had to: the kingpin's look wasn't icon-homage. It wasn't inspired by Scarface, it *was* Scarface: a direct quotation to the point of being a Halloween costume.

Many of the women's shoes in Queens wouldn't look out of place in Manhattan's Christian Louboutin boutique. They are, in essence, the exact same style of shoe—a five- to seven-inch "fuck me or else" stiletto, known in fetishistic eBay galleries as "Pleasers." In both neighborhoods, women's shoes look right at home in the rarefied air betwixt chrome poles and mirrored ceilings. In Manhattan, these shoes cost around $900. In Jamaica, the same shoe is available at a fraction of the price. However, Jamaica offers more options for the lady who wishes to be slightly more overt about her goals. It's all in the details: one store featured over-the-knee, black vinyl platform *Pretty Woman* boots, the spitting image of a pair I had recently seen in the window of Jimmy Choo—these, however, had large white dollar signs appliquéd on the sides. An alternative Pleaser with clear Lucite platform heels had elasticized fabric uppers, reaching like stockings to mid-thigh, printed with an illustration of red cherries on a white background. I didn't think anyone would have a problem selling these for $900 in Manhattan, given the right show window.

The major differences between the two neighborhoods aren't

in their looks, but in their presentation. In the context of Madison Avenue, women's shoes are *implicitly* sexy. In the context of Jamaica Avenue, virtually the same shoes are *explicitly* sexy.

Dresses in Queens, in large part, are much shorter, much tighter, much more low-cut than they are in mid-range neighborhoods—even for girl children under the age of eight. Also, on Jamaica Avenue, mannequins are crazily *stacked*. One, wearing a low-cut white sweater in a small women's boutique, had enormous DDD cups with erect nipples the size of walnuts. (Similarly endowed mannequins are also used in bikini shops in South Beach.)

The fashion libidos of both Jamaica Avenue and Madison Avenue seem to tie their bandannas together and shake hands under a flag bearing one particular brand logo: Gucci. I visited the Gucci Fifth Avenue flagship when it opened in 2008.

The designer Tom Ford had an enviable run with Gucci. The wealthy old blue-blood brand finally had its overdue sexual awakening in 1994 when young playboy Tom swung in, with his snare-drum-tight slacks and groin-deep necklines. The pairing couldn't last, of course; the markets and egos involved were too volatile. Still, Tom, for all his flaws, really understood Gucci. When Frida Giannini took over in 2008, she gave Gucci a brassy youth injection, adding bigger hair and breasts to the old luxury standby (Tom Ford had a nervous breakdown and/or made a movie). The print ads were upbeat and bosomy: a jailbait nymph with pouty lips clambering on rocks with an oily haired boyfriend—very (ahem) Guess by Georges Marciano . . . a flirty, slutty cowgirl style a wee bit tackier than one expected of the ol' Gucci, Connecticut golf-bastard legacy.

Today, Gucci seems to understand that it owes much of its ongoing popularity to the hip-hop community's affection for the brand. In Gucci's menswear section, the music is bass-thumpy; young brothaz in purple lambskin bomber jackets and jeans belted just over the knee glide around in tinted eyeglasses, greeting one another with knuckle bumps over large shopping bags. Hip-hop's romance with Gucci isn't for the Connecticut country-club loafers of classic Gucci. Hip-hop has coopted the brand and redefined Gucciness itself. Gucci has been successfully kidnapped and brainwashed by hip-hop, and, like Patty Hearst, it has succumbed to enough Stockholm Syndrome to have fallen in love with the revolution.

On the first floor, the Heritage Collection of handbags and luggage seems aimed toward those who aspire to inherited wealth. The centerpiece is a caramelized alligator sarcophagus of a steamer trunk with shiny brass locks such as the viscount might take on a steamship to the colonies, surrounded by smaller components, such as a matching jewelry box ($33,250).

The handbags are perfect for jungle doctors bringing quinine and gin to desperate indigenous housewives: muted crocodile and pocked ostrich with lacquered bamboo handles ($3,650). Matching ankle-strap pumps have a bamboo dowel embedded into the perilous needle-spiked heel ($1,980). These items are decidedly not pre-distressed; these are new family heirlooms, purchased with your freshly minted lucre.

Madison Avenue traffics in all the silk and cashmere basics necessary to outfit a young socialite for her life of international resort-hopping and trophy wifery. The headless mannequins in Madison Avenue's shop windows house the fantasy costumes of what rich girls may aspire to be when they grow up: red-carpet actresses, professional socialites, countesses, Ladies Gaga, First Ladies of the United States.

The young women of Jamaica, Queens, are encouraged by the contents of their shop windows in exactly two occupational directions: medical technician and sex worker. Medical scrubs, indeed, are often sold in the same store as Pleasers. Stretch vinyl and metallic spandex minidresses of a size and body-consciousness ordinarily reserved for Miami swimwear—including an over-the-shoulder gold alligator-print G-string—are featured in a window directly behind a row of orthopedic white nursing shoes.

(Scrubs come in the strangest, most surreal array of prints conceivable; I have become a somewhat obsessed connoisseur of medical scrub prints. One set that I found particularly thrilling featured a print of the Warner Brothers Tasmanian Devil character dressed as a doctor, wearing an old-fashioned medical head-reflector and wielding an axe-shaped mallet, savagely baring his fangs with his tongue hanging out, and riding a skateboard on which the word "AMBULANCE" was written. If I awoke from surgery and the nurse leaning over to adjust my drip was wearing that particular garment, it is possible that I would immediately need to go back into surgery . . . and perhaps this is the point.)

⚎

FROM 2008 TO 2012, Manhattan was host to an ongoing retail bloodbath. Many beloved Manhattan restaurants, boutiques, and art galleries surrendered their leases.

When the windows of Yohji Yamamoto's venerable landmark at the corner of Grand and Mercer were papered over in 2010, something intangible but precious was also lost: the last cigarette wisps of the downtown mood of the 1980s—the intellectually louche, Zen art gallery vibe that animated the customers, who built their social personas around Yamamoto's postmodern, asymmetric, post-gender tailoring. In the fashion Darwinism of this new economy, Yamamoto's irreverent, creative attitude didn't survive; to remain in business, designers had to embrace new looks for the apex predators on the rise. There was no more time to waste on subtlety or individual vision. The new look was *raw power*. There would be no more leisure time, no more middle class. The guns

STYLE: IT'S ALL IN THE SILHOUETTE

This guy made such a great shape walking down the street in Anchorage I had to run him down and chat him up. He's a human exclamation point.

were drawn; the writing was on the wall in the form of "going out of business" banners citywide.

There were other interesting ways in which fashion mirrored the political zeitgeist; for instance, handbags seemed to shape-shift overnight.

Shortly before the crash, the "It" bag of Manhattan ladies tended to be some variation on a midsize, slouchy, leather hobo-pouch in a severely distressed, even victimized, patina, as if it had been crafted to match the heartbreaking stacks of collapsed shoes at the Holocaust Museum. After the crash, all the hippie bags were firehosed away. Boho chic was sent back to rehab, and handbags were suddenly super-*new*—violently glossy, and utterly monstrous in size. This new handbag seemed to be responding to cues from a survivalist alarm that had collectively gone off in women's reptile brains in response to the collapsed economy: they were bags that spoke to secret fears of sudden poverty, and a subliminal desire to *hoard wealth*.

They were essentially patent-leather suitcases, should a lady need to discreetly Netjet in the dead of night to take refuge somewhere safe and foreign. These trend-endorsed carryalls were massive enough to carry several gallon Ziploc bags of old family jewelry and silverware, small artworks, any incriminating business records, wigs, sunglasses, three pairs of shoes, multiple passports, theatrical makeup, a laptop, a prosthetic leg full of prescription painkillers, ski boots, and a buckwheat neck pillow. They reinforced a secret *überklasse* paranoia, to wit: *You may need to flee in the dead of night, honey, because angry mobs of working-class yahoos might try to Occupy Uptown, hell-bent on throwing your hedge-funded, Pilates-dented ass into a dirty little tumbrel cart.*

Variations on this wealth-hoarding emotion were evident in many popular handbags. When I went to Madison Avenue to review the reopening of Chloé, after designer Paulo Melim Andersson took over the reins, their purses, also morbidly oversize, had another telling feature: heavy, Chloé-trademarked brass padlocks of the size and density normally used to secure storage lockers in iffy neighborhoods.

The libido of New York is primarily driven by greed, so fashion statements generally tend to express one's relationship with money: *I have Money / I need Money / Don't take my money / I am taking your money.* The New York fashion statement is, essentially, a bank statement.

Case in point: The Louis Vuitton bag.

With so many of the bags in circulation thanks to the recent "democratization of luxury" (not to mention Chinatown knock-offs as indistinguishable from the "real" thing as to be as existentially bewildering as *Battlestar Galactica* cyborgs), a Louis Vuitton bag is so recognizable, so unmysterious, so profligate, that it is

ADORABLE TEXAS TEEN is SO NOT VICTIMIZING ANYBODY with HER FABU-
LOUS NEW HANDBAG! YOU'RE JUST JEALOUS.

arguably way more of a bank statement than a fashion statement.
It makes no declaration of style, in and of itself: it only defines
who you are inasmuch as it draws a line in the sand to say who
you are defining yourself against in economic contrast. In its banal
way, it is as class-divisive as the freeway built to separate a ghetto
from a white shopping district.

Thus, luxury items that are not intended to have any particular
"message" often contain great payloads of semiotic class hostility. A
$3,200 handbag is more than just an accessory. By buying one, you
are essentially declaring your voting preference, your tax bracket,
your gang colors. This level of fashion symbolism is rarely acknowledged outside of wonky academic circles. A girl who buys a Louis
Vuitton bag isn't thinking, *This bag will really declare that I uphold
the consumer myths of the imperialist status quo by visually distancing me
from the moral quagmire of entrenched poverty and the gross, lazy subway*

people who brought it on themselves. She is certainly not committing a *conscious* act of symbolic violence. She's merely *accessorizing.*

Still, there are casualties. The Vuitton bag is a symbolic drone that drops unaccountable megatons of class resentment luggage on anyone lacking the means to vanquish their desire to own one by yielding to the temptation to buy one.

⊰⅊⅊⊱

IT WAS EQUALLY EDUCATIONAL to observe, while so many beloved retail businesses perished, which businesses survived the global economic meltdown, and how they did it.

Despite the wide financial mood swings of the mid-seventies through the early nineties, Calvin Klein always seemed to effortlessly rise. His brand vision opened an infinity of clean white space in an overcluttered design world. Everything his brand touched was reflective of spare architectural minimalism (which had yet to be mass-produced and exhausted by places like West Elm). His sumptuously erotic black and white Herb Ritts ads created a nostalgia for an easy utopian future, full of startlingly intimate moments— snapshots from crystal-clear dreams of seaside romps with surreally beautiful, multiracial lovers in various stages of undress. The designer's then wife (invariably described by magazines as "the leonine Kelly Klein") was always publicly admired for her ability to look casually ravishing with loose hair, natural makeup, and little or no jewelry. The Calvin Klein brand was a heady mix of white sand, cloudless skies, stressless luxury, and urgent passion.

I asked my fashionista friend Johanna Cox to accompany me to the flagship store, because I hadn't figured out Calvin Klein since Francisco Costa became the company's creative director in 2003. The looks had softened from their usual iconic sharpness into a mood I hadn't quite deciphered.

"Ah, but it's all so simple," Johanna cooed, gravitating to a black wool jersey dress which I thought it looked like something Jackie O might wear to the funeral of either husband—a time-lessly somber thing with three-quarter sleeves, short hemline, high neckline.

I examined a short dress spun from a fine nylon mesh ($1,495). "This looks like mosquito netting."

"Yeah," Johanna agreed, "but the *best* mosquito netting."

Next to this was a large, shapeless, cashmere-silk hoodie, ostensibly for haute dog-walking ($1,295), and a cashmere tank ($350). I found these puzzling, mainly because these basic items can be found virtually anywhere, in similarly conservative cuts, and generally at a fraction of the cost. I kept adjusting my antennae but could not get the big picture.

On the way in, I had passed a futon-like flat on the floor dis-playing the season's new sandal. These were not dissimilar to the sporty platform sandals Prada is beloved for in the summertime. The Calvin Klein version, however, was noticeably huge, with a very wide, square toe, and a rounded base like the bottom of a rowboat. My first thought was that they were bold and commend-able: metallic T-strap sandals for men!

A saleswoman breezed by with a pair.

"What size are those?" I asked, expecting an answer in the gen-tleman's footwear range.

"This is the last 38," she said. "They're really popular."

I had that vertiginous wah-wah feeling one gets when plunged into cognitive dissonance.

The sandal, detailed with silver mesh, was more or less my size, but looked like it would fit my dad, and seemed to weigh around three pounds ($1,695, or $795 for a marginally lighter, leather version). I was told they were very comfortable, which made me think that Shelley Winters might enjoy wearing them to assist in her own drowning by Montgomery Clift.

Upstairs, I found a very literal, white, asymmetrical goddess gown, difficult to envision outside of a toga party or the very beginning of a Columbia picture. Another rack of offerings in sea-foam green and soapy mauve were equally bewildering—they were so timidly undersexed and overpolite as to be impossible not to associate with mothers of brides. They were ostensibly intended to be worn in non-wedding contexts—but how? And *where*?

Johanna and I gathered armfuls of garments and scuttled off to the dressing rooms.

I was excited to try a sleeveless tank dress in shimmery liquid satin ($1,095), but it didn't provide the chrome hood ornament effect on my body that I'd hoped for. There was an asymmetrical bunching at one side that made me resemble a wet sock scrunched the wrong way down a rain boot.

Johanna was confident that a particular pewter cocktail dress would win my love once I put it on. It looked like a roiling mass of angry grey pintucks, swooping in conflicting directions for a kind of crosscurrent-undertow effect. I was willing to be won over . . . but the dress was not kind.

I staggered out to show Johanna.

"I am your lung after five years of chain-smoking," I said in the affectless voice of a disembodied organ.

I was even more confused.

We had great hopes for a teal silk jersey dress with a lovely, open mandarin neck detail ($600). "Nope," Johanna called from the dressing room. It was clingy in all the wrong places—too tight over her curves, loose and baggy in the middle—basically the same problem I'd been having with all the stuff I tried on: knit numbers which had a kind of kicky Zelda Fitzgerald look on the hanger, but tended on the body to evoke the wrong years of Brigitte Nielsen. Nothing curved in the right places; everything was straight where it should bend, and overcompensating in zones where nature already provided attractions.

Killer Beehive Attacks Waitress in the East Village, NYC . . . (and she gives YOU a big tip on how to slay demons using nothing but bobby-pins and a rattail comb . . .)

I cornered our salesman, and asked him as delicately as possible, "Is Calvin Klein primarily being designed for the Asian market now?"

He smiled serenely. "Calvin Klein does a lot more business in Asia and Europe than it does in the States."

Suddenly, it all made sense: the baby-pinks, too-polite cashmeres, proper necklines, and modest sheath cuts dropping straight from the shoulders to the knees, with none of the usual feminine detours. These dresses were not made with Western bodies in mind, at all.

What Calvin Klein revealed to me, with all this unrevealing clothing, was *the end of America's global dominance.* We no longer had the spending power to keep Francisco Costa interested.

I took it wholly for granted when America was rich and respected. I had no idea there were so many subtle perks to being a functional superpower. I never realized how much everything buyable had been attuned to American cultural preferences— from candy and yogurt flavors to comedy films to electronic beeping sounds. We were once the gravitational center of the aesthetic universe, and at Calvin Klein, for the very first time, I realized we weren't anymore.

Who would have ever predicted that the one thing that would eventually come between Brooke Shields and her Calvins was . . . *China?*

The American dream has apparently already shredded at the seams.

⊰꙳⊱

THE ODDEST SPECTACLE OF ALL, once the recession became a depression, were the strange new boutiques that were bold enough to *open* brand-new luxury flagships in Manhattan, in the midst of this dark financial march toward whatever it was we were approaching. The opening of a palatial luxury retail venue on the priciest stretch of Madison Avenue during an unrelenting down-turn begged questions. Who were these people? Were they from an alternate dimension? Could they fly?

As the executive creative director and president of Coach Inc., Reed Krakoff raised the accessories brand from a $500 million company to a ubiquitous $3 billion monolith. But apparently, he really wanted to sing. I mean direct. I mean, he wanted to be a legendary fashion designer. So, he made the very nervy move of opening massively expensive boutiques for his eponymous new fashion label in New York and Tokyo, a mere shoe-toss away from the boutiques of the historic design houses that Mr. Krakoff apparently regards as his peer group: Prada, Gucci, Lanvin, et al.

Fashion reviewers struggled to be kind about Mr. Krakoff's sartorial talent, which wasn't quite ripe yet. Commenter James Earl Jones, on Eric Wilson's "On the Runway" blog, articulated this general nonplussedness: "You can't buy your way to relevance in this arena of fashion just because you made a lot of money elsewhere." Well—ding-dong—apparently, in this brave new world, you *could*.

Mr. Krakoff casually described his ambitious new look

as "luxe punk." Indeed, one could not accuse the line of being too feminine. Everything looked sturdy, thick, armored, and unbreakable—even the sweaters. "It's a very interesting time to re-embrace American design," Mr. Krakoff was quoted as saying, on his website. "That ability to take something industrial and utilitarian and elevate it."

My interest was first piqued by a thick little black dress that I assumed was wrought out of Kevlar seatbelt material; only between my fingers did it reveal itself to be a particularly butch gauge of linen. I was not convinced that the designer was aware that the safety-regulation appearance of the dress made the mannequin (which was jointed, like a posable drawing model) resemble a crash test dummy—an impression reinforced by orthopedic-looking accessories nearby, such as an ivory fur and wool whiplash collar ($1,900).

I began to wonder if the heaviness of Reed Krakoff's materials was a psychological reaction to how thin-skinned he must feel about his spontaneous self-generation into the highest echelons of fashion designerdom. Despite my tendency to disregard artistic prestige obtained via the vulgar mechanisms of brute wealth, I did like some stuff. Much of the heavy metal jewelry would be ideal for hand-to-hand combat: shiny gunmetal chain-links of a girth normally seen around the waists of bicycle messengers, bracelets resembling the hardware required to break a psychotic horse. Perhaps the most puzzling accessory were the "beaver suspenders" ($3,200)—a strappy black lederhosen-like contraption with wide beaver-pelt mudflaps on either hip. I couldn't make sense of it, but it would certainly keep your kidneys warm while you were out poaching mastodons. The video of Mr. Krakoff's runaway show, projected on a wall, was of dubious value. When model Karlie Kloss, who is nine feet tall and has thighs the circumference of a tangelo, wears this totalitarian beaver-enforcement garment and looks like the box her dishwasher came in, there is little doubt that if I wore it, people would call me Mr. Baggins and beg me to destroy the Ring.

"It's definitely a conversation starter. Or a conversation ender," quipped the saleswoman, aware of the garment's difficulties. In struggling to envision a context in which these incredibly dense garments could exist, I eventually came up with a movie plot. The time: a not-too-distant future, post-environmental collapse, as seen through the limited technologies and styles of 1979. Kurt Russell stars as a tough Yukon cop in an Arctic dystopia. He stumbles upon a glacier and finds, encased within, a living room set, with a perfectly preserved group of four wealthy women from Long Island in long, thick, beige sweaters with built-in elbow pads ($940), tall, lizard-skin spectator boots ($1,895), and massive amber-tint sunglasses, flash-frozen around an enormous chrome coffee table. He thaws them out and takes them as wives, only to refreeze them a short time later when it becomes evident that they entirely lack any and all survival skills, and their resurrected conversation bores his favorite sled dog to death.

I tried one of the utility-inspired numbers—a buckled kimono jumper ($1,190) made of the kind of gabardine that auto mechanics wore in the 1950s. I liked its perverse combination of massive expensiveness and pseudo blue-collarness, for all the wrong reasons . . . but it didn't quite fit. Neither did the black seatbelt dress I had liked on the hanger—a racer-tank back, heavy as a vintage overcoat ($1,390). A long black leather gown in a similar cut also showed spunk and promise ($3,700), but I couldn't envision a human female who could fit in it properly; the model walking on the wall in the same dress seemed to be fighting it for normal movement. Rich people are not like us. The most compelling luxury at Reed Krakoff, really, was the rare spectacle of enough capital to squander on a learning curve that most people would prefer to master privately, before inflicting their genius on an unsuspecting public.

But this was the Brave New America. CEOs and movie stars had already bought their way into politics. Now, anyone with the means to stick a boutique on Madison Avenue was officially a fashion designer. Reed Krakoff planted a 60-pound leather flag right on Coco Chanel's grave, giving her something luxuriously utilitarian to turn over and over under.

—❦—

IT WOULD BE ENTIRELY wrong for me to suggest that all luxury items in the fashion world are inherently evil. Every once in a while, a smart design proves cost-effective because it changes the game, and reinvents its own medium.

Alexander Wang cut his teeth on the fashion world at the zenith of the bust—he was the right mind at the right time. He knew that cool rich kids wanted a new highbrow/lowbrow haute casual that could be worn to the prestigious day gig (modeling, interning, etc.), and would require no change whatsoever to go out dining and dancing all night (lather, rinse, repeat).

An $80 T-shirt should seem like a grotesque plutocratic sin. But when you put on one of Alexander Wang's, you realize: oh. This would be equally appropriate for work, bowling, lawn darts, gnocchi fights . . . and it drapes well enough to be worn as rebellious eveningwear. It connects dots you hadn't imagined were connectable before. However, regardless of its versatility, an $80 T-shirt is still a grotesque plutocratic sin.

There is an economic equation by which one may calculate surplus value. Let's take, for example, a $118 tank top.

If this tank top is made in a sweatshop in the U.S. protectorate Sai Pan (where, at least until recently, it was technically legal to affix a tag that said "Made in America"), let's say that it cost the manufacturer $3 to make, and he sells it to retailers for $10.

But one must calculate the amount of value that actual human labor contributes to the product—assembly, detail—and subtract the amount of money actually paid to the sweatshop worker by his slave-driving industrialist, who is paying the worker somewhere around $80 a month. The workers are paid pennies for each shirt; the retailer makes around $6 on each of them.

The conventional name for this difference is profit. The whole capitalist system is based on "expropriating" surplus value (i.e., stealing labor) from exploited workers.

By 2011, the whole idea of "work" had become as abstract as the concept of "leisure" to many New Yorkers (like myself), who found that their incomes had been slashed to the roots, while the executive class were earning unprecedented bonuses.

In 2011, Manhattan's hot young rich girls were going berserk for Isabel Marant, the young Frenchwoman whose label mastered the jet-set bohemian look associated with carefree Parisian chicks: that thrown-together, cigarette-hanging-from-pouty-mouth style that pretends to shrug off effort: "*Quoi*, this? Pff. I slept in this shirt, you silly child, and these pants were on the floor."

The environment of Ms. Marant's SoHo retail space is reflective of the finished-yet-unpolished look of her clothing: artsy structures in raw wood, acoustic French folk music.

I liked the inventory instantly. Then again, it all seemed very familiar—it was very reflective of play-clothes I've been collecting in thrift stores for years: solid, timeless, casual stuff. I gravitated over to that most basic of basics: a long grey sweatshirt. The price tag sank its fangs into my wrist: $400. After recovering from my initial recoil, I discovered it was made of silk.

Everything has a soft, overwashed weightlessness about it— the artificial patina of an item long loved. Cowboy shirts with snap buttons ($335) come in an array of delicately wrinkled plaids. A bleached and battered denim shirt with a smattering of metal studs was $215. A silk military jumpsuit: $530.

What I figured to be platonically ideal Isabel Marant customers were milling around in full force: tall, rich, willowy blondes wearing big mod army jackets and chunky high heels.

I was wearing a boy's plaid rodeo shirt with snap buttons (eBay, $12) a charcoal-grey Hanes zipper hoodie (Walmart, $12), skinny-legged Levi's I'd bought at one of those loud discount places on Lower Broadway (under $40), and a old wool army jacket (eBay, under $20). Coincidentally enough, I looked, in texture, shape, and substance, more or less like I got dressed right in the store. One of the iconic blondes, wearing what I reckoned was head-to-toe Isabel Marant, was dressed more or less like I was: military

WORLD-CLASS STYLE ICONS MAY BE ANYWHERE

This gorgeous specimen of soul-cholo was managing to rock that classic brim with a light flannel, white V-neck tee, thick leather watchband, and wooden Buddha-beads . . . all while keeping customers happy at the cash register (and fashion-savvy customers DELIGHTED) at his work-station at La Guardia Airport, New York City.

jacket, high clog boots, skinny pants—only the grand total of my outfit cost approximately what she had paid for parking while buying hers.

Sumptuous textiles are key to Ms. Marant's looks; the text of these suggests the international rock-star traveler aesthetic adopted in the early 1970s by the filmmaker Nicolas Roeg: rich, comely hippies recently returned from hashish-smoking and soul-seeking in exotic locales, laden with tribal weavings and hand-made ethnic trinketry they could still pick up on the cheap in freshly (if only theoretically) decolonized lands.

The blonde I was staring at purchased one of the season's signature blazers. These have a cottony thickness I visually associate with old tribal men in East Asia, but they're tarted up with fancy, dark-hued metallic prints ($850). I stared for a while into a kaleidoscopic pair of chiffon harem pants ($850) that seemed to be made of cubist peacock feathers and pixellated oil slicks.

In stores such as these, I can't help but ask myself: "Can I duplicate this look for exponentially less?"

This thought beat my head like a gong when I realized that the selections I had taken into the dressing room were a distressed denim pencil skirt and the aforementioned $400 sweatshirt. I pulled my own jeans and grey sweatshirt back on and hustled out of the store—an act of self-preservation that saved me nearly $600. Was my own wardrobe achieving parity or parody? Only my hairdresser knows for sure.

It's not that the store was without merit: Isabel Marant has a very keen flair for easy elegance. I had to admit it would be quite difficult to duplicate the feathery lightness or rich geometric prints of the silky harem pants.

Running across Canal Street a few minutes later, I passed another chic young Isabel Marant type wearing a battered green military parka over her otherwise black ensemble. Serendipitously, twenty feet past the crosswalk, I saw the exact same army jacket hanging in window of Church Street Surplus, an Army–Navy/vintage store that has been peddling such wares since 1971. The jacket in question: $45.

I strolled in. A handwritten cardboard sign read, "Beautiful Scarves $5." My hand went straight to it—a long silk foulard covered in army green, slate grey, teal, and dark-purple rectangles—the same palette I had just admired on Isabel Marant's $850 pants.

"Shall I put that in a bag for you?" asked the cashier, a young lady in a fifties pillbox hat.

"No thanks, I'll eat it here."

I looped the scarf in a slow sail around my neck; it did precisely the weightless, colorful thing I hoped it would.

"That looks great," she said. I believed her, because she wasn't smiling and I'd already paid for it.

"A fool sees not the same tree that a wise man sees," said William Blake. I stood underneath a tree on Church Street that was having a riotous outburst of pink flowers, and I may be far from wise, but I eventually noticed that no matter how much money I threw at it, it wasn't going to get any prettier. It wouldn't have been prettier if I replanted it on 86th and Madison, either. The point is to recognize a meritocracy in things of value, regardless of their low points of origin, current reigning trendiness, or future invisibility. Quality is quality, period. All else is corporate fear, hype, vanity, and vexation of the spirit.

Foolish is as foolish does—and the same goes for pretty.

14

NEVER-NEVER LAND /
THE EMPEROR'S NEW BELT

You Can't Always Get What You Want

$\rightleftharpoons$

I had a hunger for things I knew realistically
I didn't actually care for.

—TAMA JANOWITZ, *SLAVES OF NEW YORK*

If poor people knew how rich rich people are,
there would be riots in the streets.

— CHRIS ROCK

The whole previous two decades have been a weird and uncertain time for fashion, for reasons that are difficult to pin down. Nobody is really clear on what fashion is supposed to be, anymore.

I first heard this idea voiced when I interviewed the remarkable Karlo Steel, co-owner (with his partner, Constantin von Haeften) of Atelier, a cutting-edge New York men's store on Crosby Street. In 2008, Messrs. Steel and von Haeften collaborated with Rick Owens to build his New York flagship store on Hudson Street.

I interviewed Karlo Steel because he possessed a secret weapon that gave him fashion-cognitive superpowers and a razor-sharp cultural overview: a collection of sacred texts he calls "the Archive"—three decades of obsessively curated fashion magazines, to which he devotes an entire walk-in closet of his Tribeca apartment.

Mr. Steel showed me a number of editorial spreads by ingenious and influential stylists, pinpointing turning points in the fashion history of the last three decades, documented at the precise moment they occurred. Late in the interview, he disappeared into the Archive for a moment, then returned with an open magazine.

"Don't look at the cover," he said, putting it in my lap. "Just look at the spread."

On the pages were images of fairly benign current looks—some Rick Owens–esque drapy stuff; an oversize contraption that wouldn't look wholly out of place in the first Comme des Garçons look book; a girl with texturized bleach-blonde hair wearing a tissue-T under a distressed sequin minidress.

"Are you ready for this? This magazine is from 2000. This was *eleven years ago.*"

Gasp.

"Is it my imagination," he asked, "or has fashion *stood absolutely still for the past ten years?*"

He was absolutely right. I thought he could argue that nothing had changed in twenty-plus years, even.

Before the late 1990s, there were big obvious style paradigms that came around and subverted the silhouettes of the previous decade. These shapes eventually became a kind of visual shorthand, e.g., the extreme shoulder pads of the 1940s (or their comeback in the 1980s), the bell-bottoms of the seventies (or their comeback in the late 1990s). Now, these big shifts don't seem to be happening anymore. There is no recognizable "look"—the only noticeable changes between the late 1980s and the present, in fashion mag-

DEPRESSION? NO THANKS

On a sunny Easter morning in Brooklyn, this young man revealed the secret to his fashion success: He declared that he wears no clothing item that costs over $5. Economy-proof Flair.

azines, are in hairstyles. Fashion itself, he said, appears to be in a state of stasis.

I recalled reading about when the Visigoths sacked Rome, and progress stood still for a thousand years. Has our fall already happened? Are we only just noticing because we're seeing the same fall collections over and over again?

"If you look at a spread from 1970, and then one from 1980, there would be no way!" exhorted Mr. Steel. "They are *universes* apart. Completely different worlds!"

So . . . what happened?

"I think there's too many people invited to the party. Too

many designers. Too much of everybody doing everything, bringing everything back, all the time."

Fashion had frozen like a deer in the headlights—paralyzed by too much information. Even the most perishable styles—hypersexual, feminine cheesecake looks that usually have little more fashion shelf life than an actual cheesecake, are now lasting to the point of creating odd new phenomena like mothers and daughters dressed indistinguishably alike from a unified closet of shared slut-wear.

It seemed that all of New York's leading fashion intellectuals were attempting to articulate fashion's sudden escape from the whiplash shifts that had always previously governed it. Shortly after interviewing Mr. Steel, I noticed that Kurt Anderson had written about the same subject in *Vanity Fair*. When I interviewed Dr. Valerie Steele at the Fashion Institute of Technology, I discovered that all these heavyweight fashion intellects had essentially drawn the same conclusion:

There had been no big paradigm shifts in fashion for the last twenty or more years because all the previous decades and their mutually exclusive style signatures were, now, *all happening simultaneously.*

"This, in a way, is actually a terrific thing for fashion," Dr. Steele quipped, "because no matter what you look like, there is an era in which you are the magnificent ideal."

(Or alternately, as I have thought to myself many times: no matter what you look like, there is absolutely no way to *ever* be the magnificent ideal.)

IN THE OLDEN DAYS, before you could simply buy yourself a couture fashion house, a designer's ingenious new approach to style was what built a brand. Every once in a while, someone with a rare eye discovers a new simplicity or a new shape that immediately feels familiar and essential. Daringly creative new designs navigate new understandings of masculinity and femininity, and create a sense of being in alignment with the better thinking of their time: they are of a piece with all of the new thoughts, books, architecture, and social rules (or lack of them) that inspired them.

Great designers still exist, even in the luxury price range. This type of luxury—the really smart, actually beautiful stuff—can make New York a very difficult city to live in if you are vulnerable to the temptations of luxury and you don't happen to have the limitless discretionary funds of, say, an international arms trafficker.

"I was at Les Deux Cafés in Los Angeles a few years ago," my friend Nancy Balbirer enthused before our visit to the new Rick Owens flagship store on Hudson Street. "I was sitting by the door in a halter top, shivering a little. And this drop-dead fabulous older woman comes in: tiny-skinny, smoking; wild, black witchy-woman hair, wearing this very clingy Morticia-Addams-meets-Ginger-Rogers look, with her skirt dragging on the floor. Gobs of big wonderful rings. She looks at me and asks in her French accent, 'Are you cold?' And she rips this absolutely incredible leather jacket off her body and throws it around my shoulders."

"Wow."

"Then she sashays away, looks at me over her shoulder, wags her finger and says, 'Don't forget, on your way out!'"

"Did she instantly become your role model for life?"

"Completely. So, she turns out to be Michèle Lamy, the owner of Les Deux. Everything she's wearing is Rick Owens, because he's her *lover*. She's his *muse*. She's significantly older, but he fell madly in love with her when he was a crazy twentysomething bisexual. I never wanted to take that jacket off!"

Rick Owens's designs are drapy, rough-looking creations in

gorgeous materials, wrought into a style he has dubbed "glunge" (grunge plus glamor), which tends to give the wearer an appearance of emerging from the lips of a huge, black, slightly tattered orchid. The boutique—big, white, and stark—is, like a lot of Owens creations, unfinished around the edges. But this blind spot has been turned into an advantage. If Mr. Owens were an architect, he would make beautiful ruins.

When I arrived at the shop, Nancy, in the spirit of Madame Lamy, was already swaddled in a long, lean sable coat, moaning with pleasure.

"How much is it?" she asked Antino Angel Crowley, one of Mr. Owens's willowy, tattooed, beautiful employees. "It's an apartment, right?"

"Basically," Mr. Crowley replied. "It's $65,000. Which isn't bad, if you think about it."

I tried it, and agreed: not bad. Actually, it was a poem.

"You wouldn't need an apartment," I said, half-joking. "This coat is like youth and sex and butter all at the same time. You could sleep on the sidewalk and you would never feel a lack. You wouldn't even need love."

In 2003, Mr. Owens became the designer for Revillon, a label that has been wrapping women in fur since 1723. Later I read an Owens quotation encapsulating his approach to Revillon:

"It's about an elegance being tinged with a bit of the barbaric, the sloppiness of something dragging and the luxury of not caring. At Revillon, I felt it wasn't about displaying one's wealth, but rather giving the woman a selfish pleasure. It is about using sable as the lining under a very humble jacket, the luxury is all hers."

A mink cave-girl stole ($22,344) and a sheared mink coat with amorously wrapping tentacles ($43,610) echoed this sentiment (and made me gnash my teeth for want of such selfish pleasure).

Rick Owens designs are decidedly kinetic; the pieces are made to elongate lines of movement in three dimensions, whereas most clothing is spatially flat—conscious mainly in front and back, and best when standing still. The store employees, hanging around in these slouchy, body-conscious shapes, resemble a modern dance company.

I tried on a smoky brown, flared coat with a cowl neck and wobbling zipper that Bea Arthur might wear in *The Matrix IV* ($4,214). It inspired fooling around in the mirror; the perfect swing-weight of the coat added billowing slo-mo effect to my bullet-dodging Keanu backbend.

Nancy tried a pair of bias-cut trousers ($995)—very sexy and sharp for something as comfy as loungewear. The hemless hem was dragging around the unswept stone floor collecting dust, to the admiration of the staff boys, who approved of this Kate Hepburn-in-a-vacant-lot spectacle.

I tried a pleated art deco Egyptian goddess skort. It took three tries to get both legs through the proper holes in the light-free dressing room, but once on, it was very tempting to refuse to take it off until the price ($1,136) came down.

Mr. Owens's aesthetic sometimes requires more hippie élan than one might be capable of. William Streng, another tattooed sales beauty in unlaced combat boots, pulled the mohair sleeves of a $568 V-neck sweater down over my fingers.

"But I can't see my watch!" I complained.

"Who cares?" he shrugged. "Time stops."

He had a point.

Mr. Streng was wearing a sheer rayon tank top ($245), frayed into hanging clots at the hem. I've always thought it sound to buy good clothes and wear them until they rot. With Rick Owens, this is especially true, because entropy is built in as a plus factor: the tatters look better with age. Like a security blanket, the holes are proof of enduring love.

The mystique of Michèle Lamy, a chanteuse with two gold front teeth, is evident all over, but especially in a shelf full of little vicious-looking rat monsters made from sable scraps.

"Those are stash bags," Nancy whispered.

"How much?" Mr. Crowley asked Mr. Streng.

"They are five, I think."

"Hundred?"

"Thousand."

Formidable.

Rick Owens clothes, for all their Gothic fury and barbaric elegance, are deliriously feminine. Mr. Owens has said he is inspired by Lou Reed's music. This makes sense: crudely simple melodies sung in an unpretty voice, but suspended in the excruciating tension of an almost unbearably delicate softness and sensitivity.

This mood can create anxiety, like sitting under a lead-glass chandelier that would crash down if not for the brilliant efforts of a single heroic spider. But unsettling settings also inspire relaxed inhibitions, creating the possibility for sudden intimacies to occur between strangers.

Are you cold? Here!

The sable, *mes amis*, is on the inside.

⧉

I DO NOT CONSIDER MYSELF an envious person. I have always managed to live a rather fortunate bohemian life, by living beyond my means and employing a lot of magical thinking. Nonetheless, there have been moments when I have been made painfully aware of how great it might be to have an obscene amount of money. I have on occasion seen an object so covetable, it cramps my soul not to own it. Photos of Cher's infinity pool in Malibu overlooking the Pacific made my spleen wail like a theremin for nearly five years.

I discovered while reviewing the Alexander Wang store in SoHo that after lying on a fur hammock for about forty seconds, an internal paradigm shift happens. You may have thought that fur hammocks were absurd, meaningless bourgeois luxuries. Actually, they are what you've unknowingly spent your entire life searching for.

I once involuntarily gasped watching Nigella Lawson breezily savage five passion fruits, spooning their pulpy guts onto a Pavlova tart in a manner so sloppy as to be almost violently sensuous. The rapacious advantage she took of those luxury fruits corkscrewed right into my uptightness. *My God*, I thought, *those things are four bucks each*. I have always been afraid that if I let go of the wheel like that, I would never stop shucking passion fruits, and I'd end up in the gutter surrounded by a powdery residue of illegal Canadian meringue.

I have excellent reasons for not trusting myself with prohibitive tropical produce. I have been victimized in the past by wanton consumer desires too powerful and overwhelming to fight. I have been exhaustively prepared my entire life to make disastrous financial decisions. In fact, unless you grew up in deep space, or somewhere else where you were incapable of watching TV, reading magazines, or looking at billboards, so have you. We have all been conditioned this way.

Professional brainwashers (a.k.a. government propagandists and advertising executives) long ago refined the dark arts of psychological mass manipulation. By exploiting our deepest, most primitive desires and fears, our consumer libidos are activated, engaged, and directed. We have been trained to embrace consumerhood as the cure for all the pain and unfairness of human life. Through monstrously powerful, encoded psychological triggers utilized virtually everywhere in the media, a "strategy of desire" has been implanted in the deepest motivational recesses of our minds. We have all internalized the pervasive message that the gratification of our immediate individual desire is our highest priority. We have been subliminally trained to buy things we merely *want*, as opposed to things we need—and to indulge ourselves even to the point of self-sabotage whenever we feel weak, unlovely, or unloved.

To quote the siren song of Peter Pan, "I have a place where dreams are born and time is never planned. . . ." Never-Never Land, to me—that magical place where you never grow old— is a place that definitely exists, in the minds of consumers. This is because the brainwashing that our commercial media has been marinating our expectations in since birth has been whispering, all our lives, that this place among the stars is *attainable*. This remote world of luxury isn't merely for those who were born to billionaires or royalty—it's a life that *you too* could be living, if only you were a better person, or you worked harder, or dieted more, or had better hair, or you gave better blowjobs, or if you *really cared* enough to wear Revillon chinchilla coats with nothing under them but twelve-pack abs and a Brazilian Vajazzling job.

This subconscious belief that you can and should have certain things you really want—this fervent gnawing sensation that you deserve things you don't have the means to possess—can really fuck with your mind, especially in New York.

Confession: never in my life had I crossed the $1,000 barrier for a dress I didn't get married in. Some outrageously tempting garments have clung to me like weepy James Deans, but I have turned and left them coldly on their racks. The Narciso Rodriguez That Got Away stands out as one of the more bitter regrets of my sartorial life; it was a 1940s-style dress with a V-neck and strategically bunched draping, possessed of an empowered, grown-up female sexuality. It was elegant and wild in all the right ways. I felt the lines of the dress contained a direction—a future I didn't know existed, but one that I could see myself in.

It fit perfectly. It was $1,485. My Better Angel of Economic Temperance was on one shoulder, and my inner Courtney Love was on the other, sobbing, "Just bu-u-u-u-uy it! It's the fifth passion fruit you've never ha-a-a-a-ad . . ."

Love was winning. Dionysus and I were about to go four-wheeling with my credit card.

Then I became aware that it was fiscal suicide, and I put it back on the hanger with trembling hands. And I have bitterly regretted it ever since.

Unfortunately, through exercising such heroic temperance over the years, I have made a dismaying discovery: there is no *win* in denying yourself the fifth passion fruit. *It will get you in the end.*

This is perhaps the most controversial piece of fashion advice I have to give: If you try on a piece of clothing that is perfect, you should buy it, even if its price tag violates your budget.

Here's why: In my experience, if you don't buy the thing you really want, you will become obsessed with it, and your subconscious will punish you by turning it into a kind of Holy Grail that you will spend the remainder of your wretched time on earth trying to find again. I calculate that every time I have denied myself a perfect garment, I have bought at least six, and sometimes up to ten different inferior versions of it, for years afterward. The desire *will not let go.*

I ignored a pair of harem sweatpants one day, because they were $172. I have been cursed ever after to find them again. Pursuit of those forbidden sweatpants has cost me approximately $1,300 in the years since—all wasted on inferior substitutes.

Because I denied myself the perfect Narciso Rodriguez dress, I was architecturally weak the next time temptation sucker-punched me.

During his lifetime, Alexander McQueen's designs struck me with such terrible love that I avoided the place, because it crowbarred the knees of my financial intelligence. Several years previously, in a fit of design intoxication, I had plonked down $500 for a perfect Alexander McQueen black pencil skirt, a reckless expenditure that launched me into an electric panic for months afterward.

Since then, I have worn that skirt so relentlessly that even with the most conservative math, it costs me about three bucks a session to wear it. It still looks new; I figure that if it doesn't rot off my body, it will, in a couple of years, officially work its way to being free. Recalling the initial layout, however, still makes me feel as if my bone marrow is being sucked out through my checking account. These things are hard enough to justify in an economy that doesn't look like an avalanche of scratched lotto tickets; now, such purchases are indefensible.

I was required by my newspaper duties to revisit the Alexander McQueen boutique, while the designer was still alive. It was then that I was attacked by the Dress.

It was a double-V-neck, Sofia-Loren-goes-to-Wellesley miniature-houndstooth wiggle number; the perfect fusion of tweedy respectability and autobahn curves. It wasn't just a dress: It was the fulfillment of my deepest desires, in wool. It was $1,230.

"It is a sound investment," said the Devil in Miss Wilson. "An inarguable classic. You will wear it for at least 150 years."

"Shut up," I told myself, prying it off.

My consumer brain damage inundated my weak mind with a cavalcade of excellent reasons. My boyfriend was ignoring me. My birthday was coming up. I had a big literary performance in San Francisco.

"Dammit!" I snarled miserably at my idealized reflection.

My credit cards were banging steel cups against the bars of my wallet. Black smoke began pouring out of my handbag.

After much weeping and rending of sensibility, I bought the

dress. There is no investment more worthwhile, I reasoned, than an investment in your own transformation into a better future self.

Naturally, this flight of rationalization would not go unpunished, because I am an idiot. I have yet to fully pay for this dress. I will probably be paying 16 percent interest on it for the rest of my life.

But it wasn't all my fault. I couldn't help it. I actually couldn't. And neither can you.

⚌⚌

ONE OF SLAVOJ ŽIŽEK'S terrific quotes in *The Pervert's Guide to Cinema* perfectly articulated this idea, for me: "The basic insight of psychoanalysis is to distinguish between enjoyment and simple pleasures. They are not the same. Enjoyment is precisely enjoyment in *disturbed* pleasure . . . even enjoyment in pain."

This is an important concept; it is the thing advertisers know about your motivations that *you don't.*

Our will toward consumerism feels irresistible—because it is intended to. As a society, we choose to remain largely unaware that *our desires* have been built *for us*, by experts who have become so insidiously successful at planting seeds in our minds that grow into giant kudzu-sprawls of unanswerable longing that by the time we act upon these desires, we are fully convinced they were organically grown by our own psyches. We rationalize big, crazy purchases as being investments in our *better selves.*

I began reading up on archetype psychology, strategic marketing, and semiotic brand analysis after I noticed, in 2010, that there were no less than eleven ads in one issue of *W* advertising luxury handbags with doppelgängers—images of zombie twin undead girls, identically dressed. The doppelgänger is a complex psychological image, but it is mainly a symbol of Thanatos, the Freud-

ian death-drive. It's an image that goes straight past our conscious minds and straight into our unconscious desire for acting out in traumatic, compulsive, repetitive patterns, or what Walter Benjamin described, when applied to fashion, as the "excess signaling death."

According to Freud, there is no motivational drive stronger than Thanatos. The life-drive, Eros, gutters out into reasonable pleasures: getting to work on time, paying your rent, caring for your children, etc. Eros is the drive to politely survive and preserve oneself through moderation. Thanatos, however, is where all the fun is—it's the will to self-destruction that brings you to your knees in pursuit of bad relationships, crack, and high-ticket items like sports cars and $3,200 handbags.

This skullduggery is deliberately exploited by ad agencies, political parties, and any other agency that seeks to sell you things you can't afford.

Thanatos-driven purchases seduce you with ideas of self-transformation: liberation from the repressive restrictions of your reasonable, Eros-guided superego (which isn't psychotic enough to pursue twisted kicks by any means necessary). There is always a pain of unfulfillment in life, an inability to realize oneself entirely—a gaping void between the opposing drives of Eros and Thanatos. The wish for an ontological self is an irresolvable frustration, and successful advertising offers a tacit promise to scratch that unscratchable itch by invoking your desire to be part of *some ineffable mood that the object represents.* That thing you want hovers somewhere in the Twilight Zone of your consciousness, in your hazy, barely formed ideas about *reward* and *destiny* and *satisfaction.*

The thing you buy—the object itself—never really scratches that itch. The Thing can't ever be had. But, like pulling the lever on a slot machine, buying it does give you the giddy, slightly sickening momentary thrill of transgression—that naughty yielding to our sexy Bad Selves which our brains interpret as *real enjoyment.*

I have wrestled with this demon often enough for it to know my shoe size and my mother's maiden name. But what is scariest of all: it knows the perverse ego fantasies that lurk so deeply in me that I am too ashamed to realize that they are a part of me. Dolce and Gabbana, for example, unleashed my inner Uday Hussein.

At the top of Dolce and Gabbana's third-floor escalator, an excruciatingly handsome Alain Delon type offered me a flute of Veuve, or a Grey Goose cocktail. That's it, I thought. This is my promised land. Hold my animal, I'm staging a putsch.

Drooling over racks of totalitarian resort finery, I began to get delusions of megalomania. I started giving noms de guerre to each outfit: Madame Subcomandantrix. La Cobra Blanca. She Who Leaves a Flaming Trail of Plastic Animal-Print Combat Garments en Route to the Glorious People's Jacuzzi.

Or simply . . . Cher.

Here's an example of superlative service: I selected over $30,000 of garments—and there were three of them, total. They were carried into the "special" dressing room (the one with—no lie—what I believed to be actual cheetah fur covering the doors). I told the guy: "I'll be in here for a while. I am going to do a pile of blow and clean my gun."

And this sterling professional, instead of calling security, said, "So, I guess you'll be needing another drink."

This is how it feels to hold a nation in fear!

I tried on a silver lamé pantsuit with cigarette legs and black magic. It had eaten young Elvis and absorbed his power. I pictured myself on an all-chrome jet-ski, catching air over a strobe-lit ocean of mercury with a Vegas horn section.

It was $3,850. Oh, for a tyranny of my own. I vowed to return with euros after selling black helicopters to Libya, and my mother, too.

I'm not saying Dolce and Gabbana celebrates brutality, but they do make me think that all my wardrobe really needs is a gold-plated Kalashnikov, an entourage of boy soldiers, and a necklace of human teeth. They pour gasoline on life's more incendiary fantasies by tempting you to submit to your moral incompetence: to indulge your most terrible defense mechanisms, to abuse power.

L'état, c'est moi, baby.

Life, she is dirty and cheap, but not my handbag. Bring me the head of St. John Sport. I am the Lizard Queen.

⧈

CURIOUSLY ENOUGH, THE SEXUAL id of Madison Avenue's ladies, while it may be repressed in their under-wardrobes, is more than evident in their oversexed footwear.

All shoes do not inspire feelings of love and derangement. Sensible shoes do not inspire the kind of shoe-lust that inspires manicure-cracking middle-aged catfights. That kind of frenzy is reserved for party shoes—feathery, mile-high, spangly things made of sex and Christmas trees.

The ladies of Madison Avenue really show their inner animal and bare their teeth when it comes to the footwear of Christian Louboutin.

Simon Doonan, the creative director of Barneys New York (and a personal hero of mine), once commented in *The New Yorker*: "Louboutin girls are very determined. You get the sense if they had an X-Acto knife and some margarine they'd do whatever they could to get that boot on." True enough: every year when the new Louboutin "Nude" comes out for spring, it's the Night of the Long X-Acto Knives on Madison Avenue, and rich white ladies may be capable of any atrocity.

Christian Louboutin shoes are nosebleed-high pumps in dazzlingly perverse shapes and textures that inspire an obsessive, almost savage devotion in the generally declawed ladies of the Upper East Side. The Louboutin boutique occupies a small black and chrome storefront on Madison Avenue. Imagine the footwear wing of Frederick's of Hollywood trying to seduce the Wonka factory: wall-to-wall red carpet, mirrors, disco sequins, and modular Lucite cubbies all showcasing pumps with a combination of raw sex and psychedelic-striptease architecture.

I once witnessed a middle-aged Teutonic couple dressed like the millionaire and his wife from *Gilligan's Island* in a Manhattan Louboutin store, seething with palpable fury amid eviscerated cardboard boxes on a battlefield of mangled tissue. "We want since two days!" the man bellowed, the brass buttons on his nautical blazer melting in fright. His wife let out a visceral moan and gnashed her perfect teeth; her eyes rolled upward in despair as she clutched in rueful hands the wrong size. For a moment she resembled the anguished Mary of Michelangelo's *Pietà*—only evil. "They're just so popular right now," droned the sales assistant à la

Wednesday Addams, in a near-sadistic monotone. "We can't keep them in stock."

A few feet away, a woman tightly wound enough to be a Tesla coil was demanding the exact same impossible shoe.

"Does everyone want the same shoe?" I asked.

"Everybody wants the Nude," said Wednesday, all drollness and cruelty.

Suddenly, a miracle: a shopper whose stature could best be described as compact and sturdy had successfully donned a variation on the unattainable Nude. The room did the math—she had to be either a size 6 or a 10. Shazam! Her legs looked instantly toned, tanned, considerably longer and gleaming as if illuminated by flashbulbs. I suddenly understood why everyone in the store was so miserable.

Caution and sobriety are similarly recommended before braving a shoe sale at Barneys, the Upper East Side's favorite department store. They are rip-roaring events that are part roller derby, part Easter egg hunt, part war zone. The room is fortified, the staff is adrenal and ready to clash with a howling maelstrom of incoming ladies: lunched, wined, and ready to ransack, loot, and pillage. Husbands are few. I did spot one luckless bastard, abandoned, sitting in the middle of a blast zone of shoe discards. In a daze, he slowly fingered a strappy orange Givenchy platform lying next to him on the couch, tipped it over to squint at the price, then shook his head in existential bewilderment as if this, finally, represented the death of his spirit.

I saw a French family, presumably emboldened enough by our lamentable currency rates to engage in an unrestrained shopping holiday. The daughter, a willowy, laconic fourteen-year-old (size 0, unruly chestnut hair to waist, white tank top, tight cigarette jeans), was hobbling around the carpet in one flesh-colored patent leather Christian Louboutin pump (five-inch stiletto heel, five bondage buckles across the instep, lurid red sole). Her father shouted something in French, to which she swung her hair around like Rita Hayworth in *Gilda* and asked, *"Quoi?"* with widely innocent eyes and a $70,000 pout. My French wasn't quite good enough to determine what the conflict was, but it was probably something along the universal lines of "No teenage daughter of mine is going to go back to boarding school wearing a shoe that is the sociological equivalent of a crossbow full of Viagra darts."

If you are either a size 6 or a size 10 the world is your oyster; virtually any shoe will be glowing and untouched before you, like a mythical elf treasure in World of Warcraft. There was, for example, a Marni pump: kelly green, with purple suede *Flash Gordon* lightning bolts across the instep and patent leather wine-stem heels. Inconceivably, it was sitting upright and unmolested on the racks. This, of course, is because it was a 6, a size not worn by decent people since 1938.

In more popular sizes like 8½, 9, and 9½, there was a surplus on the shelves, sprawled without categories into a still life that could be tabloid-headlined "Catfight Carnage at Sock Hop!" Pink satin prom pumps lay under heavy studded black clompers; yellow suede midi-boots trample wafer-thin Blahnik mules.

As for size 7½, there is scant hope. The shelves are virtual graveyards, save for a few isolated pieces too insane to be functional (eight-inch Alaïa platform wedgies made of bronzed reptile—sale price, $1,399).

Being a veteran mercenary shopper, I have learned strategies. To find 7½s and avoid injury, one must behave like a scavenger animal and avoid the racks entirely. The carpet is where the money is. For 7½s, one wades straight into the line of fire and scans the floor for shoes that have been left for dead around the seating area. I found a roughly stacked cairn next to a recently vacated seat, and there was my mother lode of 7½ Louboutins: eggplant Mary

Janes, open-toe ($529); six-inch heels that seemed to have been sewn together out of broken mirrors ($1,295); a pump that looked like a bouquet of African violets wrought in apricot suede ($559). None of this was within my recession budget, so my victory was purely academic.

The sales staff is, for the most part, unusually brave and sporting through this blitz. "Give me your name and number," one commanded in resolute tones to a woman who had sunk into an armchair in grief after receiving tragic news: the mate of the black pump cradled in her arms was officially missing in action. "I will put this on my shelf, and if it turns up tomorrow, I will call you," he said, gently prying the orphaned shoe from the shopper's manicured fingertips. "There's a fifty-fifty chance."

Triage was being performed in the shelves: large shopping bags of single shoes recently recovered from the field. Some women were digging through them frantically, before their sizes had even been identified.

NO MATTER HOW REMOTE THE LOCALE, NATIVE FASHION TREASURES MAY BE FOUND

BEHOLD: The XTRATUF boot, dubbed "the Alaskan sneaker" by locals—a cappuccino-brown, thermally insulated, unisex waterproof wonder, worn with everything from kayak-pants to swing-dancing skirts.

A very petite woman in a head-to-toe Chanel costume (who, I suspected, may have been considerably more advanced in years than her bronzed pallor and raven hair suggested) had set up a beachhead on one of the couches. Her shoes were off; her tiny, behosed feet were up on a hassock. For more than an hour, she was deep in pleasant thoughts, making no attempt whatsoever to put any shoes on her feet, new or otherwise. She was, I realized, simply *existing* in the shoe department that was also her second living room.

War, as we know, brings out the worst in humanity. A candy-pink pump lay on its side on a vast and uninhabited stretch of carpet, its vulnerable red underside helplessly exposed—an eloquent reminder of the terrible consequences of such sales.

War can also bring out the best in New Yorkers, who unite in periods of crisis. Blizzards and terrorism, too, allow for the sudden intimacies of a shared ordeal.

It is easy to love strangers when they cry in the theater; it is also easy when the Chanel lady finally rises from her couch to hobble, lopsidedly, on one ridiculously delicate, absurdly expensive, and wholly impractical shoe, wearing the same smile she has been reserving for such occasions since age six.

These extravagant shoes are flowers from the mythological garden of expansive dreams; they are the embodied hope of fabulous future events to which they intrinsically belong. The magic vested in them promises to gravitationally lead all Cinderellas to their proper mates. (However, once she finds him, divines his incurable habits, and wishes to walk out on him, she had better call a cab.)

⊰⊱

SUCH SHOPPING FIASCOS, these days, strike me with fear and awe. The people who run the planet run your brain, too—

because they can. This idea isn't just my own paranoia talking—it's one that's been around forever. Antonio Gramsci's whole concept of hegemony was based on this quote by Karl Marx:

> The class which has the means of material production at its disposal, has control at the same time over the means of mental production, so that generally speaking, the ideas of those who lack the means of mental production are subject to it.

To wit: the people who manufacture the stuff also manufacture your *desire* for the stuff. The ruling elite has mapped, colonized, and exploited that apocryphal "unused 80 percent" territory of your brain—the deep seas of your unconscious mind—and is off-shore drilling and spilling in it, 24/7. They have decided, for our own good, that they need our brains much worse than we do. Such is the manifest destiny of an imperial march to control all lands and all people. You were once a spangling, unraped frontier. Then you were a dead Indian, but you didn't know it. Now you are a zombie, with one key mandate: to help the ruling class eat the brains of your zombie children, and to pay extra for the privilege.

Not only would an effective protest movement require us to "kill the cops in our own heads"—a phrase old hippies used, meaning that we must combat all of the cultural brainwashing implanted in our minds—but at this point, our personal cultures have been so successfully colonized, appropriated, trivialized, and regurgitated that we also need to kill the cops in our own *closets*. Clothing is one of those insidious ways in which we fall into line and voluntarily police ourselves.

While I like nice stuff as much as anyone, I have never been driven by materialism. Being a writer isn't something you do if you are motivated by money. So I thought I would be safe when I was assigned to visit the jewelry boutique of Solange Azagury-Partridge.

I'm not really a jewelry person; I like to wear weird junk-store trinkets on pieces of black string. I own little more than a handful of yawn-inspiring basics—pearls, a signet ring—mostly from pawn shops. Most gold or gem-encrusted stuff looks slightly vulgar to me, as a display of conspicuous wealth. I was prepared to focus my attentions straight into the precious rocks and enjoy the little prismatic light shows on a purely aesthetic level.

I was not prepared to suffer from a raw and unquenchable envy that would make me consider extra moneymaking strategies like kidnapping, extortion, or piracy.

Ms. Azagury-Partridge, according to her publicity material, has had no formal training in jewelry design, but she didn't need it. Her work explodes with energy, brilliance, sensuality, and courage. It is thrillingly exuberant, scary-smart, and intensely personal. She has so clearly thrown every atom of herself into the creation of these pieces, you can feel the fiery presence of a remarkable woman. It's art, and I'm not the only one who thinks so; the Louvre and the Victoria and Albert Museum have acquired her work for their collections.

The shop interior, its deep red walls embedded with 630,000 Swarovski crystals, looks somewhat like an opera set for *The Magic Flute* reimagined by Marchesa Casati: Goth–Freemason with a touch of chinoiserie thrown in, just to drop-kick me over into nosebleeds of unfulfillable desire.

The pieces range from the quasi-affordable enamel Hot Lips rings, in a dark rainbow of shades ($1,500; or a studded-all-over-with-rubies version, $24,000), to the maybe-if-you-just-sold-out-an-eight-year-run-in-Vegas Galactic necklace, which looks like a diamond breastplate King Tut might have given to Elizabeth Taylor ($350,000).

But this wasn't the stuff that really got me going. I know sacred geometry when I see it, and there was a whole lot of golden ratios and fearful symmetry going on. The Platonic line, for example, looks at first like your average batch of art deco diamond creations. Closer inspection reveals more than meets the eye: the blackened gold and bead-set diamonds seem to have been modeled on a sideways variation of Johannes Kepler's platonic solid model of our solar system. (An ultra-geeky thrill.)

And the designer snuck a couple of Archimedean solids into her Platonic line. (Naughty girl. I bet she thought her shoppers wouldn't notice an extra polygon here and there.) But I was thrilled, because I can't tell you how many times I've said that there just aren't enough truncated cuboctahedrons and rhombicuboctahedrons to be found in jewelry today.

On the subway home, I noticed that the tattoo-esque logo for Solange includes a honeybee sitting in the middle of an early design by the seventeenth-century mystic Jakob Böhme: a tetractys of flaming Hebrew letters. The honeybee, of course, constructs hive cells in hexagons, which, for some people, suggests that geometry has some deep cosmic significance in the natural world.

When I got home, I noticed an enormous rainbow out my window (a nice coincidence, considering it was Gay Pride Day). The rainbow, at least, was free and democratic, and shone upon the gay, the unemployed, and those who can afford to buy exquisite jewelry by Solange Azagury-Partridge alike.

Solange's subsequent collection, "Stoned," contained a gold and enamel opium poppy bracelet that remains one of my all-time favorite pieces of art. When a button is pushed on the golden stem that wraps around the wrist, the poppy bulb (bleeding white enamel opium from a tiny razor cut) pops open to reveal a tiny, gold naked woman, crouched and weeping. She is, Ms. Azagury-Partridge explained, either stoned or being stoned to death—possibly both.

So, until the economy rebounds, I am trying to figure out how to deprive rich people of rainbows. Because anyone who can afford something that incredible and precious really should be deprived of any beauty that this earth makes affordable to the poor.

⚎

MY JOB AT THE *Times*—reviewing wealthier and wealthier stores for my journalism job, at the same time that New York was sliding visibly into financial turmoil along with the rest of the world after 2007—was starting to make me feel socioeconomically schizophrenic. After a while, the disparity between the super-wealthy stuff I was being paid to review as actual "retail"—under the pretense that actual "people" could actually "purchase" these car- and house-priced coats and handbags and brown-diamond tennis bracelets—and what my real life and 99.99 percent of everyone else's *actually* looked like—became more and more surreal, absurd, and unnerving.

On November 17, 2012, I was taking a car service into Lower Manhattan on the way to a posh fashion event I needed to write about for an independent magazine. There was an interminable crawl of traffic on the Brooklyn Bridge. Just before the exit near City Hall, I heard a woman shouting energetically through a bullhorn, and a call-and-response from a crowd of such magnitude and volume that all the hair on my neck stood up. I realized that what was stopping traffic was a tidal surge of humanity. I had never before seen so many people mobilized toward a single goal. Occupy Wall Street wasn't just stopping traffic: the feeling in the air shared by that euphoric mob of protesters was so exhilarating, I felt that all of Lower Manhattan was throbbing with a transcendental sense of togetherness, of community, of real strength in numbers, and the incredible collective excitement of *Oh my God this is history, we are creating history, we are witnessing history, we are being history.*

And I felt something I have never really felt before, as a disaffected and alienated person: actual, real, genuine hope for the future. I began sobbing uncontrollably, because it was the greatest moment I have ever experienced in my country, and the first time I have ever felt truly at home in the world.

After driving through the Occupy demonstration, I continued to the party—a very posh, private, utterly divorced-from-humanity event at the SoHo Grand, which was chock-a-block with face-lifted socialites wearing checkerboard fur coats, standing around joylessly with glasses of white wine, being squired by an ünterklasse of gay male accessory-companions.

I should have felt proud of myself, I supposed—I had "arrived," I had been invited to this posh event, where I was able to rub shoulders with the exact people the police are usually paid to keep people like me away from. But I felt like I'd come down with a case of the bends.

And it was a terrible party. It was a miserably ridiculous, disconnected, and depraved event compared to the good fight going on downtown. It made me feel sick and crazy.

More so than usual.

15

OCCUPIED TERRITORY / THE BANDOLERO

Guy Fawkes Is the New Black

The limits of my language mean the limits of my world.

—LUDWIG WITTGENSTEIN

Tom Wolfe coined the term "radical chic" in 1970 to poke fun at celebrities and other members of high society who were seduced into supporting revolutionary causes because of their innate sex appeal. Wolfe used Leonard Bernstein as his most risible example, after Bernstein threw a fundraiser in his home for the Black Panther Party (a movement which in most cases was explicitly opposed to elite personages like Leonard Bernstein).

Today, if you're an Occupy protester, and you also happen to be a topless, pink-haired lesbian protesting in a tutu or a white kid with dreadlocks, a tattooed neck, and earlobes you can stick a fist through, the elderly Viewers at Home in Omaha watching Fox are likely to regard you as The End of the World As They Liked

It. Fashions tend to be tribal, and even a batch of protesters as wildly diversified as 99 percent of the people on earth is going to be visually reduced, in media images, to its most radicalized and potentially offputting representatives.

I saw a photo on the Internet that really stuck in my gag reflex: a piggy-faced group of Wall Street insiders—men in pinstripe suits and ties, women in silk dresses and big-ass, fuck-you, 11-mm Barbara Bush pearls—sitting on balcony overlooking Zucotti Park, smugly looking down on the protestors, drinking champagne. Two thoughts occurred to me:

1. **This is exactly** why God rots tomatoes.
2. **Dressing for class warfare** can be a tricky endeavor, but it is ver-r-ry important.

"In the Battle of Ideas, Aesthetics Matter" was the impressive slogan of Suits for Wall Street, a group that was campaigning to provide suits to OWS protesters. "Suits are camouflage in the warrens of Wall Street," says their literature. "Need a bathroom? Wear a suit . . . Want to walk past a police barricade? . . . Try wearing a suit . . . In the 1960s you could fly your freak flag high. In 2011, it just looks sloppy."

Adopting the markings of the power elite is no mere sartorial prank; it is a strategy supported by significant precedents in U.S. protest history. Dr. Montgomery McFate, a Yale cultural anthropologist, suggests OWS protesters may be hurting themselves by *not* wearing suits. "The 1 percent only listens to the 1 percent," she told me, in a phone interview. Due to their radical clothing, counterculture protesters may be "structurally disempowering themselves from being heard by the people who have the power to make the policy changes that they're demanding."

Protesters in suits, she adds, could change the game by calling into question the semiotics of suit-wearing. "At worst it could be taken as jest . . . at best it could be taken as a chance to bridge the gap [between the 1 percent and the 99 percent]."

Toward the end of 2010, I saw Tariq Ali speak about the Arab Spring. He was effusive and hopeful about the fact that the accelerated disparities between the rich and the poor had finally reached a tipping point in both Tunisia and Egypt. He argued that when a populace feels sufficiently abused by an elitist, disconnected government, and such basic human needs as access to water, education, and health care have been systematically ignored for long enough, there is a point at which the demand for economic and political shifts becomes irreversible—and the world becomes a dangerous place for plutocrats. When mass movements of people "lose their fear of death," said Mr. Ali, "they can achieve miracles . . . When the mobilization reaches that stage, crowned heads fall."

I did not believe such momentum could happen here in America. I became deeply cynical, writing about politics; I thought America was too far gone: too bloody and narcissistic, acting out its own fall of Rome in thrall to its own imperial death-drive. In other countries, there is at least some dialectical opposition in the political dialogue to abuses by an elite capitalist ruling class— but the "free-market" economic policy of the last thirty years is embraced by both parties in our two-party, for-profit political system, and there is no opposing argument to be heard anywhere in the halls of power. There is no conversation about political economy. There is no check and balance. The falconer has sold the falcon. Then he repossessed the falcon after the new falconer failed to make timely payments. Then the falcon was shot and eaten, then taken to the taxidermist and sold again.

The idea that people are inherently good and capable of cooperating toward higher goals has always been an inconvenience and/or threat to the corporate state. Ruling authorities have always exercised some campaign of domestic propaganda that subtly discourages community and group empowerment. After so many years of being brainwashed—bombarded by messages encoded into a sophisticated commercial culture intent on psychologically manipulating us to the point of regulating the way we experience our own desires and fears—I didn't believe that nonviolent strategies of protest could have an effect anymore. I didn't think we still possessed the internal sensitivities as a society to respond with a sense of collective moral outrage when presented with evidence of man's inhumanity to man.

I was very grateful and glad when hardcore activists began to Occupy Wall Street, but not optimistic about their success. I attended the demonstration in Times Square and was thrilled by the number and diversity of people who turned out; still, I wasn't convinced that even such an impressive demonstration would lead to real change. The only war there has ever been has always been the war of the rich against the underclass they wish to continue to control and exploit. Superficial differences between people have

SEATTLE GENTLEMAN

Ye shall know him by his short pants, brilliantined coif, hi-top sneakers, perversified earlobes, chin-beard, and complex eyewear. The look that asks, "WHO, ME?"

always been grotesquely exaggerated to exacerbate anxieties and insecurities; absurd concepts like the War on Drugs or the War on Terror or the Battle of the Sexes or being Tough on Crime have always been concocted to vilify, control, and enslave the Other, whomever that Other may be. Divisive social engineering mechanisms have always obstructed poor people from realizing any lasting solidarity with one another.

It came home for me when a fashionista I respect invited me to join a Facebook group called Tax the Rich. I don't know if she knew what she was getting into. She had a lot of friends in the 1 percent.

Lines were drawn in the proverbial sand. "I didn't realize you were starting a group for Poor People," sneered one lovely uptown gal. "Remove me from your list, please."

I can't remember how I replied—something to the effect of how when the revolution comes, Sneery would get a VIP invite to my very exclusive trunk show and would have the only front-row seat in the trunk.

Then someone else laughed it off and called me a "fucking serf."

"Serfs up!" I replied.

⚍⚎

I REALIZED THAT A COHERENT Occupy fashion statement had yet to emerge when I got dressed to participate in the Occupy protest in Union Square. I was very consciously regressing to my anarchistic punk days. I felt all right about it, because finally I was attending an event where all my aggressive, Army–Navy surplus, Travis Bickle motorcycle apparel actually had reason and purpose. My biker gloves with no fingers made sense if I got knocked down in a riot. My leopard-print silk bandanna, I reasoned, was some kind of protection if I got tear-gassed. The yellow-tinted shooting glasses I always wear (they're "progressives")—eye protection from pepper spray. I French-braided my hair so nobody could pull it. My knee-high steel-toed motorcycle boots—in case my toes got stepped on, in a scrum. I put various survivalist doohickeys in the pockets of my cargo pants.

There is a variety of recommended "protest-sessories" for any demonstration. Comfy footwear is always a good idea. It doesn't hurt to carry a bottle of Maalox diluted with water, which can be used as an eyewash in the event of pepper spray. A flyer circulated by Egyptian protesters recommended carrying a pot lid, which may be used as a shield against rubber bullets and batons (pot lids are also effective noisemakers, if one wishes to engage in a clanging form of popular protest in known in Spanish-speaking countries as *cacerolazo*). A can of spray paint (if you can control your urge to vandalize) may also be used to obscure the vision of advancing riot police.

I cut a stencil out of a plastic notebook cover and spray-painted a white T-shirt with a hammer and sickle. I just wanted a dialogue about political economy, that's all. I didn't want communism, but it was missing in the cultural conversation as a counterpoint to rapacious capitalism. It was like voting for Nader—a futile gesture to lean the conversation leftward, to show solidarity for global struggle against rampant inequality. The world's top .00002 percent, I had just read, was richer than the lower 50 percent of all of the people on earth. This was unprecedented greed that could not go without some rebuttal. My father was a professor for thirty-seven years, and was working through his retirement as an electrician. My mother had always made a living as a professional jazz musician and piano teacher. After 2007 all our incomes all went to hell. My parents were getting old, working constantly, and I couldn't help them. They had to help my sister and her husband and new baby, because her husband (who was selling suits at Nordstrom's) kept getting his hours cut—because nobody was buying suits (not even protestors).

Outside my building in Brooklyn, on my way to another Occupy protest at Times Square, I noticed a line of cops. Drums were banging in the background and there were hundreds of people walking around looking just like me: army jackets, boots, sunglasses, righteous scowling.

For a brief, shining moment, I thought: *The revolution has finally arrived!*

And then I walked another hundred yards, and I realized that all these hardcore-looking people in boots and army jackets were filmmakers, attending a corporate "Creator Festival" block party cosponsored by *Vice* magazine.

Today, nobody knows how coopted they are, mostly. Not even
me. And shit, I thought I was *already paranoid enough.*

"If you think you're paranoid enough, you're not nearly paranoid enough," my friend Michael told me.

Germs within germs.

❧

MILITANTS ARE, STILL, incredibly sexy—and an embrace
of properly sexy militant apparel can sell a revolution just like any
great ad campaign. There are strong protest fashion statements
that have proven to be particularly effective weapons of cultural
warfare:

1. **The Beret:** For some reason, if you wanna be a militant
   leftist icon, it's all about the beret. It's the little black
   dress of revolutionary socialism. All the most comely
   and iconic spokesmodels for the global class struggle
   cocked one: the Black Panthers, Patty "Tanya" Hearst in
   her brainwashed-by-the-SLA-prime, Carlos the Jackal,
   Faye Dunaway in *Bonnie and Clyde,* and of course, Che
   Guevara, now the Hello Kitty of the international social-
   ist revolution.

2. **The Hoodie:** The hooded sweatshirt which is currently
   the garment of choice for anarchists was first produced
   in the 1930s, for New York laborers working in frozen
   warehouses. Today, the hoodie remains symbolic of the
   cultural paradigm shift inspired by hip-hop—and has
   taken on a menacing semiotic power of its own. Not for
   nothing was the hoodie banned in various shopping centers in the U.K., Australia, and New Zealand . . . or,

for that matter, was it the outerwear of choice for both Banksy and the Unabomber.

3. **Sunglasses (or paint goggles):** A common rule is to never wear contact lenses to an Occupation—getting tear gas on them apparently su-u-u-u-ucks. Eyewear is not only a decent identity concealer and protection against chemical deterrents, but it also enables a discriminating revolutionary to be cool like Fonzie.

4. **The Bandanna / The Keffiyeh:** Whether you're a Blood, a Crip, a graffiti artist, or just having your own little intifada, a cotton scarf provides a reasonable amount of bandito-style anonymity, protects against pepper spray and tear gas . . . and can be used as both a blanket and a napkin during long nights of group pizza consumption.

5. **The Guy Fawkes Mask:** Guy Fawkes was a radical seventeenth-century Englishman who is remembered for failing to blow up the House of Lords with the infamous Gunpowder Plot. The Guy Fawkes mask was popularized shortly after the release of the 2006 film *V for Vendetta* (an anti-totalitarian tale based on the comic book by Alan Moore) when the Anonymous group wore the mask during demonstrations against the Church of Scientology. Numerous Guy Fawkses have since been turning up at various Occupy locales, replete with both the anonymity and the solid punch of social history that the mask provides.

6. **The Ski Mask / The Balaclava:** Easily the scariest and most anonymizing of all headwear, the knit ski mask is not

IN SEATTLE, WA, REAL MEN WEAR SKIRTS!

The "Utili-Kilt" is a sartorial Seattle phenomenon; part utility-belt, part cargo-kilt, worn by men of the Pacific Northwest who are BRAVE ENOUGH to prance around the construction site in a kicky little number that shows off the knees, yet has enough flanges and Utili-loops and combat-ready pockets to derail hecklers with hammers, ninja-stars, complete socket-sets, rolls of duct-tape, pewter mead goblets, and Japanese tree-saws. (So no matter how pretty or lacy their underthings may be, or how Commando they may dangle . . . watch your mouths, Suit Fruits.)

only an excellent source of warmth, but has been used as an intimidating sartorial weapon since the Crimean War. It's a daring look, but one that has been successfully

rocked by the Irish Republican Army and several incar-
nations of Zapatista leader Subcomandante Marcos.

In short, any effective class war contains a style war which
needs to be acknowledged and prosecuted. The energy a protester
uses to get dressed in the morning can substantially strengthen or
undermine the cause. History has proven that if you wage an effective aesthetic propaganda campaign, you win . . . *something*. Even
if you don't succeed in changing the world for the better, for a
moment (before the fashion world gets its thieving, fingerless Karl
Lagerfeld gloves all over it) you might aesthetically articulate a new
living subculture—a recognizable style for a rebellion that still has
the power to provoke, and has yet to be coopted, mainstreamed,
desymbolized, and declawed. You might wear something that
screams in a way that nobody has seen before, that finally gets
their attention.

CONCLUSION
TO THINE OWN STYLE BE TRUE

Temet Nosce

—LATIN FOR "KNOW THYSELF" (AS SEEN ON THE
PSYCHIC LADY'S WALL IN *THE MATRIX*)

I once went to a Renaissance Faire in Maryland and was delighted to see a guy in a yellow DEVO/biohazard suit running around in a panic with a tinfoil hat, screaming, "Help! Have you seen my DeLorean? *I went too far back into the future!*"

I will never stop admiring that guy.

If the Internet has proven anything, it is the unstoppable might of a good joke. Ideas with real verve—flashes of real fun and brilliance (and there are so many) spread like daylight, with no manipulations, no hijacks, no bombs, no maneuverings, and no ad budget. Joyful stuff feeds new colors directly into your mouth. Sharing a joke (or a tragedy) suddenly erases, for a moment, all the manufactured perceptual boundaries that create illusions of difference between people. No matter what side of the war you're on, you will appreciate a video of a sneezing baby panda.

Everywhere I went in America, I was inspired by self-styled fashion rock stars who proved to me, over and over, that fashion consciousness isn't about fashion as much as it is about consciousness.

In Manhattan, I saw a gorgeous woman dragging herself up the subway stairs, clinging breathlessly to the handrail. She was thickly powdered, with enormous black-painted eyes, at least two sets of fake eyelashes, magenta-slashed cheekbones, jet-black hair, and a black flamenco shawl. Her black satin dress was side-slit over her hipbone. It was approximately 2 p.m. She had to be at least eighty years old—and this was her *day look*.

In Kentucky, I was dazzled by an older African American gentleman working in a restaurant as a busboy. He was carrying a rubber tub full of wineglasses—but despite having worked a busy shift all evening, his hat was balanced in perfect rakishness on his head; his white linen suit was creaseless and spotless, and his silk necktie looked as if it had been knotted three minutes ago. This man may have been working as a busboy, but he was first and foremost a ninja-king of style who outclassed virtually every patron in the joint.

That guy and Diane von Furstenberg essentially embody the same message in two different fonts: both are living proof that elegance comes from self-knowledge and true character. Real style is ageless. It emanates from people who have allowed themselves enough space to swing a lot of cats in the name of self-discovery, and found such a wild abundance of themselves that they effortlessly, constantly share the wealth.

If there is anything I have learned from drag queens (and I've learned nearly everything that is truly important from drag queens): life is too short to wear disguises that hide you from the world, because these choices can end up hiding you from yourself. If the phenomenon of RuPaul has proven anything, it is that your true beauty is found by boldly striding down the most daringly personal catwalk that you allow yourself to explore. By taking the guard rails off of what you allow yourself to consider to be fashionable, you may also get to know ever more subtle and illuminating colors of your true self.

Unless you're living under a Caliphate (or any similarly style-restricting ideology), you owe it to your short time on earth to represent yourself as flagrantly as possible. Dress codes are restrictions, period—but true style always finds a crack in the sidewalk, or a buttonhole to push a flower through. Even your necktie can be your personal pirate flag.

Fashion is permission. You may give it to yourself, or, if you're rich, you may entrust your choices to the care of top designers. A respectable label may inspire you to believe that your old army jacket is more cutting-edge than other army jackets—and any dry-cleaner who reads your inside tag will surely be impressed.

The fashion industry's fantasy "lifestyle" is a complete fiction. Nobody actually lives the life pictured in fashion magazines—the serving suggestions for fat-free, poreless women, the out-of-reach opulence, the nosebleed-royal status, the eternal pampering and beautifying and shopping. It doesn't really exist for anyone. The fashion world's fake version of "aspirational" (read: unaffordable) reality . . . isn't. It's smoke and mirrors and industrial fans and Photoshop and wigs. It is artifice on artifice on artifice, advertising a hazy fantasy that doesn't exist in real life as anything but more layers of artifice and advertising.

"Fashion" qua "fashion" is by robots for robots: fantasies for people who have forgotten how to have any of their own.

Style, however, is magic, connective, humanizing—and irrepressible. No matter what your tax bracket, style is your birthright.

For all their efforts to bully and humiliate you into cowering submission, the beauty and fashion industries still can't duplicate or coopt the ineluctable nuances of personal style. They can't predict it, they can't dictate it. They can only influence it, and try to sell it to you.

This idea of *real value* versus *perceived value*, or *brand-conferred value*, really came home for me—literally—when I was packing a go-bag for a mandatory evacuation from my building during Hurricane Irene. When I was looking at my wardrobe with an eye toward what I'd really be sorriest never to see again—what really wasn't replaceable—it wasn't the stuff I thought it would be.

I wasn't nearly as concerned about the stuff I'd really worked *for*, such as the Burberry overcoat or the Alexander McQueen dress—"investments" I'd shelled out and bent credit cards for. I was most concerned about the things I'd worked *on*. The jean jacket I'd found in a thrift store and sewn an old CB radio patch on, from back when I had an all-truck-music band in San Francisco. The weird black silk shirt I'd deconstructed with a pair of scissors from an old blouse from The Limited (also found in a thrift store). A belt, the hand-tooled leather of which I'd found when I was a teenager at a flea market, the buckle of which is a custom-engraved prize congratulating a cowgirl named Rhonda Fleming for her second-place rodeo performance.

These things weren't expensive, but were precious because they were impossible to replace. My most treasured wardrobe items turned out to be the weirdest, most eclectic stuff—the dumpster diamonds that had helped me define myself as I had in San Francisco.

Finding your style is like finding your God—it's utterly personal. You find your truths wherever they find you, and you recognize them because they irresistibly resonate with you.

This same love-at-first-sight principle can, and should, be applied to pants.

In the spirit of the old Mod adage—their stated intention to give, through Mod style, the impression of "clean living under difficult circumstances"—I've learned a few "how to get the look for less" tricks over the years. One really does not need to pay astronomical prices for great clothes. A judicious eye and a little working knowledge of the clothing world will serve you as well as unlimited credit.

1. **A good knockoff** can work just as well as the thing it rips off. If you are complimented on your bling, don't blurt out that it's cubic zirconium. Don't wear anything that prompts self-dismissal or apology. Just let yourself shine. Knock people's eyes out. They'll recover.

2. **If you love clothes** but you aren't Melania Trump, get over your horror of hand-me-downs and learn to buy previously owned finery on the Internet. Buy a cloth measuring tape, and know all of your (actual) lengths and widths in both inches and the metric system. Learn how to translate U.S. sizing into U.K., Italian, and French sizing for each decade—and then ignore all of these numbers entirely and go only by actual measurements. Don't be put off by any size number on any tag, whether it's 8, 38, or M or XL—these are all totally arbitrary and different for every brand, country, and era. Just buy clothes that actually *fit you*. If your clothes fit well, no matter what your body or bank account looks like, you will look like you have all the sex and money you need.

3. **Learn the look,** name and feel of quality textiles that you like. Familiarize yourself with some basic garmentosperanto. Know the difference between georgette and

organza, three-season and tropical wools. Better fabrics invariably feel and drape better, and last longer. Once you get this knowledge into your fingertips, you can virtually speed-scan a Salvation Army rack by Braille. (However, you should never, ever buy used cashmere sweaters, because only fire will get the previous owner's armpits out of them.)

4. **Learn a couple of fast,** cheap tailoring tricks. As a life-long deconstructionist, the one fashion accessory I really can't live without has always been scissors.

In a potentially meaningless universe where civilizations crumble, institutions collapse, and creatures fade into extinction, there are still a few mathematical certainties: things of genuine quality tend to eternally recur, especially if they're made of heavy cotton duck or decent leather. Nobody ever looks like an idiot in a good pea-coat, and (a trick I learned from movie wardrobe girls) people tend to notice how comfortably you rock your silhouette far more than they notice the safety pin holding your hem together or the fact that all your buttons don't quite match (in fact, these charming delicacies of distress are often mimicked by top designers, to create the illusion of character and provenance).

But most of all, forget any fashion rule anyone has ever told you, and don't censor yourself by doubting your own taste. Give yourself and your fellow human beings the contagious gift of permission to discover and declare your own style.

Whatever it is: if you feel sharp in it, it can't be wrong. Nothing you put on your body that makes you feel like your most radiant and indestructible self can be considered a fashion mistake.

Don't let life pass you by without wearing something foolish . . . and fuck 'em if they can't take a joke.

Let fashion be a means of expanding your ability to recognize the profligate and promiscuous nature of beauty. Beauty, like nature, does not discriminate. Everyone gets to have it, every day.

What my friend Tod the God taught me when he exhorted me to be Cosmetically Correct for the Cosmos, was essentially this:

Dress for eternity. Dress as if you were honoring your ancestors. Dress for your grandchildren's grandchildren.

Be the costume change you want to see. Free your ascot and your mind will follow.

If you dress exclusively for yourself, you are instinctually dressing against every form of tyranny over the mind of man (or woman, or both genders at the same time, or neither).

You are the only rare and exotic animal you will ever be, so splash out fearlessly.

If you're not wearing yourself yet—if you ain't dead, it's not too late.

alafia

ACKNOWLEDGMENTS

A project like this one doesn't drag on for so many years without relying on the kindness, skill, patience, and kindness of a whopping amount of stellar human beings.

I want to personally thank everyone who ever met or had anything to do with me, and I will surely horrify myself by failing to include friends and compadres who have been essential to this tome (and if you don't see your name here, pal, and you know I owe it to you, I will make it up to you in cocktails).

Firstly: A most resounding, chest-beating, clothes-rending shout-out to the divine Anita LeClerc of the *New York Times*, without whom this book would not exist—also to Bill Clegg, my literary agent; Jill Bialosky, my editor (who stuck with me despite the fact that I blew through deadlines like a windsock), their assistants Chris Clemans and Angie Shih, and an extra-special, swinging-from-the-chandelier-and-screaming fugue state of wild gratitude to Allegra Huston, the radiant, multi-armed, sword-wielding goddess of all copyeditors.

I would also be failing miserably if I did not heap reams of praise upon **various superb magazine editors**, who displayed superhuman patience and understanding while I struggled through this project while trying to write articles for them at the same time, particularly Glenn O'Brien and David Coggins of *Bergdorf Goodman* magazine, Adrian Mainella of the *Aesthete*, Ann Slowey and Maggie Bullock at *ELLE*, Eugene Rabkin of *Style Zeitgeist*, Michael Polsinelli of *Garage* magazine, the merciful Steve Hawk, . . . and the immortal Joan Juliet Buck, because she's Joan Juliet Buck.

I must also pay truckloads of ongoing gratitude to my friends, who accompanied me on zany adventures, listened to me cry about broken hard drives, and were absolutely essential to both my process and my sanity, particularly Dr. Amanda Parkes, Dr. Julie Steward, Dr. Montgomery McFate, The Artist Mark Johnson, Michael Gruenglas, Esq., Nick Carlin, Esq., Mr. Robbie Caponetto, Tova Cubert, Sarah Faulkner, Toby Huss, Robert Brink, Charity Ankrum, Johanna Cox, Sophie Sutherland, Charles Beyer, Dr. Adam Russell, Mary HK Choi, Dr. Kalev Sepp, Tom Pritchard and Jody Rhone, Steve and April Hewitt, Necia Dallas, Eteri Chkadua, Nico Muhly, Alex Roy, Dr. Trevor Paglen, Ted Mann, Anpo Cash, Damany Weir, Steven Felty, Wouter Deryoutter . . . and an extra special megablast of undying and eternal love to the incomparable Gaylord Fields.

I would be remiss if I did not thank certain **luminaries in the worlds of Art, Fashion, Entertainment, and Academia** who inspired me, taught me things, and became dear to my heart: Narciso Rodriguez, Gary Graham, Paola Antonelli of the NY MoMA, the Dallas Art Museum, Dr. Valerie Steele and the Fashion Institute of Technology, Randy and Fenton from World of Wonder, Harold Koda and Andrew Bolton at the Metropolitan Museum's Costume Institute, San Francisco's First Family of Fashion the magnificent Ospitals, the *Economist* (for letting me interview Tavi Gevinson), and Alec Baldwin for letting Simon Doonan and me converse with him onstage about Yves Saint-Laurent.

There is no praise too high for all of the **fabulous assistants** who helped me through this interminable process, and should have received the remuneration they deserved instead of what I could afford: Brendan Schlagel, Gargi Shinde, Danarchy Gingold, Kire Toveski, and the always life-saving Adam Sontag.

Obvious thanks to my **family**, without whom I wouldn't exist: Steve and Gini Wilson, Rick, Roscoe, and Abigail Bernard; Alex, Rafael, Charlie, and Daisy Briones, Auntie Lisa Ridgway, and my Fairy Godmother, Miss Margot Jones.

I thank all of my friends on **Facebook** and **Twitter** (follow me: @xintra) and am especially grateful to Rob Delaney and Patton Oswalt, who have occasionally reminded the world I still exist in the midst of this interminable project.

Lastly, a shout-out to all of the **top-secret cabals** I belong to: WILBERFORCE, the Hermenautic Circle, Leopards & Horses, ASH-X, and Bitch Mafia™, esp. the photographer Susan Anderson and Chef Elizabeth Faulkner.

FUCK SEX, LET'S PLAY DRESS UP